THE BATTLE FOR
MANCHESTER

ABOUT SHOOT

Shoot has been *the* choice of football's keenest fans since its launch in 1969.

In the 1980s Shoot Magazine had a readership in excess of one million and led to the launch of many rival competitors. Many have gone, but the Shoot brand lives on in many guises.

The Shoot Annual is still the No. 1 football annual and is now complimented by its popular website at www.shoot.co.uk where there is access to free sample pages of the monthly digital version of Shoot!.

The full digital magazine is now available as a download from the app store, bringing Shoot! Bang up-to-date with the digital age.

This is just one of a whole range of official products that ensures Shoot enters its fifth decade with its foot firmly on the ball!

THE BATTLE FOR
MANCHESTER

The Rivalry between Manchester City and Manchester United

JON REEVES

NEW
HOLLAND

ACKNOWLEDGEMENTS

I would like to thank Alan Whiticker and all at New Holland Publishing for commissioning this book and for their advice and support throughout the writing process. I would also like to thank Colin Mitchell for his help during this and countless other projects over the years. Also a special thank you to Fiona Schultz and Diane Ward at New Holland, and Vicki Healiss and Rob Corney at Bulldog Licensing.

It wouldn't have been possible to complete this title without the understanding of my wife and my family, who have been extremely supportive during the long nights of research, writing and proofing. I would also like to thank the family and friends who have been part of the passionate and informed football discussions that have helped to give me a more balanced view of the game and acted as inspiration for much of the tone of this book.

I have used an exhaustive list of other football titles to help supplement my research, such as *Manchester: A Football History* by Gary James, *Manchester City Ruined My Life* by Colin Shindler and *The Illustrated History of Manchester United* by Tom Tyrrell and David Meek, as well as the beautifully written autobiographies of footballing legends like Sir Matt Busby, Sir Bobby Charlton and Sir Alex Ferguson, all being particularly helpful to check facts and events.

As a passionate football fan since the tail end of the 1980s, I have witnessed huge changes in the beautiful game; some for the better and some for the worse, with many of the modern developments leaving even the most passionate fans stained with cynicism and often disillusioned with the game they fell in love with.

In many ways, writing this book has been a therapeutic experience that has reminded me of what makes football such a fantastic and universally popular sport. Discovering the more noble and sporting rivalry between the two clubs in the past has left me refreshed and with a more healthy outlook for the future of the game.

Writing a title that chronicles so many stories and characters is enjoyable but extremely challenging as both clubs have so many memorable events, great players and top class managers to consider. I'm sure that supporters of both United and City will wonder why certain games, goals and players haven't been covered, or covered in the detail they would've craved, but overall I hope that I have captured the essence and the emotion of one of the greatest rivalries in football.

I hope that you enjoy this book and the continued unfolding drama of the battle for Manchester.

Jon Reeves

Contents

Foreword

The Battle For Manchester chronicles the rivalry between Manchester United and Manchester City, from the clubs' formation at the end of nineteenth century, through the swinging sixties when both teams competed for major trophies, and up to the recent re-ignition of the rivalry.

The highs and lows of both clubs are covered in this book, from the depths of despair of the Munich air disaster in 1958 to the glory of 1968, a year that saw United lift the European Cup for the first time and City win the First Division title.

Some of the most talented and famous names in world football have an association with the Manchester giants, including the 'holy trinities' of Denis Law, George Best and Bobby Charlton at United, and City's Francis Lee, Mike Summerbee and Colin Bell; the enigmatic talents of Eric Cantona, Cristiano Ronaldo and Carlos Tevez, and managerial greats like Sir Alex Ferguson and Sir Matt Busby as well as Joe Mercer and Malcolm Allison.

Although the fire of the hostility between both clubs was extinguished for a number of years as United chased glory and City faltered, like a dormant volcano there was always a chance that it would erupt with ferocity, and that's exactly what has happened in the last three years following the injection of billions of pounds of investment at Manchester City.

The increased intensity of competition between United and City culminated in a memorable battle for the 2011-12 Premier League title, which was settled in the most dramatic of climaxes and saw the destination of the trophy remain unclear until the final seconds of the season. The theatre of that finale is covered in detail in this book.

Recent events and the rich histories of both clubs ensure that the future will continue to be captivating and headline-grabbing, and that the rivalry between United and City will remain fierce and extremely significant as the Reds and the Blues go for glory and battle for the hearts and minds of Manchester fans.

Colin Mitchell, Shoot Magazine
August 2012

INTRODUCTION

As the clock ticked into injury time there was a sense of familiarity about the final day of the Premier League season on May 13, 2012. Manchester United were again fighting for the title and doing exactly what was required of them: winning and controlling their game. After spending the last week of the season resigned to the fact that the Premier League trophy would be hoisted on the other side of Manchester, the United fans were daring to dream again. Radios were clutched to ears, mobile phones were being frantically refreshed and the sheepish grins of belief began to emerge.

At the Etihad Stadium the tension was palpable. Playing against a resilient ten-man Queens Park Rangers, Manchester City appeared to be buckling under the weight of pressure saddling their shoulders. The agony on the home fans' faces grew more conspicuous with every mistimed pass and sliced shot. Even the usually calm Roberto Mancini cut a flustered and forlorn figure. The headline-grabbing Mario Balotelli and his often combustible temperament had entered the fray as the manager's last throw of the dice and, like their neighbours had so often achieved, City needed an injury-time miracle.

After 44 years without a league title and such significant investment in the transfer market, were the Blues about to squander such a rare chance for glory? With that first title viewed as the hardest to win, the media storm would be fierce if City failed, and the fans, the players and the manager were well aware of the repercussions. If City failed, there would be much conjecture about whether Mancini's team had the required mental strength to overcome the psychological barrier of finishing top of the pile, surely leaving the manager's job and many of the players' futures in doubt.

Meanwhile, at the Stadium of Light, a Manchester United side that had been labelled a 'team in transition' during large parts of the season were edging closer to what many observers would have labelled as Sir Alex Ferguson's greatest ever achievement. With the club he'd provided almost constant glory over 30 years of near-perfect management now saddled with millions of pounds worth of debt, the wily Scotsman had assembled a team and a squad able to compete with the huge riches of City. Could he add yet another major honour to the Old Trafford trophy room and guide United to their 20th English League title?

As the clock ticked into stoppage time, desperation was the key emotion that consumed players and fans alike at the Etihad Stadium. Queens Park Rangers were defending the edge of their box with absolute commitment, throwing their bodies in front of the ball and forcing even City's most composed and skilful players into panicking and rushing. There had been plenty of shots from distance and numerous corners and crosses into the box, but QPR, showing the grit and determination exuded by their manager Mark Hughes during his playing career, continued to slam the door shut. City won another corner and with many supporters beginning to accept what would have been the ultimate disappointment, the ball was met by the powerful head of Bosnia striker Edin Dzeko at the far post and thudded into the net, levelling the scores at 2-2. The Etihad Stadium erupted, the fans dared to dream and most importantly the players began to believe again.

QPR suddenly looked physically tired and mentally exhausted as City continued to attack with purpose. Rather than fearing failure, they now sensed glory and with a minute left on the clock the Blues knew there would be one more chance to win the game and claim the Premier League title.

As City once again approached the QPR box, all of the fans crammed into the Etihad Stadium were on their feet, willing the ball into the goal with an acute intensity that can only be realised after experiencing so many years of hurt and disappointment. The ball then fell to the headline-making Mario Balotelli. During the season the Italian striker had shown the qualities of a man made for the big occasion but also one that displayed a combustible character; equally likely to lose the plot and lose the game for his team. But on this final day of intense drama, the young Italian showed composure and mental clarity. After carrying the ball into the area, Balotelli kept possession for just long enough before sliding it into the path of Sergio Aguero. The lively Argentinian caught the strike cleanly and the ball zipped towards the target. It seemingly took an age for the net to bulge and a second for the City fans to comprehend that their wildest dreams had been realised before scenes of delirium and joyous disbelief lit up the Etihad.

As the City fans celebrated, the United fans were in a state of shock-filled sorrow. They had prepared themselves for the disappointment of losing the title and losing it to their great rivals, but the manner of that disappointment and the way that the drama had unfolded made the pain and sense of loss even more intense.

In terms of City's recent statements of intent, claiming the Premier League title was by far the most powerful and one that is likely to resonate around the City of Manchester and the landscape of English football for decades to come.

The drama of that last day was the perfect illustration of the impact of the highs and lows of the tribal nature of football. The rivalry between both Manchester clubs has intensified to almost unprecedented levels, ensuring that the Battle for Manchester is one of the most intense and intriguing in world football.

1

THE HISTORY

Manchester United are now the biggest, most famous and most profitable football club in the world, but the Red Devils' glorious history, and the history of football itself, was built upon the blood, sweat and tears of the working classes. The founding fathers of the club were a group of Lancashire and Yorkshire Railway (LYR) workers who created a football team in 1878. The club, christened as Newton Heath LYR, also known as the Heathens, played their home games at North Road in Manchester and first competed against other departments of the LYR and rival railway companies.

Two years after the birth of Newton Heath, Manchester City, the club now known as one of the richest in the world, emerged from equally humble beginnings. The club was first founded in 1880 as St Mark's (West Gorton). A local church that had previously fielded a cricket team, St Mark's would eventually evolve into a football club. The Connell family, led by rector of St Mark's, Arthur Connell, played an important role in setting up the team, in an attempt to curb crime and violence by using sport to revitalise an increasingly industrialised East Manchester community.

The first meeting between the two teams took place on November 12, 1881 when West Gorton (St Mark's) hosted Newton Heath. The Heathens went on to claim a 3-0 victory during a time when other Manchester sides also existed and this particular fixture didn't hold any great significance. However, things started to change as both clubs progressed and edged closer to nomination for the Football League, when the battle to become Manchester's biggest and best club began in earnest.

In 1884, St Mark's temporarily merged with Gorton Athletic, but both clubs soon split and the St Mark's representatives named themselves Gorton AFC, with Gorton Athletic reforming as West Gorton Athletic. After seven years competing at a local level and playing their home games at various locations around East Manchester, the club evolved into Ardwick AFC and started playing at Hyde Road.

In 1888 Newton Heath became a founding member of The Combination, a regional football league, but later joined the Football Alliance when the division dissolved. Both Newton Heath and Ardwick played in very different home colours to those associated with the clubs today. The Heathens wore green and gold split jerseys while St Mark's (West Gorton) initially played in black shirts with white shorts. Ardwick AFC went on to wear blue and white stripes and the club first displayed the sky blue colours they are renowned for today, in 1894 when they reformed as Manchester City. Like City, United first stepped out in their famous red jerseys when the club was renamed in 1902.

One early fixture between the two clubs that carried some significance took place on February 26, 1898 at the Belle Vue Athletic Ground. The match was played in aid of the Hyde Coal Mine disaster, when a pit explosion claimed the lives of 23 men. The game was the first Manchester derby to be played under floodlights and Newton Heath claimed a 3-2 victory. Another notable contest between the emerging rivals took place in 1891 when Ardwick won the Manchester Cup for the first time, defeating Newton Heath 1-0 in the final. Following the victory Ardwick were accepted as a member of the Football Alliance for the start of the 1891-92 season.

With the Football League deciding its members by invitation only, it wasn't until 1892 that Newton Heath's application was accepted, when the club joined the First Division as part of a restructured Football League. At this point the club dropped 'LYR' from its name and moved to a new ground at Bank Street, Clayton. However, the Heathens struggled with the step up in class and finished bottom of the table at the end of their first season. The club only managed to preserve their First Division status by defeating Second Division champions, Small Heath (now Birmingham City) in the Play-off Test Match.

The 1893 move to Bank Street did little to improve Newton Heath's fortunes as the team again finished at the foot of the table, eventually suffering relegation following a 2-0 Play-Off Test Match against Liverpool, who had topped the Second Division.

While Newton Heath had been competing at the highest level, Ardwick had to wait a little longer to pit their wits against English football's finest. In 1892, the club were one of the founder members of the restructured Second Division, when the Football League merged with the Football Alliance, continuing to compete under the name of Ardwick AFC until the 1894 reform as Manchester City Football Club.

Ardwick had been struggling financially, but under the new dawn, manager Joshua Parlby was able to invest in the team and made 19-year-old winger Billy Meredith one of his first signings from Northwich Victoria, and the Welshman soon had a positive impact.

Newton Heath remained in the second tier of English football for the next 12 seasons, during which the first Football League meeting against Manchester City took place in the 1894-95 season, when the Heathens defeated City 5-2 at Hyde Road.

The victory proved a rare highpoint for the club who saw Manchester City gain promotion to the top flight in 1898 while they remained in the second tier. Newton Heath were also struggling off the pitch with dwindling crowds leaving them on the verge of bankruptcy, particularly after president, William Healey, sought to have the club wound up, in order to receive monies he was owed.

Bankruptcy would have seen Newton Heath thrown out of the Football League and the team disbanded, but club captain Harry Stafford had other ideas. The determined full-back headed up a fundraising campaign which encouraged the involvement of local businessmen. New funds were injected and Newton Heath, backed by breweries boss John Henry Davies – who became the club's first chairman – now had the financial clout to compete with other clubs.

In return for his investment, Davies obtained an interest in the running of the club, leading to the Manchester United re-brand in 1902. The arrival of United's first real manager came a year later, when Burnley secretary Ernest Mangnall took up the reins. Under Mangnall, United became a more professional outfit on and off the pitch, finishing third in his first full season in charge and regaining their First Division status in 1906 after second place in the Second Division signalled the end of over ten years outside of the top flight.

Manchester City had been enjoying steady progression in the First Division with crowds at Hyde Road regularly topping 25,000, as the club made their first ever FA Cup Final appearance in 1904. City defeated Bolton Wanderers 1-0 at Crystal Palace, thanks to a goal from Billy Meredith, and became the first Manchester club to win the famous trophy. The Citizens also came close to another Manchester first that season, narrowly missing out on a league and cup double after finishing second in the First Division; the highest league placing recorded by a Manchester club to that date. City were viewed as a well-backed club whose financial strength helped them attract the best players, with many clubs envious of their resources; a state of affairs that again became evident over a century later.

A shrewd judge of the transfer market, United manager Ernest Mangnall captured big names, including Charlie Roberts and highly-rated Manchester City winger Billy Meredith. Capitalising on a bribery scandal surrounding Meredith, Mangnall snapped up the Welsh wing wizard in a £500 deal and United began the 1906-07 season in good form. The first top flight fixture between United and City occurred during this campaign, as the clubs met in December 1906 in a match that City won 3-0.

English football was then hit by a bombshell that meant disaster for Manchester City, but opened the door for an opportunist United. Following claims made by former City man Billy Meredith that the club had paid players over the minimum wage, a Football Association inquiry investigating the conduct of several clubs discovered that City had been making illegal payments to their players. It was widely believed that other clubs were guilty of similar offences but none were investigated to the same extent as the Manchester side, with the Football Association seemingly relishing the opportunity to cause disruption at money-rich City.

As part of the extremely harsh punishment dished out by the FA, 17 of City's players – the backbone of their 1904 Cup winning side – were banned from playing for the club for life. Manager Tom Maley was also suspended from football for life and the club was fined a total of £250. In order to continue in the Football League, City had to sell the majority of their successful squad, and an auction of the 17 players was set up at the club's Hyde Road ground. Having previously swooped for Billy Meredith, Ernest Mangnall was waiting in the wings to entice more of City's top players across Manchester. Knowing United would struggle to compete financially with the other Football League clubs, Mangnall moved quickly to negotiate with three of City's stars, snapping up Herbert Burgess, Alec 'Sandy' Turnbull and Jimmy Bannister.

The Manchester City quartet, including Meredith, had to serve a suspension before making their United debuts in a 1-0 win over Aston Villa in January 1907. The first great Manchester United team was emerging and the club went on to claim their first Football League title in 1908. It was a feat that the highly-rated City team hadn't yet been able to achieve, but arguably would have done if they'd been able to retain their players.

Despite failing to defend their title the following season, United impressed in the 1909 FA Cup, defeating Bristol City 1-0 in the final with a goal from Turnbull, securing United's first taste of cup glory.

While everything was rosy on the field, matters off the pitch looked likely to harm United's chances the following season, as problems surrounding improved payment and conditions for players continued to arise. The Players' Union sought affiliation to the Federation of Trades Unions with matters reaching crisis point ahead of the 1909-10 campaign. A meeting was held five days before the start of the season and representatives from all league clubs agreed that any player admitting to being a member of the union should be suspended.

The following day, Ernest Mangnall and the United board called the players to a meeting with a strike seemingly the most likely outcome. Most First Division clubs had signed enough amateurs to fulfil their upcoming fixtures, but with the United players sticking to their principles and famously labelling themselves 'The Outcasts', Mangnall's men were struggling to field a team. However, on the eve of the new season, the authorities gave in and recognised the Players Union.

Amidst all of the political wrangling, United were preparing to move into their new ground; a stadium that would be the club's home for over a century and counting. Old Trafford, which would one day be known all over the world as the 'Theatre of Dreams', was built thanks to the financial muscle of John Henry Davies and the vision of Ernest Mangnall, who realised that the club needed to grow as a business off the field to improve matters on it.

On 22 January 1910, United played their last game at Bank Street ahead of a mid-season move to Old Trafford. The new stadium's opening game saw United take on Liverpool, with the Merseyside outfit spoiling the part by defeating the home side 4-3. At least the first ever goal at Old Trafford was scored by a United player, with Sandy Turnbull finding the target. Settling into their new home, complete with state of the art grandstand and a potential capacity of 100,000, United began to carve out a reputation as one of the most progressive clubs in the country and enjoyed further success on the field in 1911, claiming their second League Championship. However, storm clouds were beginning to gather around the club and a period of silverware famine was about to begin, with United experiencing 41 years without winning the First Division title.

In August 1912, after a 13th place finish, Ernest Mangnall left United to take charge of their biggest rivals, Manchester City. He was replaced by J J Bentley and United finished fourth in 1913, but with many of their better players reaching the end of their careers, the club's future looked bleak. By the end of the 1913-14 campaign, with crowds dwindling as low as 15,000, United only avoided relegation by a single point. In contrast, a Mangnall-inspired City were on the up, finishing fifth in 1915.

United had replaced J J Bentley with the club's first official manager, Jack Robson, who stayed in the post until 1921, but the majority of his time at the club was interrupted by The First World War. During the war, United played in the Lancashire Principal and Subsidiary Tournament for four seasons.

United struggled to maintain their massive overheads during the war and, by the time competitive football returned in 1919, the club was fielding a very different team. A 12th place finish in 1920 saw Jack Robson replaced by John Chapman as manager, but Manchester City continued to steal the headlines when their new ground, Maine Road, was built in 1923. The Citizens needed a new home after the main stand at Hyde Road was destroyed by fire in 1920. Initial discussions took place between City and United regarding the possibility of the clubs sharing Old Trafford, but United's proposed rent was too high, prompting the development of Maine Road. The new ground was designed by renowned architect Charles Swain and built in Moss Side, meaning the club would relocate from the east to the south of Manchester.

In 1921, United star Billy Meredith again followed Ernest Mangnall, swapping Manchester clubs once more and returning to City where he ended his playing days. City's continued progression, which included a First Division runners-up spot in 1921, was made even more galling for United as they endured a decline that resulted in relegation from the First Division in 1922. It took three seasons for the Reds to return to the top flight, thanks to a second place finish in Division Two. United's first season back in the top flight saw them finish ninth and reach the FA Cup semi-final, where they lost 3-0 to Manchester City.

City had shown excellent form in the competition, scoring 31 goals in five matches. But the Blues hadn't been the same team following Mangnall's retirement and went on to suffer defeat in the Wembley final to Bolton Wanderers. That disappointment was coupled with league despair as the Blues suffered relegation to the Second Division.

As well as the semi-final victory over United, another City highlight during the 1925-26 campaign was a 6-1 thumping of the Reds at Old Trafford. The victory wasn't enough to keep manager David Ashworth in a job, who paid the price for relegation and was replaced by Peter Hodge. Hodge almost guided the club back into the top flight the following season, but the Blues missed out to Portsmouth on goal average.

While City faltered, United were still rebuilding and wing-half Clarrie Hilditch became player-manager during the 1926-27 season. In 1927 Henry Davies, the man who had saved Newton Heath from extinction in 1902, died and was replaced at the helm by G H Lawton, while Herbert Bamlett took over as manager. Bamlett found a club saddled with massive debts and the team began to struggle, eventually suffering relegation in 1931.

In 1928, with Peter Hodge still impressing as manager, Manchester City were promoted to the First Division after lifting the Second Division title, their fourth second tier championship. City were averaging 38,000 attendances at Maine Road; the highest in the country.

While the Blues were on the up, United fought against successive relegations. With attendances at Old Trafford dropping as low as 3,507, the board took action and relieved Bamlett of his duties. Walter Crickmer, who had been club secretary since 1926, took charge, assisted by Louis Rocca. But United continued to struggle and by December 1931 the club was again close to bankruptcy and unable to pay the players' wages. Manchester United faced demise unless another saviour could be found. Step forward, James W Gibson, who owned a garment producing company specialising in army uniforms. A keen sports fan, Gibson met the United directors and invested over £30,000 in the debt-ridden club.

Peter Hodge was replaced by Wilf Wild as City manager in 1932 and, despite a disappointing league campaign, the new boss guided the Blues into the 1933 FA Cup Final. City faced a strong Everton side, featuring the legendary Dixie Dean, and were beaten 3-0 at Wembley. Blues captain Sam Cowan famously promised that his team would return to London the following year and claim the trophy.

At United, Scott Duncan was brought in as manager to improve matters on the pitch. Duncan was backed in the transfer market and United finished 12th in 1933, but were almost relegated to the Third Division in 1934, only missing out on slumping to the lowest level in the club's history by a single point, following a final-day victory over Millwall.

In contrast, a Manchester City side containing future United manager Matt Busby were on the up and won the 1934 FA Cup final in the same week as their neighbours were fighting for survival. City defeated Portsmouth 2-1 at Wembley thanks to a brace from Fred Tilson. Just as he had predicted 12 months earlier, skipper Sam Cowan lifted the trophy.

With their Second Division standing intact, United ended the 1934-35 campaign in fifth place as the crowds began to return to Old Trafford. That progression continued a season later as United claimed the 1936 Second Division title and sealed a return to the highest level. But it proved short-lived as the team were relegated the following year, leading to Scott Duncan's resignation.

While United suffered, City celebrated, claiming the 1936-37 First Division title. The Blues began the campaign in stuttering form, winning just three of their first 14 games, which included a first Manchester derby defeat since 1931. But Wilf Wild's men, inspired by the attacking prowess of Eric Book, Fred Tilson and Peter Doherty, went on an impressive run and sealed the first League Championship in the club's history with a 4-1 victory over Sheffield Wednesday at Maine Road. City clocked up over 100 goals during the campaign and enjoyed a 22 game unbeaten run.

Walter Crickmer again steadied the ship as United's temporary manager and the Old Trafford outfit's spell as a 'yo-yo' club continued with promotion back to the top flight in 1938 after a second place finish. During this period, United signed a couple of future greats in Irishman Johnny Carey and prolific goal-scorer Jack Rowley. Rowley went on to form an impressive partnership with Stan Pearson, a Salford-born inside-left who also linked up well with Tom Manley, to form an attacking trio crucial to United's promotion campaign.

The contrasting nature of both Manchester clubs' fortunes continued as United's return to the First Division coincided with City's demotion to the Second in 1937, just a year after they had become Football League Champions. The Blues began the campaign in fearsome form, particularly at home, winning their opening seven matches but away defeats saw them sink towards the wrong end of the table. City's relegation to the Second Division was confirmed on the last day of the season, following a 1-0 defeat at Huddersfield Town.

With the Second World War looming, United finished the 1938-39 campaign in 14th place, as League competition was disbanded between 1939 and 1946 during the conflict. It meant that United retained their First Division status during the war years, while City had to battle their way back out of the Second Division when the Football League programme resumed.

Manchester United's post-war development is inextricably linked with one man: Matt Busby. Possessing remarkable vision and a philosophy that shaped the future of the club, Busby ensured that United became one of the most popular and famous teams in the world.

A former captain and FA Cup winner at Manchester City, Busby also played for Liverpool before the Second World War and had been invited back to Anfield to combine his playing career with a role as the club's assistant manager, but Manchester United's offer proved too tempting for the softly spoken Scotsman.

Busby, who was also known as 'The Godfather', first took over at United in 1945 and found a club in disarray. Old Trafford had been almost destroyed by German bombers during the war, leaving the club without a home and adequate training facilities. United were again struggling financially and had to play their home matches at Manchester City's Maine Road while Old Trafford was being rebuilt. In truth, the chance to play at a ground with a larger capacity than their own helped the Reds continue to function, as they brought in increased gate receipts.

City's manager Wilf Wild remained at the helm during the war as the club played in the Northern Regional League, but by the time the Football League resumed in 1946 Wild had taken an administrative role and was replaced by FA Cup winning captain Sam Cowan. The new manager guided the Blues to an amazing run of 18 unbeaten league games and led the club back to the top flight by winning the Second Division title.

While United were struggling off the pitch, their new manager had inherited a strong playing squad, with the likes of Johnny Carey, Stan Pearson, Jack Rowley and Charlie Mitten on the books. Busby was also a shrewd judge in the transfer market and signed the vastly-experienced Scottish winger, Jimmy 'Brittle Bones' Delaney from Celtic for £4,000 in 1946.

Another of Busby's new additions was arguably his greatest ever for Manchester United. Jimmy Murphy, a former player with West Bromwich Albion and Wales, was appointed as assistant manager. The two men had forged a strong friendship while serving together in the War and Murphy's harder, more regimented exterior perfectly complemented Busby's more gentile, father-like character.

Both men were advocates of entertaining, attacking football and possessed great tactical awareness. Busby showed this by converting the likes of John Aston and Johnny Carey to full-backs and placing players in a system that maximised their strengths and compensated for their weaknesses.

English football had initially been divided into northern and southern leagues during the war. Busby inherited a team stuck 16th in the northern table but eventually guided United to a fourth place finish. Football retuned to a national league system for the start of the 1946-47 campaign and United continued to progress under Busby, finishing runners-up to Liverpool in the Championship.

Having returned Manchester City to the First Division in 1947, Sam Cowan wasn't given the opportunity to manage the Blues in the top flight. Before taking up the role he had been running a successful physiotherapy practice in Hove and elected to maintain the business while commuting to Manchester. The club's directors felt that his refusal to relocate north made his position at the club untenable. Cowan was replaced by Jock Thomson, who led City to 10th place in the First Division.

United were enjoying consistency in the First Division, achieving two further second place finishes. Although the League Title continued to elude the Red Devils, they won their first trophy under Busby in 1948, defeating Blackpool 4-2 in a classic FA Cup Final.

United were developing a reputation for playing attacking football with plenty of width, thanks to the speed, skill and showmanship of Delaney on the right-wing and Charlie Mitten on the left. In the middle, Rowley, Pearson and Johnny Morris provided even more creativity and the FA Cup brought the best out of the team, as they scored 18 goals in five games on their way to lifting the trophy at Wembley. Blackpool featured England stars, Stanley Matthews and Stan Mortensen, and proved to be worthy opponents, scoring first through Eddie Shimwell. A goal from Rowley levelled matters but Mortensen struck to give Blackpool the lead at the break. It was a lead they maintained until the 69th minute when Rowley headed home his second. Further goals from Pearson and John Anderson gave United the advantage, allowing captain Johnny Carey to lift the Cup.

Jock Thomson's Manchester City improved during the 1948-49 campaign, grabbing a seventh place finish. While the manager's reign wasn't particularly remarkable in terms of results, Thomson was responsible for making one of the best signings in the club's history. In October 1949 he brought in German goalkeeper Bert Trautmann; a decision which drew plenty of criticism.

Trautmann had been a paratrooper for the Germans during the Second World War and the memories of the conflict were still extremely raw in England. Bert had been captured on the Western Front before being transferred to a prisoner-of-war camp in Ashton-in-Makerfield, Lancashire. After refusing an offer of repatriation to Germany, he settled in the area, combining farm work with playing football for non-league St Helens Town.

Following the German's arrival, some Manchester City season ticket holders threatened a boycott and various groups in Manchester and around the country bombarded the club with protest letters. Club captain at the time, Eric Westwood, himself a veteran of the war, made a stand by famously announcing: "There's no war in this dressing room."

City were in need of a goalkeeper with ability and presence following the departure of the great Frank Swift, and Trautmann's ability soon won over the majority of Blues fans and, even though the German continued to receive abuse from opposing supporters, he was soon accepted for his sporting ability.

While Trautmann would go on to enjoy a hugely successful 15-year career at City, Jock Thomson's time at the club was much shorter, as he was dismissed two-thirds into the 1949-50 season after City had won just five games. Inevitably, the club went on to suffer relegation and the Blues once again found themselves in the second tier of English football.

Having shared City's home since the end of the war, United were able to return to Old Trafford in 1949 when the stadium reopened. Due to the war and because of the damage caused by the conflict, a league game hadn't been played at the ground in almost a decade. The club's first game back at Old Trafford took place on August 24, 1949 as 41,748 spectators crammed into the stadium to watch Busby's men stroll to a 3-0 victory over Bolton Wanderers.

Following City's demotion Les McDowall, a former Blues player, went on to enjoy more success than his fellow Scotsman, Jock Thomson, in the managerial hot seat. McDowall initially built a solid team at Maine Road, ensuring a return to the top flight in 1951 by virtue of a second place standing, but the next three seasons saw his team flirting with relegation. However, somewhat of an innovator and a keen tactician, McDowall began deploying wing-backs and a deep-lying forward behind the strikers. A player key to this approach was future England manager, Don Revie, who operated between the midfield and forwards. McDowall's revolutionary strategy was labelled the 'Revie Plan' and soon led to improved performances for City, particularly in the FA Cup.

The league title was continuing to elude Matt Busby's first great United side, who finished fourth in 1950 and claimed another runners-up spot in 1951. With the likes of Mitten and Delaney leaving the club and many of the other players reaching veteran status, Busby knew time was running out for his ageing side when United finally sealed the First Division Championship in 1952, finishing four points ahead of second place Tottenham Hotspur. It was the club's first Championship in 41 years and the success proved a watershed in United's history.

During the Championship winning campaign, Busby began to blood some of the younger players that he and Murphy had been schooling at the club. The first home-grown teenager to break into the first team was future captain Roger Byrne. Initially deployed at outside-left where he impressed during the title winning season, Busby later converted Byrne into a left-back where he went on to establish himself for both club and country.

United struggled at the beginning of their 1952 title defence, losing six of the first 11 matches. Since his appointment at the club, Busby had instructed chief scout Joe Armstrong – a man who held a similar role at Manchester City during Busby's time at Maine Road – to scour the United Kingdom and Ireland for the most talented young players. With Armstrong's eye for talent, the coaching skills of Jimmy Murphy and the trust and patience of Busby, the policy worked in spectacular fashion as United's youngsters won an impressive five consecutive FA Youth Cups between 1953 and 1957.

It was only a matter of time before such a talented group would break into the first-team picture and Busby was a man both brave and bold enough to select them. As well as introducing locally sourced talent, Busby possessed a keen eye for the abilities of youngsters based at other clubs, signing the likes of Johnny Berry from Birmingham City and barrel-chested striker, Tommy Taylor, from Barnsley.

Other talented youngsters, including the legendary Duncan Edwards, David Pegg, Bill Foulkes, Jackie Blanchflower and Dennis Violet, began to experience first-team football towards the end of the 1952-53 campaign, as a United side in a state of transition finished eighth.

It was during the 1953-54 season that Busby really began to back the youngsters, but despite the team's undoubted talent it would take them a few years to impose their abilities on the First Division. A fourth place finish in 1954 was followed by fifth a year later but the team was finding its feet and the foundations for the future were being laid.

City had also been building something special, using Jock McDowall's 'Revie Plan' to challenge for the title in 1955 and reach the FA Cup Final. The Blues lost 3-1 to Newcastle United, with Scottish striker Bobby Johnstone grabbing their consolation goal. The team's captain for the Wembley final, Welshman Roy Paul, vowed to return to London the following year to avenge the defeat, just as Sam Cowan had done 32 years earlier. Surely lightning couldn't strike twice?

Driven on by Paul's promise and with their tactics continuing to baffle opponents, City again impressed in the Cup during the 1955-56 campaign and, following a 1-0 victory over Tottenham in the semi-final, they reached their second successive FA Cup Final. This time their opponents were Birmingham City in a match that would be remembered as the 'Trautmann' final.

Joe Hayes gave City a dream start, finding the target after just three minutes, but

Birmingham went on to equalise. City dug deep in the second half and scored through Bobby Johnstone and Jack Dyson to take a 3-1 lead. It was an advantage they held onto, but not before one of the most memorable incidents in FA Cup history.

Birmingham were fighting to get back into the game, when striker Peter Murphy bore down on goal in the 75th minute. Keeper Trautmann put his body on the line, bravely saving the ball as Murphy's knee crashed into his neck. The German stopper was in great discomfort, but with substitutes not permitted during that era he played on through the pain barrier, keeping the opponents at bay and ensuring City won the Cup.

Captain Ron Paul had seen his prediction come true but, still suffering the next day, Trautmann visited St George's Hospital and was told he had a crick in his neck. Three days later, still in intense pain, he visited Manchester Royal Infirmary and was diagnosed with a broken neck. The brave German had stayed on the pitch with five dislocated neck vertebrae, one of which had completely cracked. His third vertebrae had wedged against the second, which prevented further damage and probably saved his life. Trautmann's tale of bravery ensured an immediate entry into football folklore.

Everything clicked into place at Old Trafford during the 1955-56 season as a United team with an average age of just 22, now referred to in the media as the 'Busby Babes', took English football by storm. With the likes of Edwards, Foulkes, Taylor and Viollet, all established first-teamers, the Red Devils steamrollered the Division, claiming the title by a significant 11-point margin. Other youngsters began to roll off the United conveyor belt, with the likes of Eddie Colman, Liam 'Billy' Whelan and David Pegg all making their mark.

Tommy Taylor top-scored with 25 goals, with Viollet hitting 20 and Pegg grabbing nine, as all but three of the title winning team had been nurtured through the Old Trafford youth system. Busby's vision for the club had become a reality and his reflection of that achievement filled him with pride: "From the very start I had envisaged making my own players, having a kind of nursery so that they could be trained in the kind of pattern I was trying to create for Manchester United."

While United were gambling on youth and winning, Manchester City continued to select more experienced players, but McDowall's men struggled for consistency after their famous FA Cup win and finished the following season 18th, just one place clear of relegation.

With a settled team and the strength in depth of several other youngsters, including Bobby Charlton, backing them up, Manchester United reclaimed their title in style during the 1956-57 campaign, finishing eight points ahead of runners-up Spurs. The team hit over 100 goals, including 26 from the outstanding Liam Whelan. The league title was reclaimed by Easter with United's final points tally of 64, the highest achieved in the division for 26 years. Busby's men also reached the FA Cup final where they were narrowly defeated by

Aston Villa, missing out on the elusive League and Cup double.

The 1957 final was shrouded in controversy as United goalkeeper Ray Wood sustained a smashed cheekbone after Aston Villa forward Peter McParland crashed into him after just six minutes. Half-back Jackie Blanchflower took over in goal with Wood attempting to operate on the right-flank. Blanchflower performed admirably but Villa scored twice in the second half to seal a 2-1 victory.

During the same season, United became trail-blazers when it came to European football, with Matt Busby hugely passionate about competing against the continent's finest teams. Busby and the club were met with plenty of obstruction from the English Football League. Chelsea, winners of the 1954-55 league title, had been denied the opportunity to take part in the inaugural European Cup by the Football League's chairman Alan Hardaker, who feared that European football would damage the integrity of the English game.

Busby, possessing the foresight to realise the potential of the tournament, was determined to see his team competing on the European stage. Despite Hardaker's best efforts, which would include the introduction of the English League Cup in a bid to detract from European competition, United eventually received the backing of Stanley Rous, Chairman of the Football Association, and were permitted to take part in the 1956-57 European Champions' Cup.

United became the first English team to take part in the competition and the 'Babes' soon acclimatised to the continental game, playing their first European match against Belgium's Anderlecht in a preliminary round tie in Brussels. United won the game 2-0, bringing a good advantage back to Manchester for the second leg, which was played at City's Maine Road as Old Trafford had yet to be fitted with the necessary floodlighting. The 'home' tie was a romp for the English champions as they destroyed Anderlecht 10-0; a result which remains the club's record competitive victory.

After such an auspicious start in Europe, United went from strength to strength, eventually reaching the semi-finals where they were defeated by Spanish giants Real Madrid, who had been inaugural winners of the Champions' Cup the previous season and would go on to claim the trophy in each of its first five years. The thrill of playing against the stars of Madrid and defeating the likes of Borussia Dortmund and Athletico Bilbao had exceeded even Busby's expectations and, once the team and the manager had tasted what Europe had to offer, they wanted more. With the 1957 First Division title in the bag, and the team dominating matters domestically, the club were determined to succeed on the continent by dethroning the majestic Madrid and beginning their own European dynasty.

2

THE BEGINNING OF THE LEGEND

United's Rise to Fame

With Manchester United riding the crest of a wave, Matt Busby's maturing youngsters looked set to take charge of the English and European game for the next decade. United began the 1957-58 campaign in fine form, claiming early season victories against Leicester City, Everton and Manchester City. The Babes were realising the ambitions of their manager, playing breathtakingly entertaining attacking football while achieving the desired results and scoring a remarkable 22 goals in the opening six games.

The maturing youngsters from Old Trafford went about their European campaign in determined fashion, beginning the competition with a routine victory over Irish side Shamrock Rovers and then defeating Czechoslovakian champions Dukla Prague 3-1 over two legs to secure a quarter-final tie against Yugoslav giants Red Star Belgrade. United edged a 2-1 victory over Red Star at Old Trafford thanks to goals from Bobby Charlton and Eddie Colman. The Reds continued to enjoy free-scoring form in the league, building up to the second leg with a 7-2 thumping of Bolton Wanderers and travelling to play Arsenal at Highbury in a game that would go down in United legend.

Just four days before the match in Belgrade, Matt Busby selected the same eleven that would face Red Star in the return tie. Irish international goalkeeper Harry Gregg had replaced Ray Wood between the posts and was set for a busy afternoon as United and Arsenal treated the crowd to an end to end, goal-filled encounter. Duncan Edwards put United ahead after 10 minutes with a thumping strike, with further goals from Bobby Charlton and Tommy Taylor giving the Babes a 3-0 advantage at half-time.

Arsenal hauled themselves back into contention around the hour-mark, as future

United striker David Herd beat Gregg with a fierce shot. Rather than simply providing consolation for the home side, Herd's finish acted as a catalyst and within two minutes the North London side drew level thanks to a Jimmy Bloomfield double. The momentum had firmly swung in favour of the Gunners, who looked the more likely winners, but the spirit and bravery of a young United side came to the fore as the Reds' determination to score another goal, rather than hold on for a draw, summed up the philosophy and style of all great United teams.

As the clock ticked down Dennis Viollet slammed the ball home to the amazement of both home and away supporters. United weren't finished there, and moments later, Tommy Taylor grabbed his second of the game. Arsenal pegged back a goal through Derek Tapscott but United held on to claim a famous victory that took them into their European contest in the highest of spirits.

The Arsenal victory is seen as a game that sums up the style of the Busby Babes and just how much potential the team had to realise. It was a 90 minute encounter that illustrated the very best of Manchester United, with plenty of goals, entertaining flair-filled football, late drama and the sense that the thousands that had paid to watch them had well and truly got their money's worth.

It was a style cultivated and inspired by Busby, whose team talks encouraged the players to express themselves, as Jackie Blanchflower once explained: "One of his typical team talks was to say, 'go out and enjoy yourselves. If the public see that you're enjoying yourselves then they will enjoy themselves too. We got the reputation of playing with a smile on our sleeves."

United flew out to Belgrade holding a slender 2-1 advantage, knowing that Red Star would provide a stern test in their home stadium. There had been plenty of snow in Yugoslavia but the sun shone on the day of the match, thawing out most of the pitch in time for what promised to be a classic European encounter.

Moments before kick-off, the bulbs of the photographers' cameras flashed, capturing a United team ready for action. Now known as 'the last line-up', the image of Duncan Edwards and many of the other Babes acts as a haunting reminder of what lay ahead.

Like the Arsenal match before it, the encounter with Red Star was an absorbing one that perfectly showcased the attacking strengths of Busby's team. Dennis Viollet had shocked the home crowd with a goal inside the first two minutes to make the scores 3-1 on aggregate and Bobby Charlton extended that advantage with one of his long-range specials. The young English striker wasn't finished there and soon grabbed his second of the game, leaving the home side in a state of shock, trudging off three goals down at half-time and facing a 5-1 aggregate deficit.

Red Star emerged from the interval in determined style, clawing goals back from Bora Kostic and Lazar Tasic, who dispatched a penalty he had earned following a tangle with Bill Foulkes. The home side were dominating possession and soon found an equaliser as Kostic grabbed his second of the game with two minutes left on the clock. However, Busby's men heroically held out to claim a 3-3 draw that ensured their passage into the semi-finals of the European Champions' Cup for the second successive season.

After the game, the players and club officials celebrated their progress at the Majestic Hotel in Belgrade. They were joined by the English journalists and the Red Star players; an act of sportsmanship and camaraderie that was commonplace in those days. Those connected with United celebrated long into the night before preparing themselves for the flight home and resuming their domestic campaign with a top of the table clash against Wolverhampton Wanderers just two days later. The club was under great pressure from the Football League to ensure that the European campaign didn't impinge upon their First Division commitments, with new league regulations stating that any team competing in Europe had to be back in England a full 24 hours before a league game.

Taking off from a sun-covered Belgrade for their return to England, the United playing squad and the club's officials were joined on the flight by a collection of newspaper reporters, including News of the World journalist and former Manchester City goalkeeper Frank Swift.

The chartered aircraft, a BEA Elizabethan named the *Lord Burghley*, later stopped off at Munich's Riem Airport to refuel and should have been back in the air within minutes. The weather conditions in Munich had hardened as the runway was shrouded in low cloud, rain and snow, and during the descent into Munich Captain James Thain used anti-icing equipment on the wings.

On the ground, the Manchester party disembarked for refreshments before the plane was cleared for takeoff an hour later. However, an uneven tone in the engines alarmed Captain Thain and his co-pilot Captain Kenneth Rayment, prompting an aborted takeoff. A second aborted takeoff followed and the passengers disembarked and returned to the departure lounge.

Fully expecting a night in Munich, Duncan Edwards sent a telegram home to his landlady, reporting, "All flights cancelled. Flying home tomorrow. Duncan." But the players were soon informed that there was to be a fateful third and final attempt to fly home that night. Many of those on board were greatly concerned as the plane prepared for its final surge down the runway. A selection of passengers, including Duncan Edwards, Tommy Taylor, Mark Jones, Eddie Colman and Frank Swift moved to the back of the plane, believing it to be safer.

As the aircraft sped down the runway, with the passengers sitting in fear-ridden silence, it failed to gain height despite reaching the required speed for takeoff. The plane hurtled on before crashing through a fence and into a house. The port wing and part of the tail was torn off and the house caught fire. The port side of the cockpit was shattered after hitting a tree and the starboard side of the fuselage hit a wooden hut, causing a truck filled with tyres and fuel to explode.

During an interview in 1998, Bill Foulkes recalled the moment of impact: "The plane was bouncing along and obviously not going fast enough and then suddenly there were three tremendous sickening thuds and everything was spinning around. A second later I was sitting in my seat with my feet in the snow."

The scenes in the immediate aftermath of the crash were horrific. The plane had been torn apart on impact and ferocious fires were burning, with many passengers trapped in the wreckage. Bobby Charlton had to endure the instant realisation that one of his team mates had perished before witnessing Matt Busby lying on the runway in great pain. Charlton had kept his overcoat with him for the flight and was able to lay it on Busby as he waited for medical assistance. In his autobiography, *My Manchester United Years*, Charlton recalled the scene:

"Though I had not seen the condition of my dearest friends on the team, Duncan, Eddie and David Pegg, I knew by now that there had been terrible losses. In the snow I saw one team-mate who was obviously dead, and someone told me that Roger Byrne had gone. There was smoke and grit in the cold air and a blare of sirens, and sitting beside me, having been pulled out of the seat in which, like me, he had been thrown away from the plane, Dennis Viollet was drifting in and out of consciousness."

As Harry Gregg began to regain consciousness, still on board what was left of the plane, he feared the worst. The Northern Irishman felt blood running down his face, later saying that he "didn't dare put his hand up," thinking it "had been taken off, like a hardboiled egg."

Gregg crawled towards a spark of light in the cabin and kicked open a hole to make his escape. But, seeing the other passengers trapped in the wreckage and with fire and explosions all around him, the goalkeeper heroically returned to the plane to rescue as many people as possible, including a Serbian passenger called Vera Lukic, the wife of a Yugoslavian diplomat, and her baby daughter Vesna. Lukic was also pregnant at the time of the crash, meaning that Gregg saved another life.

Gregg recalled his memories of the disaster during a BBC Radio Ulster broadcast in 1998:

"The engine and most of the wing was gone and the socket where the engine had been was hissing and blowing and sparking. I looked directly in front of me and saw five people running through the snow, shouting 'run, run, run.' I remember standing there and thinking I was the only one alive. Then Captain Thain came around from the other side of the cockpit with a fire extinguisher in his hand. He shouted, 'run you stupid bastard, it's going to explode.'

At that time I also heard a child crying and I remembered that a lady and a child had got onto the plane. I shouted at the people running away, 'come back, there's people alive'. I crawled back in and was terrified at what I would find. I eventually found the child and crawled out. I remember running away with the child, still shouting for people to come back. I went back and went further in, found the child's mother and got her out.

The next one I found was Ray Wood, who was trapped but didn't have a mark on him. Then I found Scany (Albert Scanlon) and he was in a terrible state. I started shouting for Jackie Blanchflower but I couldn't find him at first. I made my way around to the side of the plane and saw Bobby Charlton and Dennis Viollet lying half in and half out of the wreckage. I thought they were dead and grabbed them by their waistbands and dragged them about 20 yards through the snow."

Another hero to join Gregg in his search for survivors was central defender Bill Foulkes, who had seen his team-mate rescuing the baby and returned to the wreckage to help. Gregg, Foulkes and Charlton would later be transported to hospital, where they received treatment and began to fully comprehend the enormity of the tragedy and such an immediate loss of so many lives.

The biggest tragedy to hit Manchester United occurred at four minutes past three on the afternoon of February 6, 1958, as the darkest hours, days, weeks, months and years in the club's history lay ahead.

The day after the tragedy, the bodies of the deceased were flown back to Manchester and lay in the gym at Old Trafford before being collected by the families. During the various funerals and memorial services, the people of Manchester showed what the players meant to them and how deeply they had been affected by the disaster, as thousands lined the streets.

Manchester was a city united in sadness and shrouded in despair. Grief stricken fans flocked to Old Trafford awaiting news of their heroes, with many staying at the ground for days, unable to take in the magnitude of the tragedy. A team filled with such talented young men, whose spirit and exuberance had burned so brightly, bringing joy to thousands of supporters all over the country, had been cruelly taken away in an instant. A dark cloud hovered over the club with those associated with Manchester United left feeling such profound sadness that they thought the pain would never go away. The side that played with a smile on their sleeve, entertaining so many, would never grace the English game again and the sense of loss was felt deeply all over Manchester and all over the world.

Messages of sympathy poured in and clubs across the UK and Europe held two minutes of silence at games on the Saturday following the accident. Red Star Belgrade, the team Manchester United had beaten before the crash, suggested United should be made honorary champions of the 1958 European Cup, and reigning champions Real Madrid were in agreement. UEFA wanted a different resolution, requesting that Manchester City took United's place in the semi-final. City immediately refused and offered to assist United in any way they could to help the Reds field a team for the remainder of the competition.

Like teams all over the country, City's players were deeply affected by the tragedy and couldn't contemplate returning to the pitch so soon after the disaster. However, every team in the division was forced to play their forthcoming weekend fixtures by the Football League, despite the appeals of the Manchester-based Professional Footballers Association. Many of the Blues players mixed socially with their United counterparts and would go on to attend the funerals of those that perished at Munich.

The tragedy claimed 23 lives in total, including those of eight Manchester United players. The full list of fatalities is as follows:

Manchester United players: Geoff Bent, Roger Byrne, Eddie Colman, Duncan Edwards, Mark Jones, David Pegg, Tommy Taylor, Liam 'Billy' Whelan.

Manchester United officials: Walter Crickmer (Club Secretary), Tom Curry (Trainer), Bert Whalley (Chief Coach).

Crew members: Captain Kenneth 'Ken' Rayment (DFC. Co-pilot), Tom Cable (cabin steward).

Journalists: Alf Clarke (*Manchester Evening Chronicle*), Donny Davies (*Manchester Guardian*), George Follows (*Daily Herald*), Tom Jackson (*Manchester Evening News*), Archie Ledbrooke (*Daily Mirror*), Henry Rose (*Daily Express*), Frank Swift (*News of the World*), Eric Thompson (*Daily Mail*).

Other passengers: Bela Miklos and Willie Satinoff (a close friend of Matt Busby).

The survivors, including Matt Busby, Duncan Edwards and Bobby Charlton, were taken to Rechts der Isar Hospital in Munich. Duncan Edwards would lose his battle for survival 15 days after the crash but, despite the severity of his injuries, which included multiple leg fractures, fractured ribs and severely damaged kidneys, the giant of the United team remained focused on football, famously asking United's assistant manager Jimmy Murphy what time the kick-off was against Wolves, adding that he "mustn't miss that match." In his autobiography Bobby Charlton recalls visiting his great friend's bedside, where he found Edwards in good spirits, saying, "I've been waiting for you. Where the bloody hell have you been?"

Upon hearing the devastating news, Manchester City's German goalkeeper Bert Trautmann, who had succeeded Frank Swift between the posts, contacted United to offer his help with translation or contacts. City's other goalkeeper, Steve Fleet, had been close friends with United's Eddie Colman, and as Colman's family waited for news of his fate, Steve called Manchester United from a local off-licence, eventually speaking to Club Secretary Les Olive, who asked him to inform Eddie's family that he had died.

Steve Fleet recalled the experience in Gary James' 2010 book entitled Manchester: A Football History:

"I had lots of friends at United, but Eddie Colman was my best friend. Up to his death we were as close as anybody could be. He was going to be the best man at my wedding. When he died it was terrible. We all knew the United players. We'd socialise with them, and they were just like us. Bobby Charlton, when he was living in digs, would sometimes come to our house for his tea. We were all close – Red or Blue didn't come into it."

In the days leading up to Duncan Edwards's death, the German doctors feared the worst for Matt Busby. The United manager had suffered fractured ribs, a punctured lung and leg injuries and the severity of his condition led to the last rites being administered on more than one occasion, with a hospital statement reporting that they didn't have much hope of saving him. Eventually Busby stabilised and was sent to Interlaken in Switzerland to recuperate with his wife, Jean.

The cause of the crash was initially labelled as pilot error, but it was later discovered that the build-up of slush on the runway had prevented the plane taking-off, clearing the name of the pilot, Captain James Thain.

At the time of the disaster, Manchester United were attempting to become only the third club to win three successive English league titles. Busby's side were six points behind League leaders Wolverhampton Wanderers with 14 games to go. The team were also on an 11-match unbeaten run and making progress in the FA Cup. This domestic success, coupled with their continued progress in Europe, prompted speculation that United could claim all three trophies and become the first English team to win the treble; a feat the club would famously go on to achieve 41 years later.

With the world focused on Manchester United, Manchester City continued their steady progress under manager Les McDowall. Even though their achievements had been dwarfed by United's recent success and increased profile, things were looking up at City, with McDowall's men managing a fifth place finish in 1958. Despite the improvements, the Blues remained inconsistent, scoring 104 goals in the league but also conceding 100. But that relative success would prove a brief highlight for the club and McDowall, as the team failed to achieve a further top five finish again under his command.

During the 1957-58 campaign, City went on to reach the third round of the FA Cup and striker Joe Hayes finished top scorer with 26 goals. It was the third time in four seasons that Hayes had topped the club's scoring charts, having finished with 27 in 1956 and level top with Johnny Hart with 14 in 1955.

As Manchester United attempted to move forward in the days and weeks following the tragedy of Munich, with Matt Busby bed-ridden and grief stricken, it was left to one man to keep the club going - that man was Busby's trusted assistant, Jimmy Murphy. Murphy had been coaching the Wales national team for a World Cup qualifier against Israel in Cardiff and hadn't made the trip to Munich. Having been so close to all of the players, seeing them develop from boys to men and developing their precocious potential to near-brilliance on the pitch, the depth of pain felt by Murphy must have been terribly severe.

Of the survivors, both Johnny Berry and Jackie Blanchflower were both injured so severely that they never played again, while Bobby Charlton, Bill Foulkes, Harry Gregg, Kenny Morgan, Albert Scanlon, Dennis Viollet and Ray Wood would all eventually return to the United line-up, enjoying varying degrees of success.

With the squad decimated by Munich and looking unable to fulfil their remaining fixtures, there were serious doubts about Manchester United's future and whether the club would have to fold. But, after receiving special dispensation from the Football Association to play cup-tied players, and thanks to the generosity of the other clubs, including Liverpool and Nottingham Forest - two of the first to offer their assistance - United started cobbling a team together.

Jimmy Murphy began his rebuilding by signing Ernie Taylor from Blackpool and Stan Crowther from Aston Villa, who had played against United in the 1957 FA Cup Final. Three players, Derek Lewin, Bob Hardisty and Warren Bradley, were also signed on loan from non-League Bishop Auckland.

After flying out to Munich to visit the survivors in hospital, Jimmy Murphy was encouraged by Busby to "keep the flag flying" at Old Trafford and he took that spirit into the club's first competitive fixture against Sheffield Wednesday in the FA Cup on February 19. The names of the players representing Wednesday appeared in the programme as usual, but for the United line-up there were no names because nobody knew what the team would be. The front cover of the publication stoically proclaimed that "United will go on" and a recorded message from Matt Busby was played before the game. *A News of the World* report at the time stated that "women wept as the tape-recorded voice echoed across a packed and silent Old Trafford".

Munich survivors, Harry Gregg and Bill Foulkes, had returned to Manchester and lined up against Sheffield Wednesday, with Jimmy Murphy making Foulkes captain. Leading a club in complete disarray on the pitch was an honour for Bill, but it was also a burden that brought huge pressure, as he explained to the *Daily Telegraph* in 2008: "It was difficult to go on. We had some good players, but they weren't all fully fit. I don't know how the hell I carried on. I just found some strength. I had to go on."

Buoyed by the support of a capacity crowd at Old Trafford, United managed an amazing 3-0 victory over Sheffield Wednesday, thanks to two goals from Shay Brennan and one from Alex Dawson. Football had returned to the home of Manchester United and the victory and atmosphere before, during and after the game, supported the belief that the club had a future.

It was unknown whether Matt Busby would be able to summon the strength, both mentally and emotionally to resume his role as manager. His first reaction was to never have anything to do with football again, but his wife pleaded with him, reasoning that the boys who had lost their lives would have wanted him to carry on.

In his 1973 autobiography entitled *Soccer at the Top, My Life in Football*, Busby provided an insight into his mindset as he recovered in hospital: "In my consciousness I wanted to die because my tortured mind kept saying; 'Was I to blame?'. The inner voice kept on saying; 'If I had not taken them into Europe those eight Busby Babes and the other victims would be with us still.'"

On April 18, 71 days after the crash, Matt Busby returned to Manchester, making the journey from Switzerland by rail and sea. In his absence, United's scratch team of emergency signings and youthful reserves miraculously battled their way into the FA Cup Final.

Manchester United resumed European competition on May 8, beating Italian giants AC Milan 2-1 in the first leg of the Champions' Cup semi-final at Old Trafford. However, just a week later, the return leg in Italy saw the Red Devils knocked out of the competition following a 4-0 defeat.

At the end of the season, UEFA offered the Football Association the opportunity to enter United in the competition for the following season as a tribute to the players and officials who lost their lives. The FA declined, choosing to only enter the league champions Wolverhampton Wanderers, who had topped the table before Munich.

Once back at Old Trafford, Matt Busby was focused on rebuilding a club he had already revived once before, as he explained in his autobiography: "I was determined to keep the name of Manchester United on people's lips. We had always to look as if we were doing something. Having been the greatest we would not settle for anything less, and our supporters deserved nothing less."

Since the tragedy and the impact it had upon the world, United have remained one of the best supported clubs in Britain and further afield. The depth of feeling between the club and its supporters was sealed, forming an indefinite bond and ensuring a lasting legacy for the Busby Babes who perished in Munich.

Exactly what that immensely talented group of young men could have gone on to achieve will never be known. The potential lost was immeasurable and Busby believed they would have been one of the best teams ever seen, later saying: "I am convinced that I could have sat back and watched this collection of infants pile up a list of championships and cups for years to come. They were surely the greatest group of young footballers in one team ever gathered together."

3

THE GOLDEN ERA

Both Clubs Fighting for Glory

Three days after Manchester United's emotional FA Cup victory over Sheffield Wednesday, Old Trafford hosted its first post-Munich league match, as United drew 1-1 with Nottingham Forest. The remainder of the First Division campaign was predictably tough for Jimmy Murphy's men, as the patched up team could only manage one victory in their remaining 14 games, claiming five draws and eventually finishing ninth.

United saved their best form for the FA Cup as their home victory over Wednesday set up a sixth round tie at West Bromwich Albion. After a hard fought 2-2 draw at The Hawthorns, United sealed their progress into the semi-final thanks to a last-minute winner from Colin Webster.

Just one step away from Wembley and an unlikely Cup Final, United faced Fulham at Villa Park. The teams couldn't be separated after the first 90 minutes following another 2-2 draw, but United triumphed 5-3 in an enthralling replay at Highbury, with Alex Dawson firing home a hat-trick.

The Wembley final took place on May 3, 1958, less than three months after the tragedy of Munich. United faced a Bolton Wanderers team featuring the towering England centre forward, Nat Lofthouse, who would play a crucial role in the destination of the trophy.

With the exception of the Bolton Wanderers supporters, the whole of England was rooting for United. Munich survivors Harry Gregg, Bill Foulkes, Bobby Charlton and Dennis Viollet started the game, as just two of the players that played in the previous year's Cup Final against Aston Villa remained in the line-up. Jimmy Murphy led the team out under the twin towers with Foulkes captaining the side. Still on the road to recovery, Matt Busby was able to attend the game on crutches as United attempted to end the most disastrous of seasons with a glimmer of glory.

However, Bolton hadn't read the script and Nat Lofthouse gave Wanderers a third minute lead with a smart finish. The timing of the goal seemed to deflate the United players who struggled to get back into the game, despite a thunderbolt of a strike from Bobby Charlton which slammed off the upright, and Bolton went on to extend their lead early in the second half. The goal again came from Lofthouse, but it was one of the most controversial goals scored in a Cup Final.

With 55 minutes played Lofthouse bundled into United goalkeeper Harry Gregg, catching him with an elbow and sending the ball into the net, for a goal that would never have stood in the modern era. Munich hero Gregg required lengthy treatment but the goal was given and Bolton held on to deservedly win the game 2-0. It had been an emotional and exhausting afternoon for everybody connected with Manchester United. Murphy's men had done the club proud, illustrating United's determination to escape the shadow left by Munich and go on to celebrate the memories of the players who had lost their lives by continuing to achieve and continuing to entertain.

United's recovery from Munich was further aided the following season thanks to a gutsy second place finish to Wolverhampton Wanderers, who collected their second successive Championship. Busby was back in the dugout and the team were also buoyed by the return of Munich survivor Albert Scanlon, the signing of Albert Quixall from Sheffield Wednesday and the introduction of further promising youngsters.

The Red Devils enjoyed an awesome run of 11 wins in 12 games between November and February and went on to score over 100 goals in the league, including 29 from the constantly improving Bobby Charlton, and 21 from Dennis Viollet. Charlton had emerged as the team's brightest attacking spark and Busby would look to build his side around the young forward, soon identifying the perfect attacking players to complement him.

After a solid seventh place finish in 1960, in a season when United again hit over 100 goals and Viollet top scored with 32, Bubsy knew his team lacked consistency and realised that further signings were required. Tough-tackling midfielder Maurice Setters had already been added to the ranks from West Brom and Irish left-back Noel Cantwell followed later on in the year. A calming influence who played with authority and intelligence, the former West Ham United defender was soon given the captaincy. But progress remained slow as the team continued to gel and 1961 only brought another seventh place finish. Despite the addition of clinical centre-forward David Herd from Arsenal, things got worse the following season as United slumped to 15th, with the League Title looking more elusive than ever.

With the European dream still burning brightly within, Busby was determined to bring the glory days back to Old Trafford and was prepared to take swift and significant action in the transfer market to do so. The club's big name signing during the summer of 1962 would go on to became a Manchester United legend. Scottish striker Denis Law had impressed at Manchester City before leaving the Blues for Italian side Torino in 1961. Busby wanted a goal-scorer to play off Charlton and was prepared to pay a record £115,000 fee for his countryman.

Law had spent a single season in Italy, adding to his reputation with a decent goals return, but he struggled to settle on the continent and relished the chance to return to Manchester. Forming a potent strike-force with David Herd, ably supported by Bobby Charlton, Law soon made an impact at Old Trafford, using his awesome aerial ability and instinctive nature in the box to score goal after goal.

As well as expensive signings, Busby kept true to his principles and continued to blood younger players in the first team, including the hugely promising talents of Johnny Giles and Nobby Stiles. The team was starting to take shape, but the manager knew something was still missing. He needed a ball-playing midfielder to supply the ammunition for his potent attack. Busby identified that man as Paddy Crerand, another Scotsman who had been pulling the strings in the Glasgow Celtic midfield since 1958, and parted with £43,000 to bring him to Old Trafford.

The new line-up didn't click instantly and couldn't reverse the club's fortunes during the 1962-63 campaign, as United ended the season a disappointing 19th. While league consistency proved elusive, the FA Cup provided a welcome distraction for the Red Devils, as Busby's men progressed all the way to the final to face Leicester City at Wembley.

Leicester had finished fourth in the First Division and were many people's favourites to lift the trophy, thanks to their well-organised and solid defence, which was backed up by England goalkeeper Gordon Banks. But United sensed it was their day and the energetic Law was almost unplayable up front, terrorising the Leicester defence and finding space with ease.

The vision of Crerand and movement of Law was an irresistible combination, and the size of the Wembley pitch only accentuated their brilliance. The Scotsmen were responsible for the opening goal on 29 minutes as Crerand found Law with an inch-perfect pass and the lively striker drove the ball past Banks with confidence.

United continued to dominate in the second half and doubled their advantage in the 58th minute when David Herd finished smartly. Leicester rallied and managed to reduce the arrears, but United soon grabbed a third through Herd's second of the game, making the final scoreline 3-1. The victory saw United lift their first major trophy since the tragedy of 1958, as Busby finally got his hands on the Cup.

The lowest point for Manchester City during the sixties came in 1963 when the team were relegated after finishing 21st in the table, costing Les McDowall his job. McDowall's reign would be remembered for the 1956 FA Cup success and the signing of promising young striker Denis Law. A man who would go on to have a remarkable career at both Manchester clubs, the Scotsman was snapped up from Huddersfield Town for what would prove to be a bargain £55,000 fee, even though it was a British transfer record at the time.

George Poyser who had been McDowall's assistant, replaced him the dugout, but couldn't return the team to the top flight, despite a promising first season, as City reached the semi-finals of the League Cup and finished sixth in the Second Division. Poyser made some astute signings, including strikers Derek Kevan and Jimmy Murray, who went on to score 51 goals between them in their first season at Maine Road.

The situation worsened during the 1964-65 campaign with fans dismayed at the quality of football being served up, voting with their feet, resulting in the club's lowest league attendance of just 8,015 against Swindon Town. George Poyser was relieved of his duties in the Easter of 1965 and City went on to finish in 11th place in the Second Division, their lowest ever league finish up to that point. Later that year, the Blues developed a new club badge based around the central part of the City of Manchester coat of arms.

With City stagnating in the second tier, the club's board of directors knew they needed a change of approach and had identified a man they felt would take the club back into the top flight and take the first steps on the journey back to glory. That man was Joe Mercer.

The former Aston Villa manager had been forced to step down from his role at Villa Park due to ill-health. He had suffered a stroke but, despite being given a clean bill of health by doctors, he was sacked by the Midlands club. The decision would soon be seen as an error of judgement by the Villans' board and it provided City with the opportunity to approach their number one candidate. When the Blues offered Mercer the opportunity to get back into management and awaken a sleeping giant, he immediately jumped at the chance.

Mercer, a former England international as a player, had won the inaugural League Cup during his four-year spell with Villa, after beginning his managerial career with Sheffield United. One of his first and arguably most astute decisions was the appointment of highly-rated young Plymouth Argyle manager, Malcolm Allison, as his assistant. Like Busby and Murphy at Old Trafford, the pair complemented each other perfectly, with Mercer's more traditional approach benefitting from the youthful exuberance and training ground capabilities of Allison.

Mercer's first season in charge ended in glory, as City won the Second Division title and gained promotion back to the highest level. During the summer of 1965, Mercer made two of his best signings for the club, bringing in skilful winger Mike Summerbee from Swindon Town and elegant midfielder Colin Bell from Bury, and both men were influential in the team's impressive promotion campaign. The Blues clocked up 59 points, finishing five clear of second placed Southampton and only losing five games from 42, as they won a then-record sixth Second Division title. Neil Young, a Manchester-born striker who had been brought through the ranks at Maine Road, top scored with 17 goals in all competitions, proving that it wasn't just United that could successfully cultivate local talent.

The 1963 FA Cup success saw United return to European competition in the Cup Winners' Cup, but their campaign was short-lived as Portuguese side Sporting Lisbon defeated The Reds 6-4 on aggregate. The team again enjoyed an impressive FA Cup run, reaching the semi-finals before bowing out to West Ham United, but it was in the league that the greatest progress was made as Busby's men finished in second place and started to look like a team capable of returning to the summit of English football.

As well as United's improving league displays, the 1963-64 campaign is remarkable for the introduction of another precociously talented youngster; a supremely gifted young Irishman who would go on to become one of the finest players the world has ever seen. That young man's name was George Best, who was given his United debut on September 14, 1963, against West Bromwich Albion at Old Trafford. Other youngsters, such as David Sadler, were also breaking into the side but Best stood out immediately as something special. His natural ability on the ball was almost unrivalled and the crowd soon took to him. Best's second start came against Burnley at Old Trafford and he scored his first goal for the club as United romped home 5-1 winners.

Still a teenager, Best would soon prove impossible to leave out of the team and United's holy trinity of Law, Best and Charlton started to blend and produce moments of sheer footballing brilliance. Although United still struggled for consistency, they again sealed runners-up spot in 1964, as Liverpool finished 10 points clear in first place. Denis Law was at the peak of his powers and ended the campaign with an impressive tally of 46 goals in all competitions, including 30 in 30 league games. Away from first team matters, United's youngsters claimed the FA Youth Cup for the first time since 1957, confirming that the club's youthful foundations had returned.

Busby was getting closer to finding the pattern he wanted and returned to the transfer market in the summer of 1964 to add another winger to his squad, bringing in John Connelly from Burnley. It proved an inspired signing as Connelly's direct wing-play was the final elusive piece in the Championship jigsaw, as the Red Devils finally lifted the League title in 1965, nine years after their previous triumph.

United were irresistible going forward, but the creative talent was only able to flourish because of the foundations laid by an uncompromisingly solid defence. Marshalled by Bill Foulkes, Nobby Stiles, Shay Brennan and Tony Dunne, the backline conceded just 39 goals and both goals and clean sheets proved crucial as the title was eventually decided on goal average, after United and Leeds had finished level on 61 points.

While United excelled, Manchester City remained stranded in the Second Division as a decade that would eventually deliver so much started painfully slowly. In fact, City's lack of progression led to the club's Vice-Chairman coming up with an idea that would seem crazy just a few seasons later when the Blues would be competing with and beating United to the First Division title. The almost unthinkable notion of a potential merger between Manchester's two biggest clubs was raised by Frank Johnson during the 1963-64 season. Even though the rivalry between United and City was nowhere near as fierce at the time, there was still a tribal element involved as the supporters took great pride in following their own team and being part of the identity that both clubs had created. Johnson's idea wasn't made public until January 1965, prompting supporters of both clubs to send letters of complaint about the proposal and voice their opposition.

City were struggling financially but their future wasn't in immediate danger, particularly with their significant fanbase. Vice-Chairman Johnson had already proposed that the Football League should be split into north and south sections and would follow that concept with a direct approach to Manchester United regarding the possible merger. Details of what the merger may have included remain unclear, but there were suggestions that both clubs would at the very least share Old Trafford as a joint-home. A group of City shareholders, fronted by Peter Donoghue, pushed for changes at board level, demanding resignations as they attempted to counter the proposed merger. While the board wasn't entirely overthrown, Donoghue's group joined the existing board to help secure the club's future.

Although any potential merger doesn't appear to have ever been that close to taking place, it remains one of the more remarkable but lesser-known twists in the ongoing battle for Manchester. A city with a huge appetite for football, the existence of two clubs of such significant size was far from a saturating factor. On the contrary, it allowed them to feed off each other, developing a rivalry that would be embraced within the city and further afield. The thought of the two clubs joining forces was almost as unthinkable then as it is now and Manchester City will always be grateful that Frank Johnson's proposal remained just that. As the decade progressed, rather than a merger, the main element that would help bring success to Maine Road was a Mercer.

United's 1965 title victory sealed a return to the European Champions' Cup as the club were back where they believed they belonged; competing with the continent's elite for the biggest trophy in the game. The pressures and strains of European football made the defence of their First Division title more difficult, but with a strong squad at his disposal, Matt Busby was confident his team was capable of coping with the burden of expectation and making history.

Ultimately, United's first return to the tournament they wanted to win most ended with disappointment at the semi-final stage. As fate would have it, the Red Devils faced Partizan Belgrade, meaning a return to the city that staged the Busby Babes' last ever game. George Best had suffered a torn cartilage in his knee during a sixth round FA Cup tie against West Ham United and, despite starting the away leg against Partizan, the injury got worse before it got better and soon required an operation, meaning Best missed the return match at Old Trafford. Partizan held a 2-0 advantage and advanced 2-1 on aggregate after United could only muster a single goal in Manchester through Nobby Stiles.

United again reached the later stages of the FA Cup, narrowly losing to Everton in a semi-final that took place just three days after their second leg tie against Partizan Belgrade. The cup commitments impacted on the team's league form and United could only manage a fourth place finish in defence of their title as Liverpool claimed another championship, meaning Busby and his players would have to wait another year to compete for the European Cup.

The 1966 England World Cup squad included Manchester United's inspirational Bobby Charlton and his close friend Nobby Stiles, who would both go on to play prominent roles in their country's eventual success, and winger John Connelly, who didn't figure after playing in the Three Lions' opener against Uruguay. No Manchester City players were selected in the 22-man squad.

As English football was enjoying its greatest ever moment, Manchester City were still basking in the glory of their convincing return to the top flight. Mercer and Allison were building a team with great potential. But the 1966-67 season was one of consolidation for the Blues, who claimed a 15th place finish and 39 points. City made an important addition to their squad in 1966, snapping up 30-year-old right-back Tony Book from Plymouth Argyle. Allison had worked with Book, who would go on to become City's captain, at a number of clubs and was confident that his experience would be a vital ingredient to the squad. Book missed just one game during the 1966-67 campaign and became the inaugural winner of the club's Player of the Year award.

During the summer of 1966, Matt Busby made a few changes to his United squad, with his most significant addition being the signing of Chelsea goalkeeper Alex Stepney for £50,000. Since Harry Gregg had left Old Trafford earlier that year, United lacked the presence and confidence of a top class custodian, and Stepney would provide both of those qualities.

It's often said that every team needs a top goalkeeper to achieve greatness and the addition of Stepney gave United a huge boost as they went on to reclaim the 1967 First Division in style. The first Manchester derby in three seasons took place at Old Trafford in September 1966 and saw United claim a 1-0 victory. The Reds remained unbeaten at Old Trafford all season and consistently picked up points on their travels, including a 6-1 victory at West Ham United that clinched the title.

United destroyed teams at Old Trafford, with many opponents overwhelmed by the attacking talents they were up against. The team's home matches regularly sold out, as did their away encounters for that matter, with opposing fans desperate to get a glimpse of Best, Law and Charlton – a trio whose footballing excellence captured the public's imagination. As the Championship returned to the Old Trafford trophy cabinet, the club looked to the 1967-68 campaign with great anticipation. Would United finally claim what seemed to be their destiny and lift the European Champions' Cup?

David Herd left United for Stoke City in the summer of 1967, but Busby didn't rush into the transfer market for a replacement, once again putting his trust in youth by bringing Manchester-born Brian Kidd into the first-team picture. Although just 18 years old, Kidd was a powerful physical specimen and, like so many other United youngsters before him, settled in almost instantly, playing without fear and expressing himself in a team containing some of the biggest names in the game. Kidd, whose father was a Manchester City fan, would go on to represent the Maine Road club, but not before playing a major part in one of the most historic nights in United's history.

After an opening day defeat to the Toffees, United went on an 11-game unbeaten run, securing a five point lead at the top of the table for the second half of the season. Manchester City made an important signing early in the 1967-68 campaign, bringing in Francis Lee from Bolton Wanderers. Soon after Lee's October arrival, City went on an impressive 11-match unbeaten run that rocketed them up the table and into title contention alongside United.

Lee's signing helped lift the club after two successive league defeats, which included a 2-1 reverse to Manchester United, in game that saw Colin Bell put City ahead inside five minutes and Bobby Charlton bag a brace for United. Joe Mercer and Malcolm Allison believed their team was close to greatness and just lacked one player. Once that player was identified as Francis 'Franny' Lee their judgement was instantly rewarded after Lee inspired City to a 2-0 home victory over Wolverhampton Wanderers on his debut.

Midway through their unbeaten run, City faced Tottenham Hotspur in a famous contest at Maine Road. In snowy conditions, the icy pitch made things difficult for both teams, but thanks to a modification of the City players' boots, when Tony Book suggested the players loosened their studs to help provide a better grip on the slippery surface, the Blues played some fantastic football.

Spurs' England international striker Jimmy Greaves gave the visitors an early lead before Colin Bell equalised for City ahead of half-time. After the interval, Mercer's men blitzed the Londoners' defence and added three further goals to grab a 4-1 victory that left City just a point behind league leaders United.

The unbeaten run came to an end at Christmas, with back-to-back defeats as the team dropped down to fourth place before regaining their form at the turn of the year, beginning 1968 with seven games without defeat.

City's next defeat came to former player Don Revie's Leeds United, a loss that allowed the United of Manchester to reclaim top spot ahead of a highly anticipated Manchester derby at Old Trafford. United were on a poor run of form, despite their solid start to the season, but with the title at stake the Reds stormed into an early lead after George Best found the net with just 38 seconds on the clock. However, the home side were shell-shocked by the performance of their rivals, who fought back to claim a vital 3-1 victory. The defeat was one of five in eight games for United and saw the Championship initiative handed to the blue half of Manchester.

United lost further ground on City following a surprise loss to West Bromwich Albion and the Blues capitalised on the Red Devils' slip-up by beating Sheffield Wednesday, meaning that victory in their final three fixtures would guarantee the club's first League Championship in 51 years.

City sealed maximum points in the first two games thanks to a 2-0 victory over Everton at Maine Road, which featured Tony Book's first goal for the club, and an impressive 3-1 win over Spurs at White Hart Lane, setting up a last day of the season title decider against Newcastle United at St James' Park.

Going into the final fixtures, both Manchester clubs were level on points, but City held the advantage thanks to their better goal average - a tale that would be replicated the next time that both clubs challenged for the title some 40 years later—but the Blues still needed a win because third-placed Liverpool lay three points behind with a game in hand, meaning they could claim the title if both City and United faltered.

The red half of Manchester faced Newcastle United's local rivals, Sunderland, at Old Trafford on the last day. Sunderland had finished bottom of the table and United were huge favourites to claim maximum points.

City's game against Newcastle turned into a classic. The Magpies had little to play for after finishing in 10th place, but in front of a passionate home crowd they put in an impressive performance. Buoyed by 20,000 travelling Blues fans, Mike Summerbee calmed the City nerves by opening the scoring on 13 minutes but the lead didn't last for long as Newcastle soon levelled matters. Neil Young reclaimed the lead for the visitors but Newcastle pegged them back again before the interval, ensuring a 2-2 scoreline at half-time.

Straight after the break, Young grabbed his second of the afternoon to edge City ahead again, before Francis Lee provided a bit of breathing space, finding the back of the net after 63 minutes to put City 4-2 up. A late Newcastle goal set up a nervy finish, but City held on for a famous 4-3 victory that confirmed that the title would return to Maine Road. It was the club's first major trophy since the 1956 FA Cup triumph, and saw them qualify for European competition for the first time. Following the game, Malcolm Allison famously claimed that City would 'terrify Europe' and with the devastating attacking football that had taken them to the title, it was a statement accompanied by plenty of substance.

City's title triumph had been compounded by United's inability to beat Sunderland at Old Trafford, as the visitors pulled off a shock 2-1 victory, but in terms of the league it was all about the Blues. One of the stars of the season had been Mike Summerbee who played up front and finished with 20 goals, just one behind top scorer Neil Young, while the energy, elegance and goals of Colin Bell and Francis Lee in midfield were equally important.

Going into their last day decider against Sunderland, United knew they had another huge occasion on the horizon, with the European Cup semi-final second leg against Real Madrid in Spain only four days away. Clearly the players wanted to achieve a league and European double, but with the shadow of Munich still felt at the club, lifting the European Cup had become an obsession. City had been worthy league winners and deserved their title as Champions of England, but United wanted a greater crown; they were focused on becoming Champions of Europe.

United's star was George Best, who enjoyed his most prolific goal-scoring season in a red shirt, notching 28 that helped him win the Footballer of the Year award. Best had shown match-winning brilliance throughout United's European adventure, including in the 1968 final against Benfica.

During a quarter-final tie against Benfica two seasons before the '68 campaign, a spellbinding performance by Best in the Stadium of Light had seen him christened 'El Beatle' by the Portuguese press. United went into the second leg in Portugal with a slender advantage following a 3-2 victory at Old Trafford. A tight game was expected but Best had other ideas and soon took charge of proceedings. George grabbed his first goal with just six minutes on the clock, heading home a Tony Dunne free-kick, before scoring an absolute belter after 12 minutes. With the familiar close-control that made the ball appear an extension of his body, Best weaved past three defenders before slotting the ball home with the calmest of finishes. Another driving run created a goal for John Connelly before a Shay Brennan own goal gave the hosts some hope. However, it proved short-lived as late goals from Law and Charlton put extra gloss on a truly memorable performance. But the game belonged to Best and saw his profile rise, making the Belfast boy one of the most feared players on the planet.

United's opponents in the 1968 final knew all about the Reds' greatest talent, just as English clubs were well aware of the dangers posed by Benfica's world class striker Eusebio, but stopping either man when it mattered was a near impossible task. Before lining up against the Portuguese giants in the final, United first had to dispose of the greatest team in European history, Real Madrid. To be the best, United had to beat the best and it was fitting that their semi-final opponents possessed the ability, attacking philosophies and romance that had so enticed Busby to begin United's European adventure.

Real Madrid had once tried to entice Busby to Spain as manager during the Busby Babes era, but the Scotsman remained loyal to United, as he later explained: "Mr Bernabeu and the officials there said it would be a tremendous salary and they would make Madrid a heaven for me. I eventually said to Mr Bernabeu that I was very grateful but heaven is here in Manchester."

It was United's fourth European semi-final and it began with a narrow 1-0 victory thanks to another crucial strike from George Best. It was the slenderest of leads to take to the imposing Bernabeu Stadium, with Real famed for turning on the style in front of their fanatical home supporters.

Denis Law was sidelined with injury for the trip to Madrid, but Busby was able to recall the vastly experienced Bill Foulkes in defence. Madrid were playing with their usual flowing style, leaving the United players chasing shadows. 'Los Meringues' made their dominance tell with half an hour played, thanks to a Pirri header before taking the lead through Francisco Gento. A Zoco own goal brought United back into the tie, but moments later Amancio Amaro scored to put Real 3-2 ahead at the interval.

With United facing another semi-final exit, Busby's half-time words did the trick as United surged forward with wave after wave of attack. The Madrid defence remained stubborn, but United retained the belief and the courage to play under extreme pressure and, when Paddy Crerand's free-kick was nodded down by Bill Foulkes, David Sadler flicked the ball home to level the tie. An unlikely provider for the goal, Bill Foulkes went one step better as United pressed for a winner. The centre back began a run forward after seeing George Best receive a throw-in and dribble down the right wing. Perhaps knowing that his team-mate would beat his man and create space for a cross, Foulkes continued forward, and when Best's near-post centre fell into his path the experienced Englishman finished emphatically to level the scores at 3-3 to send United through to the final with a

4-3 aggregate win.

Seeing Foulkes pop up in the area and stroke the ball home shocked and delighted his team-mates in equal measure. Foulkes was the only survivor of the other semi-final between the two clubs some 11 years earlier and it was fitting that he would play such a big role in the outcome of the tie. Matt Busby was now just one step away from realising his European dream.

The build-up to the final at Wembley was filled with reference to the Munich air crash and how Busby had rebuilt the club. With so many people all over Britain rooting for a Reds victory, no matter who they supported, the country was united.

Stung by the memories of George Best's brilliance in Lisbon, Benfica attempted to man-mark the United winger. This allowed his team-mates more freedom on the ball, including the lively David Sadler who created United's opener with a devilish cross that was guided home by a perfectly timed Bobby Charlton header.

United created plenty of golden chances, but a top class team like Benfica are always likely to have a spell of dominance, and just ten minutes from time, the Portuguese pressure finally told as Jaime Graca slammed an equaliser past Alex Stepney. Benfica sensed victory and surged forward for a late winner and when the ball fell to Eusebio, who had been largely kept quiet by the close attentions of Nobby Stiles, it looked as though the dream was over.

The powerful striker, nicknamed the 'Black Pearl', burst into the box and looked certain to score as Stepney advanced from his line to close him down. Eusebio hammered a strike towards the goal, but Stepney showed catlike reflexes to catch the ball and keep United in the contest. It was a world class save that left Eusebio aghast at what he'd seen, so much so that he patted the English stopper on the back and generously applauded.

Benfica's potential match-winner had been denied but, as the game went into extra-time, United's danger-man soon had his chance for glory. Just a minute into the first period, Alex Stepney launched a clearance up field to Brian Kidd, who flicked the ball into the path of George Best. Surging into a rare few yards of space, Best dribbled towards goal, leaving defenders in his wake and finding himself one on one with Benfica goalkeeper, Henrique. With a drop of the shoulder and quick shimmy, Best showed the composure Eusebio had lacked to dance around the advancing stopper and clip the ball into the back of the net with his left foot.

On this emotion-filled night, United displayed the focus of a team that believed in destiny rather than one burdened by it, and while the goal ignited Busby's men it completely deflated Benfica. Sensing blood, the Red Devils continued to attack at pace, stretching their opponents' defence thanks to the expert wing play of Best and Aston. It wasn't long before the net was bulging again, as Brian Kidd was afforded enough space to aim two headers at goal, the second one bouncing in off the cross-bar to put United 3-1 ahead. There was time for Bobby Charlton to add extra gloss to the victory as he flicked Kidd's right-wing cross into the roof of the net to spark scenes of jubilation.

Busby had realised his dream of seeing Manchester United become the first English club to lift the Champions' Cup. The emotions of relief and joy were also tempered by sadness and reflection by both Busby and Bobby Charlton as the two men hugged each other on the pitch before the captain climbed the Wembley steps to lift the trophy.

After the game, Busby spoke emotively to the media, attempting to sum up the gravity of the players' achievement: "They've done us proud. They came back with all their hearts to show everyone what Manchester United are made of. This is the most wonderful thing that has happened in my life and I am the proudest man in England tonight."

Ten years after the sadness of Munich, the club had finally conquered European football. It was fitting that Brian Kidd, a 19-year-old local lad, would play such a significant role in the final, scoring a goal on his birthday and showing such youthful exuberance throughout the contest. Following the glory of Wembley, Matt Busby was knighted and George Best was named both Footballer of the Year and European Player of the Year, the youngest to have received the accolade. United had dominated the Ballon d'Or award in the 1960s, as Denis Law was given the accolade in 1964 and Bobby Charlton enjoyed the same honour two years later.

Bill Foulkes, the other crash survivor, who also shared a moving embrace with the manager at the final whistle, later reflected on his feelings when the achievement was realised: "I had come the whole way with the Boss trying to make Manchester United the champions of Europe. I thought the destruction of our team at Munich would have been the end of it, but he patiently put together another side. I'm proud to have been part of it, and for those of us who lost our friends coming home from a European Cup tie in 1958, our victory seemed the right tribute to their memory."

United's victory meant that both Manchester clubs would participate in the European Cup during the 1968-69 season, and the city became the first in Britain to have two sides competing for the biggest prize in club football.

Denis Law had to watch the final from hospital following surgery on the knee injury that blighted the second half of his season, but the Scotsman's absence meant that, of the starting eleven, only two of the players had been signed for transfer fees, with Busby bringing the rest of the team through the Old Trafford ranks. His methodical attention to detail, as well as his trust in the players and having the patience to wait for the team to gel, was key to the manager's ability to create collective greatness on the pitch.

4

THE HEROES

Part 1

Throughout their history, both City and United have seen hundreds of players labelled as legends and heroes, but a select few transcend their generation, going on to be remembered as all-time greats. Part 1 of a tribute to some of the most successful, talented and committed players to have appeared for either club, focuses on the men that made their mark between 1900 and 1970.

Billy Meredith

POSITION:
Outside Forward-Winger
BORN:
July 30, 1874 in Chirk, Wales
DIED:
April 19, 1958
CITY CAREER:
1894-1906 and 1921-1924
APPEARANCES:
394
GOALS:
151
HONOURS:
Second Division Title (1899, 1903), FA Cup (1904)
UNITED CAREER:
1906-1921
APPEARANCES:
335
GOALS: 36
HONOURS:
First Division Title (1908, 1911), FA Cup (1909)

A natural-born footballer whose close-control and dribbling ability made him one of the most entertaining and effective players of his generation, Billy Meredith excelled at both Manchester City and United during his career. Known for constantly chewing on a toothpick, the Welsh wizard possessed the end product to back up his nimble footwork; able to swing in a dangerous cross or thump a shot on target. He remains one of City's record scorers, and while he wasn't as prolific at United, he created countless goals and was an influential part of a Red Devils side that won two First Division titles. Meredith was one of the British game's first superstars.

TRIVIA

Meredith's career was also remarkable because of its longevity. He ended his second spell with City by playing his final game for the club just 120 days short of his 50th birthday.

Frank Swift

POSITION:
Goalkeeper
BORN:
December 26, 1913 in Blackpool, England
DIED:
February 6, 1958
CITY CAREER:
1932-1949
APPEARANCES:
378
HONOURS:
FA Cup (1934), First Division Title (1937)

THEY SAID ...

"For a big man Swifty was phenomenally agile. He narrowed the angle for an opponent to shoot in as if he had made a science of it. His showmanship was not exhibitionism. He wanted to demonstrate that football could include a bit of fun. He was immensely popular everywhere he played, as popular with the opposition and opposition supporters as with his own team and his own team's supporters. If any footballer could be termed lovable, Big Swifty was the man." Matt Busby.

One of the finest goalkeepers in Manchester City's history, Frank Swift spent his entire career with the club and was a major factor in the Blues' FA Cup and Championship successes during the 1930s. He went on to make over 200 consecutive first team appearances for City, and was ever-present as the club claimed the 1937 title. Swift's giant presence between the posts, as well as his agility and bravery, made him one of the most talented keepers of his generation and, alongside his larger than life personality, helped him make the England number one jersey his own. Frank may have gone on to become the club's record appearance holder had the Second World War not interrupted his City career. He retired from the game in 1950 and became a football writer. While reporting for *The News of the World*, Frank was killed in the 1958 Munich air disaster.

Peter Doherty

POSITION:
Inside-forward
BORN:
June 5, 1913 in Magherafelt, Ireland
DIED:
April 6, 1990
CITY CAREER:
1936-1945
APPEARANCES:
133
GOALS:
81
HONOURS:
First Division Title (1937)

A key element of City's 1937 title winning team, the hugely gifted inside-forward played with boundless energy and equal measures of flair. Excellent in possession, both in terms of dribbling technique and passing ability, Doherty joined City in a club-record £10,000 deal from Blackpool and soon proved to be value for money, scoring 32 goals in 45 matches during the Blues Championship winning season. The skilful Irishman would have surely added to his impressive scoring record if the Second World War hadn't taken seven years of his career.

THEY SAID ...

"Of all the opponents I faced I particularly remember Doherty, who was unplayable on his day. He was built like a greyhound, very fast and elusive but with stamina, too. He had a Rolls-Royce engine in him." Joe Mercer.

Bert Trautmann

POSITION:
Goalkeeper
BORN:
October 22, 1923 in Bremen, Germany
CITY CAREER:
1949-1964
APPEARANCES:
545
GOALS:
0
HONOURS:
FA Cup (1956)

The perfect replacement for departing legend Frank Swift, Bert Trautmann went on to enjoy a hugely successful 15-year spell as Manchester City's first-choice goalkeeper. Unlike the modern game, it was almost unheard of for a player outside of the British Isles to line up for an English team during the 1950s, particularly one from Germany, but Bert's swashbuckling displays between the posts ensured that he was soon accepted by the City fans as well as the British public. Trautmann was a genuine athlete, using his strength, speed and bravery to sniff out countless attacks and make match-winning saves.

THEY SAID ...

"There have only been two world-class goalkeepers. One was Lev Yashin, the other was the German boy who played in Manchester - Trautmann." Lev Yashin

Roy Paul

POSITION:
Central Defender
BORN:
April 18, 1920 in Ton Pentre, Wales
DIED:
May 21, 2002
CITY CAREER:
1950-1957
APPEARANCES:
293
GOALS:
9
HONOURS:
FA Cup (1956)

The inspirational Roy Paul led by example during his Manchester City career. A versatile defender who could play anywhere across the backline, Paul was a good reader of the game and an adept passer of the ball. The Welshman gave excellent service to City during his seven years at Maine Road, which included the FA Cup success of 1956 and is still remembered as one of the club's most influential players.

TRIVIA

When Roy Paul joined Manchester City from Swansea City in 1950 the £19,500 fee was a British record for a half-back.

Joe Hayes

POSITION:
Striker
BORN:
January 20, 1936 in Kearsley, England
DIED:
February 4, 1999
CITY CAREER:
1953-1965
APPEARANCES:
364
GOALS:
152
HONOURS:
FA Cup (1956)

A reliable goal-scorer for City during his 12-year spell at Maine Road, hard-working striker Joe Hayes was always comfortable in front of goal and had the knack of finding the net when the Blues needed it most. A man for the big occasion, Hayes scored in City's 1955 FA Cup Final defeat but also bagged the opening goal of the 1956 Final, putting City on the path to a 3-1 victory over Birmingham City. Joe is still regarded as one of the best all-round strikers to have played for the Blues.

TRIVIA

Joe Hayes is Manchester City's fourth highest goal-scorer of all time.

Mike Summerbee

POSITION:

Right winger-Forward

BORN:

December 15, 1942 in Preston, England

CITY CAREER:

1965-1975

APPEARANCES:

452

GOALS:

68

HONOURS:

Second Division title (1966), First Division title (1968), FA Cup (1969), League Cup (1970), European Cup Winners' Cup (1970)

A skilful and ultra-competitive winger or striker, Mike Summerbee was a crucial part of an extremely dangerous Manchester City attack that fired the Blues to the most successful period in their history. Much like the holy trinity of Manchester United, the names Bell, Lee and Summerbee are synonymous with that era. An excellent crosser of the ball who could beat men with both pace and technique, Summerbee also knew where the goal was. Nicknamed 'Buzzer' by his team-mates, the former Swindon Town man was also known for a fiery temperament, which led to Francis Lee describing him as 'retaliating first'. Mike has been Manchester City's Club Ambassador since 2009.

TRIVIA

Summerbee starred in the cult football film *Escape to Victory* alongside Sylvester Stallone, Michael Caine and Pele.

Francis Lee

POSITION:
Forward
BORN:
April 29, 1944 in Westhoughton, England
CITY CAREER:
1959-1976
APPEARANCES:
330
GOALS:
148
HONOURS:
First Division title (1968), FA Cup (1969), League Cup (1970, 1976), European Cup Winners' Cup (1970)

The catalyst for the 1968 title win, Francis Lee was a stocky centre forward who played as though his life depended on it. A prolific scorer for City, Lee was a classy finisher who instantly developed a telepathic understanding with the likes of Bell, Summerbee and Young. Franny scored the winning goal as the Blues claimed their first ever European trophy and his addition is seen by many as the crucial ingredient of the 1968 title winning team. Lee was a penalty expert and holds the English record for most spot-kicks converted in a season, having notched 15 for City during the 1971-72 season; a campaign that saw him hit 35 goals in 46 games.

THEY SAID...

"He was very confident. He knew he was a good player; you didn't need to tell him. He used to take penalties and aim them at the goalkeeper, and the goalkeeper would try to get out of the way. He used to take a right run up it, and then whack. He was some player." Joe Mercer.

Tony Book

POSITION:
Right-back
BORN:
September 4, 1934 in Bath, England
CITY CAREER:
1966-1974
APPEARANCES:
311
GOALS:
3
HONOURS:
First Division Title (1968), FA Cup (1969), League Cup (1970, 1976), European Cup Winners' Cup (1970)

A real athlete of a footballer, Tony Book was extremely fit and possessed deceptive pace and plenty of stamina; qualities he continued to show during his City career, despite joining the club in his 30s. An inspirational captain who used his experience and personality to cajole some of the Maine Road club's younger players into a winning team, Book remains the Blues' most successful captain thanks to the five major trophies he lifted during his eight-year spell with the club.

THEY SAID ...

"He worked miracles for us, Tony Book. He was so quick and a great tackler."
Joe Mercer

Neil Young

POSITION:
Striker
BORN:
February 17, 1944 in Fallowfield, England
DIED:
February 3, 2011
CITY CAREER:
1961-1972
APPEARANCES:
412
GOALS:
107
HONOURS:
Second Division Title (1966), First Division Title (1968), FA Cup (1969), League Cup (1970), European Cup Winners' Cup (1970)

Manchester-born and a lifelong City supporter, Neil Young enjoyed a fairytale career during his 11-year stay at Maine Road. Top scorer during the 1968 title-winning season, 'Nelly' also grabbed crucial goals during the European Cup Winners' Cup campaign, including strikes against Schalke in the semi-final and Gornik in the final. Young was blessed with a cultured left foot and the ability to glide around defenders and hit the target with great power and accuracy. He was inducted into the Manchester City Hall of Fame in 2008.

THEY SAID ...

"Young was a very talented player with great skill and he scored marvellous goals. He never really got the recognition, but he was some player." Joe Mercer.

Colin Bell

POSITION:
Midfielder
BORN:
February 26, 1946 in Hesleden, England
CITY CAREER:
1963-1980
APPEARANCES:
492
GOALS:
152
HONOURS:
Second Division title (1966), First Division title (1968), FA Cup (1969), League Cup (1970, 1976), European Cup Winners' Cup (1970)

Widely regarded as Manchester City's greatest ever player, Colin Bell was arguably the star in City's most successful team. Nicknamed 'The King of the Kippax' and 'Nijinsky' – after the famous racehorse, thanks to his awesome levels of stamina – the English midfielder combined technical excellence with consistency and the ability to control matches. Bell was as close to the complete player as the Blues have ever had and his consistently high levels of performance were accompanied by awesome longevity. The Etihad Stadium's West Stand is named the Colin Bell Stand in his honour.

THEY SAID...

"Colin Bell is probably the best player I ever worked with. He was so gifted and had so much talent. He could score goals from midfield, was good in the air and had great pace; he had everything." Malcolm Allison.

Manchester United

Sandy Turnbull

POSITION:
Forward
BORN:
July 30, 1884 in Kilmarnock, Scotland
DIED:
May 3, 1917
CITY CAREER:
1902-1905
APPEARANCES:
110
GOALS:
53
HONOURS:
Second Division Title (1903), FA Cup (1904)
UNITED CAREER:
1906-1915
APPEARANCES:
247
GOALS:
101
HONOURS:
First Division Title (1908, 1911), FA Cup (1909)

A prolific goal-scorer with both Manchester clubs, Sandy Turnbull would have been one of the biggest names in football had he performed in the modern era. Playing with skill, bravery and fierce commitment, while popping up with crucial goals, the Scotsman also courted controversy both on and off the pitch. Sandy first joined City as a 17-year-old and his goals helped inspire the blue half of Manchester to their first FA Cup win. Following the payments scandal involving the club, Turnbull was snapped up by United and remains one of the few men to have reached the 100 goal mark for the Old Trafford giants.

TRIVIA

Sandy Turnbull was the first Manchester United player to score at Old Trafford, hitting the target against Liverpool when the ground was opened in 1912.

Johnny Carey

POSITION:
Full-back
BORN:
February 23, 1919 in Dublin, Ireland
DIED:
August 22, 1995
UNITED CAREER:
1936-1953
APPEARANCES:
344
GOALS:
17
HONOURS:
FA Cup (1948), First Division Title (1952)

Converted from an inside-forward to a full-back by Matt Busby, Johnny Carey was a consummate professional during his time at Old Trafford. Carey joined United as a 17-year-old, signing in a £200 deal from St James's Gate. A fantastic reader of the game, possessing boundless energy and good technique on the ball, the Irishman was appointed club captain by Busby and went on to lift the 1948 FA Cup and 1952 First Division Title. Also known as 'Gentlemen John', Carey was named Footballer of the Year in 1949.

THEY SAID...

"Carey knew the game well and was a captain by example as well as technique. He was an immense player and a great help to me, and a great captain." Matt Busby.

Jack Rowley

POSITION:
Striker
BORN:
October 7, 1920 in Wolverhampton, England
DIED:
June 28, 1998
UNITED CAREER:
1937-1954
APPEARANCES:
424
GOALS:
211
HONOURS:
FA Cup (1948), First Division Title (1952)

Nicknamed 'The Gunner' due to his explosive shot and prolific goal-scoring record, Jack Rowley is one of only three players to have scored more than 200 goals for Manchester United; the other two being Bobby Charlton and Denis Law. Powerful in the air and on the ground, Rowley joined the Reds as a 17-year-old, signing from Bournemouth in a £3,000 deal in 1937. A fine servant for the club, both before and after the Second World War, Jack scored 30 league goals as United won the 1952 First Division title, the club's first Championship since 1911, and bagged a brace in the 1948 FA Cup Final victory over Blackpool.

THEY SAID...

"He (Jack Rowley) must rank as one of the greatest players it has been my good fortune to handle. His confidence on even the greatest occasions amounted almost to disdain." Matt Busby

Jimmy Delaney

POSITION:
Outside Right
BORN:
December 3, 1914 in Cleland, Scotland
DIED:
September 26, 1989
UNITED CAREER:
1946-1950
APPEARANCES:
184
GOALS:
28
HONOURS:
FA Cup (1948)

Although famed for the younger players he acquired and brought through at Manchester United, Matt Busby knew when he needed to add experience to the side, and veteran winger Jimmy Delaney was the perfect example of that. Signing for the club as a 31-year-old in 1946, Delaney added guile and know-how to the Red Devils attack, providing the ammunition for the likes of Stan Pearson and Jack Rowley. Fleet footed with excellent close control and an eye for a pass, the skilful Scotsman played a crucial role in the success of Busby's first great United side.

THEY SAID ...

"Jimmy was brimful of boyish enthusiasm. He would chase the unlikely and sometimes even the impossible ball just in case. He always put himself into places that hurt the opposition, and in all was a source of great inspiration to others."
 Matt Busby.

Charlie Mitten

POSITION:

Left Winger

BORN:

January 17, 1921 in Rangoon, Burma

DIED:

January 2, 2002

UNITED CAREER:

1946-1950

APPEARANCES:

162

GOALS:

61

HONOURS:

FA Cup (1948)

THEY SAID ...

"Charlie Mitten could land a corner kick on a sixpence at will. He was a penalty taker who would ask the opposing goalkeeper which net stanchion he would like him to hit, with as accurate a left foot as ever graced the game." Matt Busby.

Charlie Mitten made a huge impact at Manchester United during his four years at the club. A breathtaking dribbler with deadeye delivery from crosses, corners and free-kicks, Mitten was one of the most exciting players in an extremely attacking United side. Also a penalty specialist, Charlie became an important part of Matt Busby's team but went on to disappoint his manager by controversially signing for Colombian side Independiente Santa Fe, of Bogota. The move, which earned Mitten the nickname 'The Bogota Bandit', came after United had toured South America and played in front of huge crowds. Dismayed with the comparatively poor wages that British players could earn because of the maximum wage restrictions, Charlie was determined to try his luck in Colombia once he realised the type of money available there. Mitten later returned to United, turning down the chance to join Real Madrid in the process. But the skilful winger found Old Trafford a much less welcoming place and soon left the club for Fulham.

Roger Byrne

POSITION:
Full-back
BORN:
February 8, 1929 in Manchester, England
DIED:
February 6, 1958
UNITED CAREER:
1951-1958
APPEARANCES:
280
GOALS:
20

THEY SAID ...

"He (Roger Byrne) had the aura of a true captain. If you did well, scored a good goal, say, you would not expect more than a cursory pat on the back, yet from him it was a gesture you would prize very highly indeed."
Bobby Charlton.

Manchester-born and still regarded as one of the greatest United captains in the club's history, the ultra-committed Roger Byrne was an inspirational character. Converted from a more attacking role, Byrne excelled as a full-back who used his huge reserves of energy and great desire to summon the very best from his team-mates. Byrne was an excellent defender and a fantastic leader, something Matt Busby soon realised, making him club captain at the relatively young age of 24. A regular with his country, Roger would appear in every England international that took place after he made his debut against Scotland in April 1954 to his last match against France in November 1957. Aged just 28-years-old, Roger was one of eight United players tragically killed during the Munich air disaster.

Tommy Taylor

POSITION:
Centre forward
BORN:
January 29, 1932 in Barnsley, England
DIED:
February 6, 1958
UNITED CAREER:
1953-1958
APPEARANCES:
191
GOALS:
131
HONOURS:
First Division Title (1956, 1957)

THEY SAID ...

"I went to see him play for Barnsley against Birmingham. After half an hour I had seen enough. He was the boy to complete my pattern."
Matt Busby.

Another of the players whose life was cut short in Munich, Tommy Taylor was a natural centre forward. Full of goals, capable of finding the net with both feet and his head, Tommy also possessed excellent close-control and was dubbed 'Magnifico' by Real Madrid legend Alfredo Di Stefano. Aged 21, Tommy signed for United from Barnsley in a £29,999 deal, with Matt Busby reluctant to burden the youngster with the label of a £30,000 player. Taylor enjoyed a prolific goal-scoring record, bagging 131 in 191 appearances for United and hitting the target 16 times in 19 games for England.

Duncan Edwards

POSITION:
Wing Half
BORN:
October 1, 1936 in Dudley, England
DIED:
February 21, 1958
UNITED CAREER:
1953-1958
APPEARANCES:
177
GOALS:
21
HONOURS:
First Division Title (1956, 1957)

THEY SAID ...

"There is no doubt in my mind that Duncan would have become the greatest player ever. Not just in British football, with United and England, but the best in the world. George Best was something special, as were Pele and Maradona, but in my mind, Duncan was much better in terms of all-round ability and skill." Tommy Docherty.

Widely recognised as the most talented of all the Busby Babes, the all-action Duncan Edwards was the complete footballer. Strong in the tackle, skilful on the ball and with the ability, mental strength and confidence to dominate games, the Dudley-born teenager was a remarkable talent. Duncan possessed boundless energy and a ferociously powerful shot, and was nicknamed 'Manboy' after making his first team debut for United at the tender age of 16 years and 185 days, before making his England debut two years later. Most often deployed as a defensive midfielder, Edwards excelled in every position he played and was described by Matt Busby as "the most complete footballer in Britain–possibly the world." Duncan was seriously injured during the Munich air disaster, eventually losing his brave battle for life almost two weeks after the crash, aged just 21-years-old. Despite the short length of his career, Edwards made an indelible mark on Manchester United and English football.

Dennis Viollett

POSITION:
Inside Forward
BORN:
September 20, 1933 in Manchester, England
DIED:
March 6, 1999
UNITED CAREER:
1953-1962
APPEARANCES:
293
GOALS:
179
HONOURS:
First Division Title (1956, 1957)

TRIVIA

The 32 league goals scored by Dennis Viollett in the 1959-60 season remains a Manchester United record.

An expert finisher, Dennis Viollet remains one of Manchester United's most prolific goal-scorers. Another Manchester-born footballer who first made his mark at Old Trafford as a youngster, Viollet struck up an impressive partnership with Tommy Taylor during his early United career, with the two strikers ideally suited and receiving excellent service from an extremely attacking team. Dennis was lightning quick and used to expertly time his runs to finish off the knockdowns from the towering Taylor. A survivor of Munich, Viollet remained at the club for four years following the disaster, signing for Stoke City in 1962.

Bill Foulkes

POSITION:

Central Defender

BORN:

January 5, 1932 in St Helens, England

UNITED CAREER:

1951-1970

APPEARANCES:

688

GOALS:

9

HONOURS:

First Division Title (1956, 1957, 1965, 1967), FA Cup (1963), European Champions' Cup (1968)

THEY SAID ...

"Bill Foulkes was a natural born pillar at the heart of a defence. He was maybe the hardest physical specimen I ever encountered on a football field. If he happened to clip you with his arm during training it was like being hit by a rock." Bobby Charlton.

Third in United's all-time appearance list, only behind Bobby Charlton and Ryan Giggs, Bill Foulkes gave excellent service to the club during his 19-year stay at Old Trafford. An extremely reliable defender, Foulkes was almost an ever-present during Matt Busby's reign at the club, having graduated from the famous United youth team and established himself alongside many of the other Bubsy Babes. Bill survived Munich and went on to play an influential role as the Red Devils finally claimed the European Cup, scoring a crucial and unlikely goal against Real Madrid in the semi-finals. Strong and brave in the air and on the ground, Foulkes was a no-nonsense defender who read the game well and provided a bedrock of leadership as the club rose from the ashes of Munich.

Harry Gregg

POSITION:
Goalkeeper
BORN:
October 25, 1932 in Tobermore, Northern Ireland
UNITED CAREER:
1957-1966
APPEARANCES:
247

TRIVIA

Harry Gregg was United's goalkeeping coach for three years, between 1978 and 1981.

One of the best goalkeepers to have pulled on the Manchester United jersey, Harry Gregg played with bravery, agility and style. The Northern Irishman was a real presence between the posts, organising defenders and dominating his area. Signed for a world record £23,000 fee for a goalkeeper just three months before the tragedy of Munich, Gregg endured more than his fair share of misfortune with injuries, missing out on winners' medals in the FA Cup and First Division. Capped 25 times by his country, Harry was voted as the 1958 World Cup's best goalkeeper.

Bobby Charlton

POSITION:
Forward
BORN:
October 11, 1937 in Ashington, England
UNITED CAREER:
1956-1973
APPEARANCES:
758
GOALS:
249
HONOURS:
First Division Title (1957, 1965, 1967), FA Cup (1963), European Champions' Cup (1968)

THEY SAID ...

"The greatest thing for a manager is to trust the talent. Bobby Charlton never betrayed that trust. It was a privilege to have him play for you." - Matt Busby.

A name synonymous with Manchester United and a player held in the highest of regard all over the world, Bobby Charlton is an Old Trafford institution. One of the original Busby Babes, Charlton had to endure the agony of Munich, admirably carrying the burden of the disaster and what it meant to the club for the majority of his career, before finally achieving the ecstasy of winning the European Cup in 1968. As a player, Bobby had few equals. One of the cleanest strikers of the ball the game has ever seen, Charlton could seemingly score from any distance and angle, as both his left and right foot were blessed with devastating power and accuracy. Able to play as a centre forward, but more often deployed as an attacking midfielder, the 1966 World Cup winner was a sublime passer of the ball and extremely skilful, dovetailing quite brilliantly with the remarkable talents of Best and Law. Despite hanging up his boots 40 years ago, Charlton is still both England's and Manchester United's top scorer. Whether or not those records remain intact, he is likely to retain the recognition of being England's greatest ever footballer.

Denis Law

POSITION:
Striker
BORN:
February 24, 1940 in Aberdeen, Scotland
CITY CAREER:
1960-1961 and 1973-1974
APPEARANCES:
67
GOALS:
37
UNITED CAREER:
1962-1973
APPEARANCES:
404
GOALS:
237
HONOURS:
FA Cup (1963)

Denis Law was a Manchester United icon. Affectionately known as 'The King of the Stretford End', the former Manchester City man is fondly remembered for his exploits at both clubs. One of the first players to salute the crowd when celebrating a goal and with the ability to score spectacular strikes, bullet headers and clinical tap-ins, the Scotland international was the complete centre forward. More than just a prolific goal-scorer, Law was an excellent passer of the ball and had a fantastic awareness of what was around him on the pitch. 'The Law Man' is often wrongly credited with scoring the goal that relegated United in 1974 while playing for City, but despite the significance of seeing their former hero score against them for their local rivals, Reds fans continue to worship Denis as one of their all-time favourites.

THEY SAID ...

"He was the quickest-thinking player I ever saw, seconds quicker than anyone else. He had the most tremendous acceleration and leapt Olympian heights. He headed the ball with almost unbelievable accuracy and with the power of a shot. He had the courage to take on the biggest and most ferocious opponents. No other player scored as many miracle goals as Denis Law." Matt Busby.

Paddy Crerand

POSITION:
Midfielder
BORN:
February 19, 1939 in Glasgow, Scotland
UNITED CAREER:
1963-1971
APPEARANCES:
401
GOALS:
19
HONOURS:
FA Cup (1963), European Champions
Cup (1968)

THEY SAID ...

"With his passion for Manchester United he became an integral strength of the team. It was also a great help that he could put the ball on a sixpence from fifty yards. He passed the ball quite beautifully." Bobby Charlton.

While Charlton, Law and Best would grab the majority of the headlines during the 1960s, one of the most crucial performers in Matt Busby's second great team was the combative yet elegant ball-playing midfielder Paddy Crerand. So much so that United fans often remarked that "If Pat Crerand plays well, United play well." After joining the club from Celtic on the fifth anniversary of the Munich air crash in 1963, Crerand went on to pay a major part in United's bid to finally win the European Cup in 1968. The Scotsman's vision and ability to express himself under pressure ensured he was perfectly suited to life at Old Trafford.

George Best

POSITION:
Winger
BORN:
May 22, 1946 in Belfast, Northern
Ireland
DIED:
November 25, 2005
UNITED CAREER:
1963-1974
APPEARANCES:
470
GOALS:
179
HONOURS:
First Division Title (1965, 1967),
European Champions' Cup (1968)

THEY SAID ...

"Boss, I think I've found you a genius."
Manchester United Chief Scout, Bob
Bishop.

"George Best was gifted with more
individual ability than I have seen in
any other player, certainly unique in a
number of his gifts. He had more ways
of beating a player than any other
player I have seen. Every aspect of
ball control was perfectly natural to
him from the start." Matt Busby.

The most naturally gifted player in United's history and one of the game's all-time greats, Georgie Best was a phenomenon. His close-control was on another planet to anything the British game had seen before, and combined with his pace, balance, ability to change direction in an instant and the courage and trickery to tantalise some of the game's toughest defenders, it made him a nightmare to mark. A swashbuckling winger, Best was equally impressive on either flank and when pressing forward to join the strikers. He also boasted a prolific scoring record, with his goals rarely anything other than spectacular. One of the first footballers to transcend his sport and become a household name, George loved life off the field but he shone brightest when gliding across the Old Trafford surface, with his feet caressing the ball and swaying around defenders. In full flow, the Belfast Boy was spellbinding poetry in motion.

Nobby Stiles

POSITION:
Defensive Midfielder, Central Defender
BORN:
May 18, 1942 in Manchester, England
UNITED CAREER:
1960-1971
APPEARANCES:
395
GOALS:
19
HONOURS:
FA Cup (1963)

One of the most tenacious players to ever pull on the Manchester United shirt, Nobby Stiles's energy and commitment to the cause made him crucial to the club's major successes throughout the 1960s. Capable of playing in defence or in a deeper midfield role, Nobby was a fierce tackler and an almost telepathic reader of the game sniffing out danger, regaining possession and setting United back in attacking motion. Diminutive in stature but with a huge heart, Stiles was also an expert man-marker.

THEY SAID ...

"Nobby Stiles did things for United, and England, that no one else could have done. He read the game as though he was equipped with a radar. No one I would ever know in football was prepared to do so much for his team-mates." Bobby Charlton.

Alex Stepney

POSITION:
Goalkeeper
BORN:
September 18, 1942 in Mitcham, England
UNITED CAREER:
1966-1978
APPEARANCES:
539
GOALS:
2
HONOURS:
First Division Title (1967), European Champions' Cup (1968)

An extremely reliable stopper and excellent communicator, Alex Stepney's presence in United's starting eleven was crucial to their 1968 European Cup success. The Londoner possessed lightning-quick reactions and accurate distribution and was an extremely safe pair of hands between the posts for the Red Devils. Stepney famously scored twice for United, and will always be remembered for the match-winning save from Benfica's Eusebio that helped the club claim their first European Cup.

TRIVIA

Despite the occasional attacking instincts of Peter Schmeichel, Alex Stepney remains Manchester United's record scoring goalkeeper.

Brian Kidd

POSITION:
Striker
BORN:
May 29, 1949 in Manchester, England
UNITED CAREER:
1967-1974
APPEARANCES:
203
GOALS:
52
HONOURS:
European Champions' Cup (1968)
CITY CAREER:
1976-1979
APPEARANCES:
98
GOALS:
44

Another local youngster who made the grade at United, Brian Kidd established himself in the team as a teenager, going on to score a goal in the 1968 European Cup Final victory on his 19th birthday. A quick striker who possessed good movement and real composure in front of goal, Kidd enjoyed seven years with the Reds before spending two years at Arsenal and then signing for Manchester City. Brian enjoyed a good goals return at Maine Road and is fondly remembered at both clubs for his efforts on and off the pitch, having assisted Alex Ferguson during the 1990s and now being part of Roberto Mancini's backroom staff at the Etihad Stadium.

5

SILVERWARE FOR CITY
AS UNITED STRUGGLE

As the swinging 60s drew to a close, Manchester United would go on to endure an extremely damaging and long-lasting European hangover. With so much energy focused on reaching the summit of Champions' Cup glory, the long-term vision of the club had been neglected.

United still possessed some of the brightest young talents in the country, but with established stars Denis Law, Bobby Charlton, Paddy Crerand and Bill Foulkes approaching the veteran stages of their careers, the Red Devils were about to lose some of the most influential footballers to have played for the club.

A lot of expectation would be placed on the shoulders of George Best, as Matt Busby attempted to find yet another successful formula at Old Trafford, but facing up to a further rebuilding exercise and having to part with some of the players that had served him so well proved difficult for the Scotsman.

Ahead of the 1968-69 campaign, Busby moved to fill arguably his favourite position on the pitch by signing Scotland international winger Willie Morgan from Burnley. Morgan soon settled into the team but United started the season in sluggish fashion.

The Red Devils took part in the Intercontinental Cup as a result of their European Cup success but a two-legged tie against Argentinian side Estudiantes proved a chastening experience. Estudiantes had won the South American equivalent of the European Cup, the Copa Libertadores, and were a formidable team, both in terms of ability and physicality. The first leg took place in Buenos Aires in September 1968 and, despite a cordial welcome for United upon their arrival, all pleasantries were forgotten once the game began.

The ignition of a huge smoke bomb before kick-off set the tone for what would be an extremely uncomfortable afternoon for the visitors as the Argentinian players put them under tremendous physicalforth

pressure, with most of it outside of the rules. Nobby Stiles, a man whose reputation for mixing it with opposing players had been grossly exaggerated by the South American press, was targeted throughout. A particularly violent member of the Estudiantes side was combative midfielder Carlos Bilardo, whose behaviour would later lead Matt Busby to conclude that, "Holding the ball out there put you in danger of your life."

The only goal of the game was scored by Estudiantes forward, Marcos Conigliaro, after 28 minutes but that wasn't the only noteworthy statistic of the game as Nobby Stiles saw red for an apparent gesticulation to the linesman after disagreeing with an offside decision.

The return leg in Manchester was another bad-tempered affair and United's attempts at retrieving the contest were made significantly harder when Estudiantes took an early head through Juan Ramon Veron's header. Veron was known as 'La Bruja' (The Witch) and his son, Juan Sebastian Veron, a hugely talented midfielder known as 'La Brujita' (The Little Witch), would one day play for United.

Veron senior's goal was equalised in the 89th minute by Willie Morgan but it proved too little too late, as the Argentinians held on for 2-1 aggregate victory. The game had again been marred by dismissals, as a minute before Morgan's goal, George Best, who had been kicked to pieces throughout the game, finally lost his cool and was sent off following a violent scuffle with José Hugo Medina.

Following the drama of the Intercontinental Cup, United faltered in the league but they weren't alone, as Manchester City struggled to defend their title and compete in Europe. Following a slow start to the season, winning just four of their opening nine games, the Blues eventually finished two places below the Reds in 13th position. With both Merseyside clubs, Liverpool and Everton, getting stronger and the emerging threat of Leeds United, Manchester's temporary dominance of the domestic game appeared to be at threat.

With Malcolm Allison's supremely confident proclamation they would 'terrify Europe' ringing in their ears, City began their first season in European football against Turkish champions Fenerbahce. City's opponents were a well-drilled, tactically sound outfit, illustrated by the performance they offered at Maine Road, frustrating the Blues in a scoreless draw.

The second leg, which took place in Turkey a fortnight later, proved an even tougher test for the English champions, who went on to lose 2-1 despite taking the lead through Tony Coleman. City had failed at the first hurdle, but the players and the management were determined to experience European football again and, with a team possessing suchgreat potential, it would only be a matter of time before the Blues were competing on the continent again.

United began their defence of the European Cup with a thumping 10-2 aggregate victory of Ireland's Waterford, with seven of the goals coming from Denis Law. The second round tie against Anderlecht was nowhere near as comfortable for the Reds. Despite a convincing 3-0 win at Old Trafford, thanks to two more goals from Denis Law, a man on a mission after missing the 1968 triumph through injury, United stumbled to a 3-1 defeat in Belgium. Recent addition, Carlo Sartori – an Italian born youngster who had grown up in Manchester – scored the crucial goal that assured United's passage into the quarter-final.

Next up was Rapid Vienna, who were dispatched 3-0 at Old Trafford and a 0-0 draw in Austria set up a semi-final tie with Italian champions AC Milan. A 2-0 deficit from the first leg at Milan's San Siro stadium gave United a mountain to climb in the return tie. Milan defended stoutly in Manchester despite incessant attacking pressure from the Reds. The deadlock was finally broken in the 70th minute when Bobby Charlton converted a George Best pass, to score United's 100th goal in European football. However, it was the only goal of the game, despite United claiming the ball had crossed line on two occasions, following efforts from Denis Law and Paddy Crerand. The club's defence of the European Cup was over and signalled the start of a barren period for the club, as the Reds failed to qualify for European competition for the next eight years.

City's league form eventually improved, particularly at Maine Road where they crushed Burnley 7-0 and West Brom 5-1, but the team's away displays let them down. In fact, the Blues only managed two away victories during the defence of their title, one at Sunderland and one against Manchester United.

By the turn of the year, with United adrift from top spot and suffering consecutive defeats, Busby decided it was time for a new man to take charge of the team as he moved upstairs to become the club's general manager. His replacement would not be one of the big names linked to the job, which included Don Revie, Brian Clough and former player Johnny Carey, but rather a young coach already working at the club named Wilf McGuinness.

The 31-year-old former Busby Babe, whose career had been cut short by injury, had been Busby's recommendation as the legendary former manager continued to hold significant sway; a factor that wouldn't always be entirely positive, as McGuinness struggled to stamp his authority on such an established and talented squad of players.

United went on to finish the season in 11th place but never provided a title challenge to eventual champions Spurs. Despite a slightly improved eighth place finish in 1970, where one of the highlights of the season had been a 4-0 victory over Manchester City, the managerial changes at the club signalled the start of an alarming decline.

Despite the disappointments in the league and in Europe, Joe Mercer and Malcolm Allison maintained the momentum of success by leading Manchester City to the 1969 FA Cup Final where they faced a Leicester City team licking their wounds from relegation. Inspirational Blues captain Tony Book was back in the side, having missed the first-half of the season through injury and his presence helped transform the club's fortunes.

The final was tight but Manchester City always had the upper hand and scored the goal their dominance deserved through Neil Young's spectacular effort. It was the Blues' second major honour in less than a year and the club's fourth FA Cup success in 13 years.

The 1970s were significantly more successful for Manchester City than Manchester United, particularly the early part of the decade when the Mercer and Allison bandwagon continued to roll. Following consecutive trophies in 1968 and 1969, the Blues began the 70s challenging on four fronts, attempting to reclaim the First Division title they had lifted two years previously, progressing in the domestic cups and, most importantly, attempting to give a better account of themselves in Europe.

A hard trainer who demanded physical excellence from his players, Malcolm Allison continued to work tirelessly on the training ground to extract the absolute maximum from what was still a supremely gifted squad. The hard work soon paid off in Europe as City went on to win their first continental fixture, defeating Athletico Bilbao of Spain 3-0 in the Cup Winners' Cup at Maine Road following a 3-3 away draw.

The second round of the competition resulted in straightforward progression for City, who thumped Belgium's Lierse SK 8-0 over two legs. A quarter-final tie against Portuguese side, Academica Coimbra, followed and provided a much sterner test. A bruising first leg in Portugal ended 0-0 and the scores remained blank after 90 minutes in the return tie at Maine Road, before Manchester-born Tony Towers grabbed the only goal of the game in extra-time to ensure City's progress to the semi-finals.

With just two games and German side Schalke 04 standing between Manchester City and their first ever European final, the Blues started the semi-final tie slowly, losing 1-0 in Germany. But, with Maine Road rocking for the return leg, City recaptured some of the form that had made them the best team in England and tore into their German opponents from the first whistle. Goals from Mike Doyle, Francis Lee, Colin Bell and two from Neil Young inspired the Blues to a memorable 5-1 victory.

The final would be held in Vienna against Polish side Gornik Zabrze, but first City had another Wembley final to contend with, but this time it wasn't the FA Cup. United had put paid to City's hopes of retaining that trophy by knocking them out in the fourth round, but the Blues avenged that defeat by beating their local rivals over two-legs in the League Cup semi-final, edging the first-leg at Maine Road 2-1 and holding on to that narrow advantage thanks to a 2-2 draw at Old Trafford.

City faced West Bromwich Albion in the League Cup Final on a pitch that lacked the usual perfection of a Wembley surface. Rather than a green carpet, the pitch was a muddy bog as the Horse of the Year Show had been held under the twin towers just a few days earlier. Joe Mercer described it as a 'pig of a pitch' and it proved far from conducive for a footballing spectacle. In a slog of a game, West Brom took the lead through England striker Jeff Astle, before Mike Doyle levelled matters for City and Glyn Pardoe guided home an extra-time winner. It was the club's third trophy in three years but the Blues weren't finished there.

Just a month later, City travelled to Austria for the 1970 European Cup Winners' Cup final to face Gornik Zabrze, who had defeated Italian giants AS Roma in the semi-finals. It would be the third straight cup final that saw the Manchester club lining up in their red and black striped away kit, and it again proved a lucky omen as City claimed an early lead thanks to the man for the big occasion, Neil Young. In the driving Vienna rain, Franny Lee doubled the team's advantage with a customary penalty kick in the 43rd minute, helping City complete a 2-1 victory, despite a late rally from Gornik and a goal from Stanislaw Oslizlo. City had indeed dominated Europe, but just a year later than Malcolm Allison had predicted.

The post-match reaction of Mercer and Allison provided a perfect insight into the contrast in the the characters of both men. Mercer was quick to thank City's travelling fans; "Our supporters, about 4,000 of them, stood in the pouring rain in Vienna to cheer us on. We are only sorry the rest of them were unable to watch on television." Allison revealed how the team celebrated: "It was a great night. Perfect! Back at the hotel Harry Godwin, our Chief Scout, was playing the piano – all the old songs – while Francis Lee was on top, dancing away in his underpants. It had to be seen to be believed."

Allison would later revel in the club's success in a speech to the City fans who had gathered to celebrate the victory in Manchester's Albert Square, and was quick to point out what The Blues European victory meant to the landscape of Mancunian football, stating: "We are the greatest club in Manchester. I am only sorry, ladies and gentlemen, that we were unable to win more than two cups this year. We decided to let a London club (Chelsea, who claimed the FA Cup) win something this year."

Under Wilf McGuinness, Manchester United did little to challenge Allison's view, finishing eighth in 1971 and lacking consistency. Both teams were struggling to recreate the glory years of the 1960s, having slumped to mid-table finishes in the 1969-70 season, but despite City and United not competing directly for trophies and titles, Manchester derbies developed a real edge during the 1970s, as the atmosphere on the terraces started to sour and tempers on the pitch often boiled over, emphasised during a 4-1 victory for City at Old Trafford in December 1970 when George Best was sent off after a late 50-50 challenge with Manchester City left-back, Glyn Pardoe. It was a damaging tackle and resulted in a double fracture and Pardoe almost losing his leg due to the severity of the injury.

Francis Lee scored a hat-trick in the game, showing every bit of his tenacity in a Manchester City shirt. Lee had been a constant menace to the United defenders throughout the game and continued to be a good luck charm for the Blues.

After United went on to lose the League Cup semi-final to Third Division Aston Villa, the writing was on the wall for Wilf McGuinness and, following a 4-4 Boxing Day draw with Derby County, he was relieved of his first-team duties and Matt Busby returned to the dugout for the remainder of the season. Busby's influence saw an upturn in form, but United could again only manage an eighth place finish.

Having made just three new signings in six years, the Red Devils needed new blood both on and off the pitch. The experience and influence of Bobby Charlton was heavily relied upon, as was the brilliance of George Best, although that brilliance was becoming increasingly fleeting as off the field distractions began to take hold.

One of Best's great friends off the field of play was Manchester City winger Mike Summerbee. In fact, a lot of City and United players socialised away from the pitch during the era. Best and Summerbee struck up an instant bond in the late 60s, holidaying together and chasing the fairer sex both at home and abroad. The profile of professional footballers was changing with the times and companies began to use top class sportsmen, particularly those like Best who were easy on the eye, to endorse their equipment and services. Players were becoming more commercially savvy, signified by a fashion boutique called 'The Edwardian', which was opened by Best and Summerbee in Manchester in 1967. A year later, George would be the 'Best' man when Summerbee married his 20-year-old fiancée in Mottram.

As United stuttered, Manchester City also endured another disappointing league campaign during the 1970-71 season, eventually finishing 11th, and this time there was no cup consolation, as Joe Mercer's men suffered their first trophyless season since 1967. City came closest in the European Cup Winners' Cup, again reaching the later stages of the tournament, before fellow English club Chelsea put paid to their hopes in the semi-finals.

City's fans and players had become accustomed to success and the disappointment felt in 1971 showed just how much the club had progressed under the Mercer-Allison partnership. But, as the trophies began to dry up, cracks appeared in the pair's relationship as the once great chemistry and understanding started to dissolve.

Increasingly popular with the players, supporters and the media, the enigmatic Allison was often seen as the figurehead of the club, with the more traditional approach of Mercer starting to fade into the background. 'Big Mal' had become a regular in the tabloids due to his captivating personality and his relationships with a string of women. He was also famed for smoking huge cigars and for his fashion attire, which included a sheepskin jacket and a fedora hat. In a time when the profile of football was continuing to rise, Allison's exuberant nature saw him revel in the media attention.

In many ways Mercer and Allison were polar opposites, but where in the past their vision for Manchester City had bound them together, it was now beginning to tear them apart. Allison felt betrayed by Mercer after turning down the opportunity to manage Italian club Juventus on the understanding that his partner would step aside and allow him to take charge of City. Mercer was enjoying the success that both men created and was reluctant to step down.

Allison was determined to back up his belief that he could be the best manager in the country and a power struggle for control over team affairs ensued. Mercer remained manager for the start of the 1971-72 season, but the speculation surrounding the club's future, and that of its manager and assistant manager, continued. Joe Mercer was supported by the existing Manchester City Board, led by the respected Albert Alexander, but Allison - now entirely disgruntled with matters in the dugout - threw his support behind a rival group of businessman attempting a takeover of the club that had promised him the managerial job if their bid succeeded.

Following plenty of political wrangling and boardroom manoeuvring, the board was split over which path to take and a compromise was reached that saw Albert Alexander's son, Eric, take charge. The board had to choose between Mercer and Allison, and with Mercer's age potentially a factor, as well as Allison's more modern approach to coaching and tactics, it wasn't long before 'Big Mal' was effectively the boss, as Mercer moved upstairs to take a general manager's role. The former manager's relationship with the new City board began to sour, not helped by the fact that his office and car parking space at Maine Road had been removed. The rift left a bitter taste in the mouths of both men and was arguably the beginning of the end of the greatest period in the club's history.

In future years both men would regret the way their partnership dissolved, but remained acutely aware of how their combined strengths brought so much success to Manchester City, as later encapsulated by Allison: "Joe and I were a perfect partnership. Apart from the tenseness of those last few months, I think we had barely two disagreements in all the time we worked together. I never for one moment regretted working with Joe Mercer, and I know he felt the same way about working with me. We had some fabulous times together and built some fabulous teams. The Mercer-Allison years at Manchester City were the best years of my life."

Mercer, who retained his dignity throughout the controversy, would also appreciate Allison's attributes: "Mal and I were a good combination. Mal was marvellous, he really was. He was a character but he was fanatically keen on football. I needed Malcolm, no doubt about that, but he needed me, and the combination was right. With my experience and his adventure, that was what worked."

On the pitch, City were showing some of the best league form since winning the 1968 Championship, as the old attacking swagger returned on a more regular basis. Perhaps influenced by Allison's adventurous nature, the Blues played with more freedom and stormed to a four-point advantage at the top of the table by March. The last time City had claimed the Championship, the management team had brought in Francis Lee in a move that gave the Blues a new attacking dimension, turning them into genuine title contenders. As the 1972 run-in approached, Allison saw the signing of the supremely gifted Rodney Marsh from QPR as an addition that could make a similar impact.

Marsh was a genius on the ball but his integration into the team didn't have the desired effect and rather than add a new dimension it disrupted the flow. City's form slumped as they managed just four wins in the last nine games and eventually finished fourth, just a single point behind surprise Champions Derby County. Marsh was made a scapegoat for City's failure by the media, with many believing his slower, more technical style prevented the Blues from playing their customary counter-attacking football.

The disappointment of losing the title was compounded in the summer of 1972 when Joe Mercer left the club to become general manager of Coventry City. The majority of City fans were appalled at the way a man who had achieved so much for the club had been treated and doubts over whether Malcolm Allison could lead City to glory without Mercer began to surface.

Over at Old Trafford, Matt Busby's next successor was announced in the summer of 1971 as the experienced Frank O'Farrell was enticed from Leicester City. Learning from the mistakes made during Wilf McGuinness's time in charge and stung by the media's criticism of his continued active presence at the club, Matt Busby decided to take a seat on the board of directors.

O'Farrell brought in his assistant at Leicester, Malcolm Musgrove, as both men tried to reawaken a giant that, while not fast asleep, had certainly been snoozing. With O'Farrell a supreme organiser who was astute in the transfer market, and Musgrove a forward-thinking coach in the same ilk as Manchester City's visionary assistant manager Malcolm Allison, there was reason for optimism around Old Trafford.

However, the challenge would prove too much for both men, as they started with a third successive eighth place finish in 1972 before United slumped to an unthinkable 18th in 1973. The talents of George Best were rarely available to O'Farrell as the United icon went AWOL for club and country on several occasions. When focused on his ability and training properly, Best remained one of the most talented and influential players in England, but despite an aborted retirement, the Northern Irishman's days at Old Trafford were numbered.

With Malcolm Allison the main man at Maine Road, Manchester City were hoping to improve upon a fourth place finish but the 1972-73 campaign proved one to forget for the manager and the club. The team's performances started badly and got worse, leading to Allison's resignation halfway through the campaign.

Johnny Hart stepped into the huge gap left by Allison's departure, attempting to stabilise a team that had lost its way on the pitch and a club still reeling from the loss of the most talented managerial team in its history. Hart made a significant and shrewd move in the transfer market, snapping up Manchester United striker Denis Law on a free transfer and also guided the Blues to an 11th place finish.

A tough season went from bad to worse for Frank O'Farrell and Manchester United when a 4-1 home defeat to Tottenham Hotspur was followed by derby day defeat to City. The United board began the search for another new manager, and when the Reds suffered a 5-0 drubbing at Crystal Palace, O'Farrell's tenure at the club came to an end.

Scotland manager at the time, Tommy Docherty, was appointed and inherited a team struggling on the pitch, but a club still in a strong financial position off it. The fiery Scot had both the hunger and the ambition to make his mark at Old Trafford. He wasted little time, ringing the changes to his playing squad in an attempt to address United's worrying league form.

Despite his determination to succeed, it would take time for 'The Doc' to make an impact at Old Trafford. His first game in charge ended in a 3-1 reverse to Arsenal, which left the club marooned at the bottom of the table. Docherty again entered the transfer market signing the combative yet highly-skilled Lou Macari from Celtic, despite the attentions of Liverpool manager Bill Shankly.

United began to turn defeats into draws and eventually claimed their first win under Docherty's stewardship against Wolves on 10 February 1973, but it was followed up with a 4-1 hammering to Ipswich Town and the almost unimaginable threat of relegation to the Second Division loomed large. But just when they needed it, the Reds found some form, picking up victories over Newcastle United, Southampton, Norwich City and Crystal Palace, eventually finishing 18th, just seven points away from the drop.

Docherty, who had brought in former Busby favourite Paddy Crerand as his assistant, was preparing to put faith in some of the emerging youngsters on the books at Old Trafford, including Sammy McIlroy, as the club prepared for the 1973-74 season. But, with United in need of an instant improvement, one of the biggest names in the club's history made an amazing return, as George Best decided to come out of retirement and resume his United career. But, despite Docherty's best efforts, the reunion didn't work out and the supremely talented winger made just 12 more appearances for the club.

There were also plenty of changes at Manchester City during the early 70s, as established performers like Tony Book reached the twilight of their Maine Road careers. Peter Swales took over as Chairman in October 1973 and was soon faced with the task of finding a manager to replace Johnny Hart, whose deteriorating health made it impossible for him to continue at the helm.

Many of the players wanted former captain Book to take over as manager, in a move that would have been extremely well-received by the City support, but Swales opted for Norwich City boss Ron Saunders and appointed his man in November 1973. Saunders lasted less than a year at Maine Road with the two high-points of his City reign being the signing of Sunderland winger Dennis Tueart and leading the club to the 1973 League Cup Final.

City's third Wembley final in four years ended in disappointment after Wolves defeated them 2-1, with Colin Bell registering for the Blues. Despite still possessing a front-line that included Lee, Law, Marsh and Summerbee, Saunders opted for a more cautious style of play. It didn't go down well with the players or supporters, and Swales showed Saunders the door before the season's end.

Tony Book, who had been Saunders's assistant, was brought in as his replacement and helped steady the ship to ensure that City weren't embroiled in a relegation scrap as the last months of the 1973-74 season approached.

A dramatic early season clash between the Manchester rivals saw Lou Macari and City defender Mike Doyle trade punches, leading to a mass brawl between players and staff from both clubs, and the eventual sending off of both players. The game finished 0-0, securing a point that neither team really wanted, but the venom on the pitch had led to ferocious scenes on the terraces as fighting broke out between rival supporters. Hooliganism was beginning to become a more prominent problem in the English game, ensuring that the tribal rivalry between supporters was developing more passion and ill-feeling.

On the pitch Docherty's men continued to flirt with relegation and their fate would soon be sealed during another hugely significant Manchester derby, this time at Old Trafford. United would still have another game to play following the clash with City, but their relegation rivals, Southampton and Birmingham City, were playing their last fixtures of the season that weekend. The Reds needed to win their last two games and hope that

Birmingham would slip up.

In the 80th minute, with the scores deadlocked at 0-0, Francis Lee played the ball to United legend Denis Law, who instinctively back-heeled the ball past Alex Stepney and into the net. As his team-mates rushed to congratulate him, the consequences were not lost on the Scotsman, who refused to celebrate, later summing up how he felt after the game. "I have seldom felt so depressed in my life as I did that weekend. After 19 years of giving everything I had to score goals, I have finally scored one which I almost wished I hadn't."

While the goal was crucial on the day, it wasn't the decisive factor in United's relegation, as the other teams fighting survival had achieved the results they needed. Despite United's demotion, there had been signs of improvement under Tommy Docherty and the club's board of directors gave the Scotsman time to turn things around.

United began their first Second Division campaign since 1938 against Leyton Orient at Brisbane Road, and a comfortable 2-0 victory would set the tone for what was ultimately a very successful season. Positive results away from home were the norm and United's home record, buoyed by fantastic support, provided the backbone of their promotion bid.

On the other side of Manchester, Tony Book was beginning a long reign as Manchester City manager, but the popular former captain would struggle to recapture the glory days he had experienced as a player. Book made several changes during the summer of 1974, allowing Francis Lee to leave for Derby County and bringing in Asa Hartford from West Brom as he attempted to shape a side that could again compete in the upper echelons of the First Division.

Despite a good start to the 1974-75 Second Division campaign for United, which saw the team on top of the table at the turn of the year, Docherty again made moves in the transfer markert signing flying-winger Steve Coppell from Tranmere Rovers, who helped supply the ammunition for United to continue dominating the division. The Reds eventually sealed promotion back to the top flight as Champions at the beginning of April thanks to a Lou Macari-inspired victory over Southampton.

United were back where they belonged, and like so many promotion-winning sides they managed to maintain the momentum of the previous season and began the 1975-76 campaign in excellent form, winning five of their opening six games and topping the First Division for a five week period. A slight loss of form saw the Reds drop to fifth and Docherty's men endured an alarming eight games without victory which saw them slip to 17th place before a much-improved run-in ensured a credible third-place finish.

At City, Tony Book's first full season in charge ended with an eighth place finish, a feat he repeated in 1976. All the time, the promising manager was adding to his squad, acquiring the likes of Joe Royle and Dave Watson as Mike Summerbee and Rodney Marsh departed. Another legend of the 1968 title-winning team, Colin Bell, also left the club following a knee-injury sustained against Manchester United in a 1975 League Cup tie. Bell was crocked following a challenge from Martin Buchan, and on-pitch incidents of that nature began to further fan the flames of the rivalry between both clubs. The friendly banter that existed between Blues and Reds decades before was replaced by a more tribal and personal enmity that began to verge on hatred in some quarters, particularly as football hooliganism continued to develop into a major problem in the game.

Throughout the 70s, United's supporters, known as the 'Red Army', were notorious for their behaviour at away games and became the focus of many negative headlines in the media. In truth it was a minority of fans involved, but it had a big impact on the club's reputation. Old Trafford was often the venue for such activities, prompting the club to install perimeter fencing around the ground in 1971, as United's stadium became the first League ground in England to take such measures.

Docherty assembled a United side capable of achieving progress in the FA Cup and the Reds faced Second Division Southampton in the 1976 FA Cup Final. A Gordon Hill brace against Derby County booked United's place at Wembley and the Red Devils were made huge favourites to take the trophy, but Docherty's emerging team froze on the big occasion and a plucky Southampton claimed a shock victory thanks to Bobby Stokes's solitary strike in the 83rd minute. Docherty vowed to avenge the loss by leading United to future Cup Final success and he was true to his word as United reached the Wembley showpiece the following year.

Manchester City also made the trip down Wembley way in 1976, reaching the final of the League Cup. The competition that had seemingly finished Colin Bell's career would go on to have a happier ending for the Blues as City defeated Newcastle United 2-1, with goals from Peter Barnes and Dennis Tueart, who found the back of the net with a spectacular overhead kick. It was Tony Book's first trophy as manager and the club's first major honour in six years.

After being widely tipped in the 1976 FA Cup final, United went into the 1977 showpiece as underdogs against Liverpool but after a gutsy performance, and goals from Stuart Pearson and the combination of Lou Macari and Jimmy Greenhoff, Docherty and his players finally got their hands on the trophy. It was the club's first major success since 1968 and prevented Liverpool from claiming an unprecedented treble of winning the First Division Title, FA Cup and European Cup; an achievement that United would go on to realise themselves, just over two decades later.

As the players and supporters celebrated victory, Tommy Docherty was in pensive mood during what should have been one of the most satisfying moments of his managerial career. The manager was about to break some controversial news, revealing an extra-marital affair he'd been having with the wife of club physio Laurie Brown.

The affair soon became front page news, as both Docherty and Brown's marriages ended and the controversial couple maintained their relationship. With concerns about the club's reputation, the Scotsman was called in front of the United board of directors who requested that he tender his resignation. Docherty refused and was sacked, despite guiding United to the FA Cup just 44 days earlier and being the club's most successful manager since Matt Busby. Tommy and Mary Brown later married and remain together to this day, but the way divorce was looked upon in the 1970s, and the fact that the affair directly involved another member of staff, had seemingly forced the club's hand.

Despite cup success, United's league form remained inconsistent, confirmed by their 10th place finish in a season where they were again topped by City, who finished fourth, a full 12 points behind Champions Nottingham Forest. Following Tommy Docherty's controversial exit, the red half of Manchester were once again seeking a new manager. The board wasted little time appointing a replacement by bringing in Chelsea boss Dave Sexton just ten days later.

Inspired by their 1976 League Cup victory, Manchester City started the 1976-77 campaign in Championship winning form and lost only two of their first 25 games in a run that included 13 clean sheets. Back in Europe, thanks to their League Cup victory, City again struggled as Juventus knocked them out in the first round of the UEFA Cup.

Early exits followed in both domestic cups, allowing Book's side to concentrate on the league as they entered a two-horse race alongside Liverpool. City eventually lost out on the title by a single point, with two particularly damaging defeats coming against Manchester United, as the Reds completed a league double against their closest rivals. Despite the end of season collapse, City could take consolation from again being involved in a title race and securing a runners-up spot – their highest league finish since winning the Championship nine years previously.

While City enjoyed managerial consistency with Tony Book, Manchester United's players and supporters were adjusting to another new man at the helm. Dave Sexton was a very different character to Tommy Docherty. The Englishman was more pragmatic and enjoyed the coaching and tactical side of the game. The team that Docherty built began the 1977-78 season in fine form under Sexton, thumping Birmingham City 4-1 at Old Trafford on the first day. The new manager soon stamped his mark on the side, signing Leeds United pair Joe Jordan and Gordon McQueen during the season.

City added just one new player to their squad for the 1977-78 campaign, signing England striker Mike Channon from Southampton. The Blues again enjoyed consistency in the league and disappointment in Europe, once again falling at the first hurdle in the UEFA Cup.

Tony Book's men were again in contention for the title with Dennis Tueart in fine form, bagging three league hat-tricks before Christmas. On Boxing Day a 4-0 home victory over Newcastle United was a statement of the team's intentions. It was a match that provided a huge boost to the club, not only due to the result, but because the legendary Colin Bell had made an amazing return to action after an agonising fight to save his career.

The win and Bell's return helped set City on a run of six successive victories as they maintained pressure on league-leaders Nottingham Forest. But, inspired by the managerial genius that was Brian Clough, Forest would not be caught and the Blues finished fourth. It was to be the club's last title challenge of the century and, with the free-scoring Dennis Tueart soon sold to New York Cosmos, there were signs that the Tony Book inspired bubble was about to burst at Maine Road.

Manchester United had spent most of the 1977-78 season marooned in mid-table, eventually finishing 10th, and with the team not playing the most entertaining brand of football, the Old Trafford faithful began to question Sexton's suitability.

Like United, City endured a slow start to the 1978-79 season and the team's below-par performances would eventually cost Tony Book his job. The signing of Polish World Cup captain Kaziu Deyna gave supporters a boost, as did an impressive run in the UEFA Cup where City overcame the might of AC Milan en route to a two-legged quarter-final defeat to Germany's Borussia Monchengladbach, but it was a quarter-final that Tony Book wouldn't oversee.

In January 1979, a larger than life figure from the recent past returned to Maine Road when Malcolm Allison was named as manager. Book remained at the club on the coaching staff as the romance of Big Mal's return proved irresistible for club Chairman Peter Swales.

Allison had been a good judge of player during his first spell at the club alongside Joe Mercer and was soon given a substantial transfer war chest by his chairman. To make room for his new additions, the new manager controversially sold fans' favourites like Peter Barnes and Gary Owen, bringing in Michael Robinson and Steve Daley, the latter for a then British transfer record of £1.45m.

Burdened by the huge price tag and playing in a team struggling for confidence and form, Daley failed to make an impact and was soon dubbed an expensive flop by the media. Later Allison would claim that he'd agreed to a much lower fee with Wolverhampton Wanderers for Daley, but following Swales's interference in the transfer, the price tag was increased. Another former terrace hero returned to Maine Road in 1979, as Dennis Tueart ended his short spell in the United States, but the team's form didn't improve. A shock FA

Cup defeat to Shrewsbury Town and a 15th place finish, the club's lowest in the league since 1967, were a sign of things to come, as Allison battled to save his and the club's reputation.

Adjusting to another new manager, United again struggled for league consistency, but FA Cup progress would again provide salvation as they overcame an impressive Liverpool side in the semi-finals following a replay to set up a clash with Arsenal at Wembley. However, despite playing in one of the most memorable finals in the modern era, United lost to the Gunners in the most painful of circumstances, maintaining the pressure on Dave Sexton and the United board. The game would be known as the 'five minute final' due to the incredible, late drama of the final five minutes. Arsenal had led the game through first-half goals from Brian Talbot and future United striker Frank Stapleton but, with just three minutes remaining, towering defender Gordon McQueen gave the Reds hope with a powerful finish before Sammy McIlroy showed fleet of foot and ice cool composure to level the scores a minute later. United readied themselves for extra-time, but Arsenal surged up the pitch and Graham Rix's lofted cross was turned home by Alan Sunderland. It was a crushing blow for United and Sexton, as silverware would have provided much-needed breathing space. The manager continued to shape a team in his own image by signing classy midfielder Ray Wilkins from Chelsea in the summer but the 1979-80 campaign again proved one of frustration.

At least United provided something of a challenge to Liverpool at the top of the table, spending most of the season within touching distance of their Merseyside rivals. But embarrassing results, such as the 6-0 defeat to Ipswich Town, and a hardening relationship with the media, made it almost impossible for Sexton to win over the fans and his critics. His team finished in second place to Liverpool, just two points behind the Champions, but despite achieving the club's most successful league finish since 1968 Sexton's days at Old Trafford were numbered, and as a new decade approached, United would go on to appoint one of the most charismatic managers in the club's history.

City were led into the 1980s by another charismatic character as Malcolm Allison continued his second spell at the club, but whether he would be able to summon any of the old magic remained to be seen.

6

MANCUNIAN MEDIOCRITY

Malcolm Allison's second spell as Manchester City manager would last less than a year. Further expensive signings had been made, such as the £1m capture of Kevin Reeves, but City were struggling in the league and Big Mal's fractious relationship with chairman Swales was worsening. The money spent on Daley and Reeves would have helped rebuild an entire team and, with many of their better players approaching the veteran stages of their career, the lack of judgement by both men in the transfer market would prove costly in both the shorter and longer-term.

Swales kept faith with his appointment throughout the summer of 1979, but the task of overhauling a team that simply wasn't in the same league as the one he'd enjoyed such success with during the 1960s and early 70s proved too much for Big Mal. Without the guidance and experience of Joe Mercer beside him, Allison was half the managerial force he had been and some of the displays his City team served up during his second spell at the club were so poor that he was in danger of undoing all the good work he had put into place a decade earlier.

Allison's struggles continued at the beginning of 1980 when Fourth Division Halifax Town knocked City out of the FA Cup. Things went from bad to worse in the 1980-81 season, and with the Blues failing to win any of the first 10 games Allison and Tony Book paid the price in October 1980 and John Bond took charge of team affairs.

The writing was also on the wall for Dave Sexton whose United side were struggling for form and goals – emphasised by a run of six games without scoring. The fans were losing patience as the poor results, which were not helped by an increasingly large injury list, continued. The Reds weren't losing many games, but they weren't winning enough either, drawing eight of the first 12 fixtures. Sexton made a bold move in the transfer market, signing the prolific Nottingham Forest centre-forward Gary Birtles for a then club record £1.25m.

United's form improved slightly but, plagued by the pressure of the fee and playing in a team lacking confidence and the full-backing of the Old Trafford faithful, Birtles struggled to find his feet in front of goal. With key players still missing, the Reds went over a month without a win in the league, leaving them in mid-table and many supporters calling for Sexton's head.

Sexton remained at the helm and with more players back to fitness the team went on a nine-match unbeaten run, including seven victories, towards the end of the season, but it would prove a temporary reprieve for the manager who was dismissed just five days after a final day victory over Norwich City in front of one of the lowest crowds seen at Old Trafford for years.

Perhaps Sexton's perceived lack of charisma and warmth contributed to his downfall. The United supporters never really identified with his approach and with such impressive characters as Matt Busby and Tommy Docherty setting the tone of what was expected of a Manchester United manager, in terms of presence and personality, it was becoming clear that coaching ability, experience and football knowledge weren't enough to ensure success at one of the English game's box office clubs.

In direct contrast to his predecessor's extravagance in the transfer market at City, John Bond was far more frugal and obtained Tommy Hutchison, Gerry Gow and Bobby McDonald for what would prove to be bargain fees. The three Scottish veterans cost less than £500,000 and the experienced trio would play a major role in stabilising the team. Bond had an instant impact at Maine Road, and like Allison the former Norwich City man was a flamboyant and extremely confident character.

A new-look City were transformed, as Bond brought more width to the side and an impressive run of victories ensured that the team soon edged away from the bottom of the table. City also went on to reach the 1981 League-Cup semi-final where they were denied by Liverpool over two legs, but Bond's men went one better in the FA Cup, reaching the Centenary Final.

The Blues' road to Wembley included a 6-0 thrashing of Bond's former team, Norwich City, and a 4-0 victory over Malcolm Allison's Crystal Palace. City's impressive form in the FA Cup continued with a quarter-final replay victory over Everton, thanks to two goals in a minute from full-back Bobby McDonald and an extra-time victory over Ipswich Town in the semi-final.

The Blues faced Tottenham Hotspur in the final, drawing the first game 1-1, with City's Tommy Hutchison famously scoring for both clubs - his second, a bizarre own goal,

The Football League Division One trophy is paraded around the pitch before kick-off at Old Trafford in August 1952, celebrating Manchester United's title victory the previous season (1951/52).

Left: Legendary Manchester City goalkeeper Bert Trautmann before the FA Cup Semi-Final between City and Tottenham Hotspur in March 1956.

A photo of the Busby Babes 1956-57 team sits in a book alongside a signature from Matt Busby in front of a 1958-2008 commemorative flag

The Manchester United team line up before their game against Red Star Belgrade in 1958, after which their plane home crashed in Munich.

IN MEMORY OF THE OFFICIALS & PLAYERS WHO LOST THEIR LIVES

WALTER CRICKMER   TOM CURRY

BERT WHALLEY

ROGER BYRNE

GEOFF BENT   MARK JONES
EDDIE COLMAN   DAVID PEGG
DUNCAN EDWARDS   TOMMY TAYLOR
BILLY WHELAN

IN THE MUNICH AIR DISASTER ON THE 6TH FEBRUARY 1958

The memorial dedicated to those who lost their lives in the Munich Air Disaster on 6 February 1958, unveiled in 2008 to mark the 50th Anniversary of the tragedy.

Roger Byrne (right), captain of the 'Busby Babes', gets changed after the European Cup tie against Red Star Belgrade on 15 January 1958. Roger died in the Munich air crash disaster.

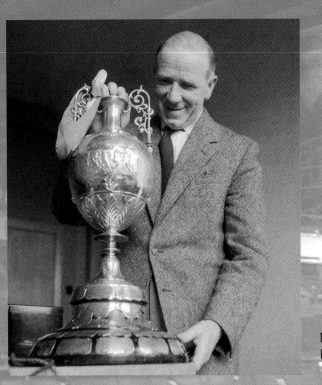

Matt Busby with the 1957/58 League Championship trophy.

The United team strip off their tracksuit tops which are collected by manager Matt Busby (left) prior to the 1963 FA Cup Final against Leicester City. United won 3-1.

The Manchester United team line up before kick-off against Leicester City ahead of the FA Cup Final on 25 May 1963.

Manchester United captain striker Denis Law raises the League Championship trophy in front of the crowd at Old Trafford in May 1965.

Bobby Charlton shoots past the Fulham defence in an English Football League Division One match in February 1967.

George Heslop (left) and Colin Bell celebrate in the changing room after Manchester City's victory against Newcastle United in May 1968 to secure the Division One title.

Left: Manchester United's Bobby Charlton (left) celebrates with George Best during the 1968 European Cup Final against Benfica, which United won 4-1.

Below: Manchester City players about to board the train at Piccadilly station on their way to Wembley for the FA Cup final against Leicester City on 24 April 1969. (From left) Alan Oakes, Mike Doyle, Colin Bell, Neil Young and Tony Coleman. City won 1-0.

Newcastle United v Manchester United. Nobby Stiles (left) shouts at an injured Newcastle player while Wyn Davies (centre) pushes Denis Law and George Best aside in a Division One match in April 1969.

Manchester City's Mike Summerbee (right) in a Division One match against Middlesbrough in September 1974.

Arsenal v Manchester City at Highbury City, 4 October 1975. Defender Willie Donachie challenges Alan Ball (centre) during City's win at Arsenal.

Manchester United boss Alex Ferguson in 1987.

Manchester United's Norman Whiteside in the Division One match against Ipswich Town in January 1988.

Manchester City pair Steve Redmond and Ian Bishop win the ball from United's Brian McClair in the local derby in September 1989.

Peter Schmeichel (left) stands with his United team mates as they celebrate victory in the 1991 European Super Cup Final against Red Star Belgrade.

David White in action for City in 1993.

Denis Irwin misses the tackle on City's Nicky Summerbee in a FA Cup match in 1996.

Two controversial players, (above) Eric Cantona wearing the captain's armband for United in a 1996 FA Cup encounter. (Left) Manchester City's Mario Balotelli.

A large poster of Peter Schmeichel is flanked by flags of other Manchester United players on the road to Old Trafford in 1998.

Manchester United capture the 1999 Champions League trophy after defeating FC Bayern Munich in the final. The suspended United pair of Paul Scholes and Roy Keane celebrate by lifting the trophy.

Sir Alex Ferguson (right) applauds his teams efforts as Ronaldo and Wayne Rooney prepare to come on as substitutes in the Premier League match against Fulham in March 2008.

A panorama of the City of Manchester Stadium, also known as the Etihad Stadium'
Credit: Liam Duffy

The statue outside Old Trafford of the United trinity George Best, Denis Law and Bobby Charlton.

The statue of Bobby Charlton, Denis Law and George Best outside Old Trafford.

Wayne Rooney holds the Sir Matt Busby (Manchester United Player of the Year) Trophy in 2010.

Manchester United captain Nemanja Vidic is carried off on a stretcher following a tackle with FC Basel's Marco Streller in a December 2011 UEFA Champions League match.

Mario Balotelli of Man City is fouled by Man United's Anderson in a 2011 FA Cup Semi-Final match.

Manchester City manager Roberto Mancini celebrates City's win over Stoke in the 2011 FA Cup Final.

Manchester United manager Sir Alex Ferguson and his one-time Manchester City counterpart Mark Hughes.

The Manchester United players celebrate their win in the 2010-2011 Premier League title at Old Trafford.

Carlos Tevez lifts the trophy high and celebrates with the rest of the Manchester City players following their 1-0 win over Stoke City.

Manchester City captain Vincent Kompany keeps an eye on the ball in a 2012 pre-season match against Arsenal.

kept Spurs in the game. But City went on to lose the replay 3-2 in a classic FA Cup Final encounter. The game was settled by a sublime solo effort from Argentinean international Ricky Villa, whose weaving run mesmerised the City defence before he kept his balance and his composure to drive the ball home. The Blues had more than played their part in an absorbing encounter and led the game with just 15 minutes remaining thanks to goals from Steve MacKenzie and Kevin Reeves, but late strikes from Garth Crooks, and then Villa, meant the Cup would stay in London. It was a fitting spectacle for the 100th Cup Final, but that provided little consolation for City.

In the summer of 1981, City made the most high-profile addition since the signing of Rodney Marsh when they captured England international striker and European Cup Winner Trevor Francis from Nottingham Forest. A proven goal-scorer who led the line with poise and purpose, it was a signing that excited the City supporters, who turned out in their numbers to witness Francis bag a brace against Stoke City on his debut. John Bond had fought tooth and nail to bring Francis to the club, even threatening to resign when Chairman Peter Swales showed reluctance at parting with such a significant transfer fee. However, City's financial instability continued and the club was forced to sell the striker to Italy after just one season.

City began the 1981-82 season in fine form, eventually reaching top spot over the Christmas period after a 3-1 victory at Liverpool and a 2-1 win over Wolves. But it would prove a season of two halves for the Blues, who lost their way after the turn of the year and saw their title challenge fold following a run of just five wins in 22 matches, resulting in a 10th-place finish.

Following Dave Sexton's exit, United needed a man that could carry that mantle of the job while also putting his own stamp on the club, and the United board appointed the charismatic Ron Atkinson, who had enjoyed success with limited resources at West Brom.

Atkinson brought in his own backroom staff and started to make significant moves in the transfer market. Atkinson's first addition was Arsenal and Ireland striker Frank Stapleton, a hard-working target man with a smart finish, but 'Big Ron's' next bit of business would be his best, as he captured a man who would become one of the club's all-time greats, as the manager returned to his former club to seal the £2m double-signing of midfield duo Remi Moses and the much sought after Bryan Robson. Robson became the heartbeat of the team and soon developed into the Red Devils' 'Captain Marvel'. The fee for Robson was £1.5m, making him the most expensive signing in British history at that stage.

Other clubs, including Liverpool, had been linked with the Durham-born England international but Atkinson and United had persuaded Robson that his future lay in Manchester, prompting a high-profile on-the-pitch signing of his contract ahead of

United's October clash against Wolves at Old Trafford. United went on to win the game 5-0, contributing to an impressive start for Atkinson as the Reds stormed up the table.

Robson made his league debut in the Manchester-derby at Maine Road, equipping himself well in a 0-0 draw. As well as his early judgement in the transfer market, another of Ron Atkinson's strengths was his belief in giving young players a chance, emphasised by the emergence of two exciting attacking talents from the youth team, as first Norman Whiteside and then Mark Hughes made an impact upon the first team.

Belfast-born Whiteside made his United bow a week after his 17th birthday, coming on as substitute as United defeated Brighton and Hove Albion 1-0 in the league at the Goldstone Ground on April 24, 1982. In the process, Norman became the youngest United player since Duncan Edwards, and he shared physical similarities with the 'Busby Babe', being well-built, strong and powerful in possession. Once in the team, Whiteside proved hard to dislodge and his ability to produce the goods when it mattered would be of huge benefit to Ron Atkinson.

City's poor form continued into the 1981-82 league campaign and the team began to slip down the table and, following a shock 4-0 FA Cup defeat to Brighton and Hove Albion, John Bond tendered his resignation. Bond's former assistant, John Benson, was awarded his first managerial appointment and given the unenviable task of trying to save a team that appeared doomed. Benson couldn't inspire a turnaround and results actually took a turn for the worse as the team claimed just 11 points from his 19 games in charge.

City went into the last day of the season needing a point to survive, facing fellow relegation candidates Luton Town at Maine Road, but with a tense and nerve-jangling atmosphere inside the ground, the team slumped to a 1-0 defeat thanks to a smart volley from Rady Antic. Luton boss David Pleat famously ran across the pitch in celebration, but the despair in the stands turned to anger, and Pleat was soon joined by thousands of home supporters who vented their frustrations at the team's ineptitude and the almost inconceivable reality of relegation, just like Manchester United fans had done during their demotion nine years earlier.

A new-look United finished the 1981-82 campaign in third place and things improved the following year, as Atkinson inspired the club into two Wembley Cup Finals—the Milk Cup and the FA Cup. United lost to Liverpool in the Milk Cup, despite a well taken goal from Norman Whiteside, but fared better in the other competition as the precociously talented Northern Irishman again showed his class in the FA Cup semi-final against Arsenal at Villa Park, scoring a spectacular volley to clinch a 2-1 victory and send United into the final.

United faced Brighton and Hove Albion at Wembley and were expected to bring home the trophy against a team that had already suffered relegation from the First Division. But the Reds had already experienced an unpleasant Cup Final surprise against Southampton in 1976, and a shock was again on the cards when Gordon Smith gave Brighton the lead inside the first 15 minutes. Atkinson's men rallied and goals from Frank Stapleton and Ray Wilkins put them 2-1 ahead going into the last quarter of the game. With the trophy seemingly heading to Manchester, Brighton scored an unexpected equaliser in the 87th minute through Gary Stevens to force extra-time.

The goal shocked United and inspired Brighton, who impressed during the extra half hour and came close to a late winner when Gordon Smith had the goal at his mercy following a purposeful run and cross from former Manchester City man Michael Robinson. But despite finding himself with acres of space, Smith could only find the advancing United stopper Gary Bailey who held onto his shot to keep United in the game.

The replay was held at Wembley five days later and United began the game in dominant mood. The Reds played at pace and with confidence and blew their opponents away thanks to a Norman Whiteside brace, one from Robson and a penalty from Arnold Muhren.

Robson had since been installed as club captain, replacing Ray Wilkins, who had also lost the England armband to his United colleague, and the midfield maestro climbed the Wembley steps to lift his and Ron Atkinson's first major honour with the club.

Dismayed at the way their club was being run following the club's relegation, Manchester City fans gathered outside Maine Road to demand the resignation of Peter Swales. The thick-skinned businessman remained at the helm, but the same privilege wasn't afforded to manager John Benson who was replaced by Celtic boss Billy McNeill in the summer of 1983. McNeill had been linked with the other Manchester managerial hotseat two years previously, eventually losing out to Ron Atkinson. The pressure at Old Trafford would have been tough for any manager to contend with, but McNeill arguably faced a much harder job on the other side of the city as he attempted to resurrect the Blues.

Buoyed by their 1983 FA Cup success, United's form continued to improve during the 1984-85 season as Atkinson's men entertained the supporters with a more attractive brand of attacking football. With Norman Whiteside a fixture in the team, 'Big Ron' was ready to blood another youngster, as he promoted youth team striker Mark Hughes to the first team squad, and gave him his first start in a Milk Cup tie against Oxford United.

Despite their improving displays in the league, which saw the team lying second only to Liverpool, United suffered a disastrous FA Cup defence, losing 2-0 to Third Division AFC Bournemouth at Dean Court. It was a sobering afternoon for Atkinson and his players and the first real low-point of his United career, but with the European Cup Winners' Cup to focus on there was certainly cause for optimism.

Under Atkinson, United had stumbled in the UEFA Cup the previous season, having lost to Spanish side Valencia, but the Reds enjoyed steady progress in the first two rounds of the Cup Winners' Cup, advancing past Dukla Prague and Spartak Varna to set up a mouth-watering quarter-final tie against the mighty Barcelona.

United travelled to the awe-inspiring Nou Camp stadium to face a team filled with world superstars that included the awesome Argentinian Diego Maradona and the strength of the Catalan club proved too much as Barca brushed them aside 2-0. But the return leg at Old Trafford was a different matter entirely. With nothing to lose and roared on by their ferocious fans, United tore into Barcelona with relish. Bryan Robson was in inspirational form, raising his game to another level to dominate the midfield and drive the Reds forward. The players fed off the crowd as the excitement and anticipation continued to build with every surging attack or tenacious tackle.

United needed an early goal and it duly came after 25 minutes when that man Robson nodded home from close range to send the home supporters into raptures. With the aggregate score still 2-1 to the Spaniards, United pressed on for an equaliser and it came in the second half, again through Robson. The tie was level, but with the Barcelona defence rocking and Robson and co well and truly dominating, Old Trafford smelt blood. United went in for the kill and Frank Stapleton fired home a Norman Whiteside knockdown to almost take the roof of the famous old stadium and seal United's progress into the semi-finals.

With a fully-fit Bryan Robson in the team, Manchester United were quite simply transported to another level. His ability alone would have made him a top class footballer, but all of his attributes combined with a fierce competitive instinct, a huge desire to succeed and unflinching bravery, made him a genuine match-winner. Robson led by example and inspired the players around him to raise their game, much in the same way that Duncan Edwards had for the Busby Babes and that Roy Keane would go on to do for the great United team of the 1990s.

However, Robson's bravery and propensity to play on with niggles and sometimes more serious injuries often led to him missing games, including that season's Cup Winners' Cup semi-final against Juventus. Italy's World Cup-winning striker Paolo Rossi gave Juventus an early lead at Old Trafford in the first leg but United levelled matters through Alan Davies, setting up an intriguing return tie in Turin, but despite almost forcing the game to extra-time after Norman Whiteside equalised an opening goal from Polish star Zbigniew Boniek, United were knocked after Paolo Rossi grabbed a late winner.

United finished fourth in the 1984-85 First Division, qualifying for the UEFA Cup. Despite sound early progress in Europe the Reds eventually faltered at the quarter-final stage, following a shock penalty shootout defeat to Hungarian minnows Videoton. The tie proved to be the club's last opportunity to play in Europe for five years, after English and Italian clubs were banned from European football by UEFA following the Heysel Stadium tragedy in the 1985 European Cup Final involving Liverpool and Juventus, when 39 local fans were crushed to death in Brussels, Belgium.

An eventual fourth place finish in 1985 was hard to take as United had topped the table on occasions, but up against seasoned Championship contenders, Liverpool, to find the consistency and mental strength to maintain their challenge. As had been the norm in the 1970s, United spent most of the 1980s in the shadow of their fierce rivals from Merseyside. The Red Devils would regularly beat Liverpool both at home and away, but the battles that had been won during the campaign mattered little at the end of the season, when the Anfield club won the war and lifted the trophy. The modern day dominance of United has amazingly mirrored this from a Liverpool perspective, with the Merseysiders often summoning the quality and battling abilities to beat United over 90 minutes but rarely finding the consistency to outdo them over the course of a season. As this rivalry became fiercer, the one between both Manchester clubs became weaker and less relevant, particular when viewed from the red side of the city.

Despite the disappointment of not being able to live up to the challenge of Liverpool there were plenty of positives at Old Trafford as another youngster started to make an impact on first team matters, as Welsh warrior Mark Hughes became a regular under Atkinson. As is often the case when a young player begins their fledgling United career, the Old Trafford faithful provide immense support, even affording them a few errors to help them to realise their raw potential. Like Whiteside before him, Mark Hughes was a youngster that soon showed he was ready for the first team as his combative and powerful style almost instantly won over the home supporters.

One of Hughes' most crucial goals during the 1984-85 campaign came in an FA Cup semi-final tie against Liverpool. After a pulsating 2-2 extra-time draw at Goodison Park, which included goals from Hughes and Frank Stapleton, the contest went to a replay, which was played at Maine Road. An early own-goal from Paul McGrath handed the Merseysiders the advantage, but a customary goal from Bryan Robson hauled United back into the contest at the start of the second half. United weren't finished there, and 12 minutes later Hughes ran onto a Gordon Strachan pass to slam a beautifully struck shot into the top corner to send United to Wembley for their sixth FA Cup Final in 10 years.

Ron Atkinson's men met another Merseyside team in the final, lining up against League Champions Everton. The Toffees were a fantastic team, reaching their peak following the vision and fine-tuning of future Manchester City boss Howard Kendall, and Everton were going for a unique treble of trophies after following up their League title with the European

Cup Winners Cup. United knew they would face a battle to win underneath the twin towers and it was a battle that soon took on a more up-hill trajectory after Reds defender, Kevin Moran, made an unenviable piece of history.

Following a closely fought first-half, the game opened up in the second period and Everton's Peter Reid, who would go on to play for and manage Manchester City, intercepted a sloppy Paul McGrath pass on the half-way lane before beginning the long dribble towards Gary Bailey's area. United centre-back Kevin Moran put in a last ditch challenge but miss-timed his tackle and sent Reid tumbling.

Moran acknowledged the foul and walked off, before being called back by referee Peter Willis, who asked the player to turn around to take down his number. The United man was expecting to see the yellow card waved in his direction and could scarcely believe his eyes when the official produced a red. Just like his team-mates, Moran was completely incensed by the decision, and tried to grab the referee to reason with him. The United players and even some of their opponents appealed to Willis but he was having none of it and Moran had to be escorted off the pitch. Kevin became the first player to be sent-off in an FA Cup Final and as he trudged away from the action, the Irishman would have surely believed he was taking United's FA Cup hopes with him.

But a United team containing players of the ilk of Robson, Whiteside and Hughes would never give up without a fight, and the feeling that they could avenge an injustice gave them even more motivation to battle for the Cup. The Red Devils defended stoutly for the remainder of the second half, keeping the scores tied at 0-0 and forcing extra-time.

Everton were an extremely well-organised unit, and with United a man light it would take a moment of magic to score against the Champions, and that's exactly what the Reds created in the 110th minute. Mark Hughes collected the ball in his own half, turning on a sixpence and drawing in the challenge of four Everton players, before playing an exquisite through-ball with the outside of his boot, finding Norman Whiteside in acres of space on the right-flank.

Whiteside burst down the wing before enticing the challenge of Everton left-back Pat Van Den Hauwe and using the defender as a shield, curled an unstoppable left-footed strike around his marker and passed Neville Southall in goal. Whiteside's effort sent the United dugout, including Kevin Moran, into delirium as the Reds held on to seal Atkinson's second FA Cup in three seasons.

Over at Maine Road, Billy McNeill had managed to stabilise Manchester City during his first season in charge, guiding the Blues to fourth place in the Second Division; a finish he improved upon by one place in 1985 to ensure automatic promotion and a return to the top flight. In their first season back in the First Division, City managed to finish a respectable 15th, continuing to enjoy progression under the steady hand of McNeill. But things changed at the beginning of the 1986-87 campaign, signalling the start of a period of great uncertainty at Maine Road.

Under 'Big Ron', Manchester United were developing a reputation as a team capable of brilliance in the cup competitions but one that lacked the consistency and mental strength to claim the First Division title. The Red Devils hadn't won the league title since 1967 and the weight of expectation for Championship glory grew heavier every season. The United fans were content with Atkinson at the helm but many remained unconvinced about his suitability to build a long-term dynasty of success at Old Trafford.

United began the 1985-86 season in scintillating form, setting a new club record of winning their first 10 games in the league, which catapulted them to the top of the Division and saw many observers predicting it would finally be United's year. But as the injuries piled up, the strength of United's squad and Atkinson's resolve would be tested, with the intermittent losses of Bryan Robson proving most damaging. The Reds began to drop points on a more regular basis and although still top of the league by December, a run of just one win in five followed, causing the first stirrings of discontent at Old Trafford.

Despite their lack of consistency, United retained top spot for most of the season, eventually relinquishing first place at the beginning of February following a 2-1 defeat against West Ham at Upton Park. Further defeats followed, and with Liverpool entering the period of the season they relished, United began to slip out of the title picture, eventually finishing fourth. The fans' sadness at seeing the league title slip away turned to anger when the news was leaked that one of their favourite performers, Mark Hughes, would join Barcelona at the end of the season. A £1.8m fee had been agreed for the exciting striker, but with Hughes possessing such huge potential the fans were dismayed at the young striker's exit.

The memories of Manchester being the dominant footballing city in England seemed increasingly distant throughout the 1980s. United and City remained extremely well-supported, both in terms of the number and dedication of their fans, but neither club appeared equipped to mount a serious challenge to the Merseyside monopoly on major trophies, and the First Division title in particular.

The Red half of Manchester had come tantalisingly close at times, but continued to come up short when the season reached a crucial stage, while City seemed light-years away from achieving the required level. But, as the progress of traditionally smaller sides, like Nottingham Forest and West Ham United proved, English football remained more competitive and inclusive to all teams. While money was important in the game, it was not the be all and end all, a fact that continued to give the Maine Road faithful hope each summer that the Blues would improve. If United's target was to overcome Liverpool in a rivalry that was becoming increasingly fierce amongst the supporters, the Blues target remained United as they were desperate to keep pace with their city rivals.

Atkinson had been heavily backed in the transfer market during his Old Trafford tenure, adding to his significant yet superb investment in Bryan Robson with expensive outlays on two wingers with the potential to excite the United faithful, Denmark's Jesper Olsen and Scotsman Gordon Strachan, keeping true to the club's tradition of playing with width and pace. However, Big Ron had also recouped plenty of money through the sales of Ray Wilkins and Mark Hughes, ensuring that his net transfer spend was relatively modest. Atkinson had also brought through other youngsters, with classy Irish defender Paul McGrath also making his debut during the manager's reign. But despite his attempts to stay true to the best traditions of the club, and his two FA Cup wins ensuring he boasted the best record of any United manager since Matt Busby, Ron's Old Trafford future looked far from secure.

The Red Devils struggled for form at the beginning of the 1986-87 season as the injury woes continued and rumours about a drinking culture did little to help the perception that Atkinson didn't have the discipline and mental strength to continuously get the best out of his squad. Shock home defeats to the London trio of West Ham, Charlton Athletic and Chelsea didn't help matters, but a thumping 4-1 defeat to Southampton in the League Cup on November 4, 1986 was the straw that broke the camel's back, and 24 hours after the game, Ron Atkinson was sacked by Manchester United.

Within hours of Atkinson's role at the club coming to an end, United had identified the man they wanted to succeed him – someone who would go on to revolutionise the club and bring a level of success that the board and supporters could scarcely have believed.

While the 1986-87 campaign was shrouded with uncertainty and managerial comings and goings at Old Trafford, the same can be said of matters at Maine Road when, just a few weeks into the season, Billy McNeill left to take over at Aston Villa. McNeill's replacement was Jimmy Frizzle, who had been his assistant and previously spent 12 years in charge of Oldham Athletic. It was a steady but far from spectacular appointment and did little to inspire the supporters, but Manchester City were not the draw they had once been and, with the club struggling financially, attracting bigger name managers proved difficult.

Frizzle worked hard to improve matters on the pitch, but as City's financial woes worsened he was hamstrung in the transfer market and unable to add to a squad that desperately needed strengthening. The Blues' slump continued and they eventually finished second from the bottom in 1987, enduring their second relegation of the decade. There may have been cause for optimism at Old Trafford, but the only vibes coming out of Maine Road were drenched in pessimism.

7

THE FERGUSON EFFECT

Just three hours after dismissing Ron Atkinson as Manchester United manager, Chairman Martin Edwards was en route to Scotland to talk to the man that would transform the future of the club. Edwards had been given permission by Aberdeen to talk to their highly-rated young manager, Alex Ferguson, about taking over at Old Trafford, and would visit the former Glasgow Rangers striker at his home that evening to discuss the future. Those discussions went well and the following morning Ferguson met his new players at The Cliff, the club's famous training ground, for the first time.

Alex Ferguson had gained a host of admirers at clubs right across England following a period of unrivalled success with Aberdeen. A huge believer in bringing through young players and moulding a positive team unit while playing attacking and winning football, Ferguson had taken a provincial club to the heights of winning the Scottish First Division, breaking up the dominance of the two Glasgow clubs Celtic and Rangers in the process, while dominating domestic cup competitions and also tasting European success after beating the might of Real Madrid in the 1983 European Cup Winners' Cup Final.

As well as his record, Ferguson's attitude and philosophy appealed to the United board. The pressure on the Scotsman would be huge, particularly in the early years, but eventually he would not only realise those expectations but exceed them – and in spectacular fashion.

Ferguson was a manager that wanted an input in every part of the club. A fantastic organiser, with an incessant work ethic, the Scotsman would strive for perfection in all areas at Old Trafford. While Ferguson had a fierce reputation as being prickly with the media and a harsh disciplinarian with his players, he also had a natural way with people, putting them at ease and helping to create a family atmosphere at Manchester United. His dedication to home-grown talent was evident early on as he looked to revolutionise the club's youth setup, a decision that would later bear significant fruit.

However, Ferguson's first task was to turn around the ailing league fortunes of a team struggling for confidence. He inherited a squad filled with talented players and attempted to get the very best out of them, but knew the squad needed major surgery. Ferguson started by adding to his backroom staff, bringing in Archie Knox, who had served as his assistant at Aberdeen, while former United European Cup winner Brian Kidd was later appointed in a coaching capacity.

Under Ferguson and Knox, training began to take on a new intensity with longer and harder sessions introduced in an attempt to improve fitness and sharpness. The extra effort on the training field soon transferred into positive performances on the pitch, including a 1-0 win against Liverpool in Ferguson's first trip to Anfield. But the team was still dogged with inconsistency, as the new manager experimented with a number of players, trying to find the best solution. Ferguson's first Manchester derby came in the FA Cup and ended in a 1-0 victory after a goal from Norman Whiteside, but the Reds later exited the competition to eventual winners Coventry City and could only manage an 11th place league finish.

On the other side of Manchester, Jimmy Frizzle was shown the Maine Road door in 1987 and Chairman Peter Swales once again picked a man that had enjoyed success at Norwich City, as Mel Machin followed in the footsteps of Ron Saunders and John Bond in making the move from East Anglia to Manchester. Machin experienced an eventful first few months at Maine Road that included a 10-1 home thrashing of Huddersfield Town. Hat-tricks from David White, Tony Adcock and Paul Stewart contributed to the rout, which became the club's highest ever victory. However, City's supporters would not be treated to such entertainment every week and had to make do with a mid-table finish in 1988. Machin's City enjoyed a significant improvement the following season, as the team finished runners-up to Chelsea in the Second Division and secured automatic promotion.

During the Machin-era, a number of youngsters began to make the breakthrough into the first team, including Manchester-born players Paul Lake, Andy Hinchcliffe, David White and Paul Stewart, who had been signed from Blackpool. As well as the local lads, players from other areas that had been reared through the club's youth system, such as Paul Simpson and Ian Brightwell, also began to make an impact. With little money to invest in transfers, the progression of an impressive collection of home-grown talent was of great benefit to the manager. The players were labelled as City's 'golden generation' and went on to make history by winning the FA Youth Cup for the first time in the club's history in 1986. The majority of the youngsters went on to form the basis of the Blues team for a number of years, making a largely positive impression at the higher level.

During the summer of 1987 Alex Ferguson began to put his stamp on the Manchester

United squad as a number of players that had been regular starters under Ron Atkinson, including Gary Bailey and Frank Stapleton, left the club. The manager's first additions came with the signings of experienced England international defender Viv Anderson and Celtic's prolific striker Brian McClair.

McClair settled quickly and his goals helped the Reds climb the table. Despite his team's progress, Ferguson was still keen to strengthen, and when Paul McGrath sustained an injury the manager moved for Norwich City defender, Steve Bruce, who would prove one of Ferguson's most inspired signings.

As the 1987-88 season progressed, United found themselves in fourth place and within touching distance of challenging for the title, but disappointing results following the turn of year showed that there was still plenty of room for improvement. Most of the players had bought into Ferguson's methods and there were positive signs for the future.

During the crucial Easter period, United faced Liverpool in a memorable league encounter at Anfield. The game ended in a 3-3 draw that, in truth, didn't really damage the Merseyside club's title hopes, but nevertheless Ferguson's men had laid down a marker. Robson had fired them into an early advantage before Liverpool cruised to a 3-1 lead and United's Colin Gibson was given his marching orders. With the pressure off, United's 10 men put in an inspired display and grabbed an unlikely point when Robson and Gordon Strachan both scored late goals in front of the Kop, as the Liverpool Stadium terraces are colloquailly known. Liverpool would eventually claim the title at a canter, with the Red Devils finishing second.

Alex Ferguson's first full season in charge had ended well, but the Scotsman knew there was much work to be done and he wasted little time making further additions to his squad, signing Scotland goalkeeper Jim Leighton from his former club Aberdeen and securing the return of Mark Hughes following his disappointing two-year spell at Barcelona. Ferguson saw it as a signing that would inspire the supporters who had been devastated to see Hughes leave the club, and was confident that Hughes would provide the ideal attacking foil for Brian McClair.

The improved youth system began to bear fruit as Lee Martin and Lee Sharpe, a teenage signing from Torquay United, were thrown into the first team fray. As the months went on, Ferguson introduced further youngsters, including Russell Beardsmore and Mark Robins, a local striker who would go on to play a crucial role in the manager's United career. In reference to the famous 'Busby Babes', the youngsters were labelled as 'Fergie's Fledglings' by the media.

As more teenagers came into the team the manager allowed more experienced performers to move on, including Gordon Strachan to Leeds United, a deal that would go on to haunt Ferguson in the future. United fielded 23 players in the last 24 games of the season and again struggled for consistency, ending the 1988-89 campaign in 11th place. It was a significant drop from the previous season's runners-up spot, but Ferguson was in the middle of a major rebuild and perhaps accepted that a short-term backward step was necessary for long-term progression.

The summer of 1989 was another busy one for Ferguson, who spent heavily to bolster his midfield, capturing England international Neil Webb from Nottingham Forest and Norwich City captain Mike Phelan. The pair would provide assistance and cover to the often overworked Bryan Robson, but news of their arrival was soon dwarfed by matters off the field, when it looked as though the club would be sold to charismatic businessman Michael Knighton, who wanted to become United's majority shareholder.

Knighton submitted a £20m bid, a British record at that point, to existing Chairman, Martin Edwards, but his interest was soon fiercely examined by the media, especially by *The Daily Mirror*, owned by media mogul Robert Maxwell, an extremely powerful man who had also attempted to take charge at Old Trafford in 1984. It would not be the last time that a man who wielded huge power and influence in the media would attempt to buy a controlling stake in the club, and certainly not the last time that a controversial character would attempt to engineer such involvement at Manchester United.

Knighton had outlined grand future plans, proposing significant investment and improvements to facilities at Old Trafford, before donning a full United strip and famously juggling the ball toward the Stretford End ahead of the first game of the season against Arsenal. Despite Kinghton's bravado and vision for the club, the charismatic young businessman would never complete a takeover, failing to secure the funds required to complete the deal.

The buzz that Michael Knighton had created at Old Trafford ahead of the season's opening fixture against reigning Champions Arsenal would soon translate onto the pitch, as Ferguson's new-look United tore into the Gunners from the first whistle. The Reds eventually won the game 4-1, with goals from Bruce, Hughes, McClair and debutant Webb.

Just three games into the new campaign, Ferguson again made a bold move in the transfer market, capturing Middlesbrough defender Gary Pallister in a club record £2.3m deal. It took the future England international a little time to settle at Old Trafford, but he and Steve Bruce soon formed the basis of one of the club's finest ever defensive units. In September, two more new signings arrived at Old Trafford as Ferguson completed the much-protracted transfer of powerful midfielder Paul Ince from West Ham, as well as adding lightning-quick left-winger Danny Wallace from Southampton.

Manchester City had returned to the First Division for the 1989-90 season to find a

Manchester United side still adapting to the managerial style of Alex Ferguson. As both teams struggled in the league and the cup competitions, local pride and bragging rights were two of the only things left to play for, and the most memorable moment of Machin's reign came during that first season back in the top flight, when City thumped United 5-1 at Maine Road on September 23, 1989.

In a performance filled with tempo and determination the Blues ruthlessly tore into a below-par United after the game had been restarted following an enforced break when trouble erupted in the stands. Returning to the pitch, City seized the initiative, thanks to early goals from David Oldfield (who later grabbed a second) and Trevor Morley, before Ian Bishop and Andy Hinchcliffe ensured the scoreline was even more emphatic. United's solitary response was a belting scissor-kick from Mark Hughes, but the day belonged to City.

The defeat was an experience that Ferguson would dub the worst of his career and one that Reds defender Gary Pallister considers as the lowest point in his career. The players were left in no doubt how much the supporters were hurt by it, as Pallister explained in a 2003 interview with *The Guardian*. "When I walked from the dressing room there were four burly United fans waiting for me outside the door. They told me I wasn't fit to wear a United shirt, we shouldn't have sold Paul McGrath, I was a 'disgrace' to the club, the whole treatment. I thought it was just me but it turned out that all the lads had got abuse from these guys. They really ripped into us."

City were a team-filled with local youngsters and, buoyed by a crowd eager to relish the first Manchester derby in three years, they tore into the visitors for 90 minutes. United's expensively assembled eleven, were outplayed and outfought and Ferguson's men looked to be as far away from winning the title as they were when the Scotsman first took charge some three years earlier.

Despite giving Blues fans one of the highest points in years, Machin was shown the door just two months after the famous victory, with City languishing at the bottom of the table. Machin's successor was former Everton boss Howard Kendall. It was City's biggest managerial appointment for years and it had the desired impact as the Blues' form improved and the team soon eased away from the threat of relegation.

Kendall's time at the club was far from a long and distinguished one, however, as he tendered his resignation at the start of the 1990-91 campaign in favour of a return to Everton. Kendall's replacement would be a man that he'd managed at Goodison Park, with Peter Reid appointed City's Player Manager.

Despite the low of the Maine Road massacre and the occasional flirtation with the lower reaches of the league, United had enough quality in their squad to ensure a relegation battle was never a genuine possibility, although several crucial victories were needed to stave off the threat of demotion, including a crucial 2-1 Mark Hughes-inspired win over Millwall in February. The Reds eventually slumped to their lowest league placing for 15 years, finishing 13th in the table.

With the team cemented in mid-table at the turn of the year, sections of the Old Trafford support began to call for Alex Ferguson's head. However, the protests were far from widespread and many fans remained patient and hoped, if not truly believed, that the Scotsman would turn things around. The club directors remained calm and gave their backing to the manager privately if not publicly. The decision-makers had witnessed progression in a number of areas and remained confident that Ferguson's vision for the club matched theirs. The manager and the fans needed something positive to cling to and looked towards the 1990 FA Cup for respite from their travails in the league.

United's FA Cup campaign started with an extremely tough-looking away draw against Nottingham Forest. With the continued league struggles and the team long since out of the League Cup, the world's oldest cup competition represented the club's only chance of silverware. The Reds went into January's third round tie on the back of a run of eight league games without a win, including four defeats. The media speculated that defeat against Forest would force the board's hand and signal the end of Alex Ferguson's time at Manchester United. It was a view that remained unfounded years after the result with Martin Edwards later denying that removing the manager was ever considered, but Ferguson ensured it was a view that also remained entirely hypothetical by inspiring his team to a 1-0 victory.

United's preparations for the Forest cup tie were far from ideal, as Paul Ince and Danny Wallace joined Robson and Webb on the treatment table, ensuring a midfield selection headache for the manager. Ferguson opted to back youth, adding Russell Beardsmore and Mark Robins to his starting eleven. The contest at Forest's City Ground was far from a classic, but it mattered little to United, as the aforementioned Robins headed home the only goal from close-range following a measured cross from Mark Hughes.

The Reds were drawn against Fourth Division Hereford United in the fourth round and avoided a potential banana skin thanks to a late winner from Clayton Blackmore. Ferguson's men enjoyed further progression after knocking out both Newcastle United and Sheffield United to set up a semi-final clash against their Lancashire neighbours, Second Division Oldham Athletic.

Oldham were managed by former Manchester City striker Joe Royle, who had assembled an extremely competitive unit on a shoestring budget. The semi-final took place at Maine Road and proved to be one of the most entertaining matches of United's season, ending in a 3-3 draw after extra-time. The replay at Maine Road just three days later was another thrilling encounter, filled with attacking football and ferocious tackling, and again went to extra-time after a 1-1 draw. United needed a hero and once again young striker Mark Robins stepped forward to score the winner that ensured the team's first major final under Alex Ferguson and the club's first FA Cup final since 1985.

United faced another physical and well-drilled team in the final, lining up against former Reds winger Steve Coppell's Crystal Palace. Another replay was required in the final, following another 3-3 draw. Palace had taken a shock lead through Gary O'Reilly before Bryan Robson pegged them back to ensure the scores were level at half-time. Mark Hughes, who would go on to prove himself as a man for the big occasion, thumped United ahead, but as the trophy looked destined for Old Trafford, Palace substitute Ian Wright capitalised on some slack defending to send the game into extra-time. Another goal from Wright put the Eagles ahead during the extra half an hour, but Hughes grabbed an equaliser to force a replay.

The second match was again held at Wembley but was much less memorable than the first encounter, with the most remarkable factor, apart from unlikely hero Lee Martin's goal, being the controversial decision taken by Alex Ferguson to drop United's usual first-choice keeper Jim Leighton for the game. Leighton, who had worked under Ferguson at Aberdeen, had looked shaky in the first contest, but he wasn't helped by a defence that struggled to cope with the physicality of their opponents. However, Ferguson, showing the ruthless nature his managerial career was famed for, elected to play Les Sealey, a man he'd recently loaned from Luton Town, in Leighton's place. Sealey made a difference to the team's attitude, who felt assured by his presence and it showed the players that Ferguson wasn't afraid to take the toughest of decisions to ensure success for Manchester United.

United won the game 1-0, via a goal from Manchester-born full-back Lee Martin who found himself in the right place at the right time to smash the ball into the net after an exquisitely measured pass from Neil Webb. The victory meant that Bryan Robson lifted the FA Cup for a third time in his career. The Red Army may not have known it then, but their club was on the verge of something very special.

The FA Cup victory provided the platform that Alex Ferguson and Manchester United needed and signalled the start of a decade of unprecedented success at Old Trafford. Ferguson continued his constant development of the club, adding another key man to his squad during the summer of 1990, signing versatile Oldham Athletic full-back Denis Irwin. Irwin would be Ferguson's only major addition but his team continued to progress, particularly impressing in the cup competitions by reaching the final of both the League Cup and the European Cup Winners' Cup, as the Reds returned to continental competition for the first time since 1985.

Over at Maine Road, 34-year-old player manager Peter Reid was attempting to re-establish City as a consistent First Division club by building on the foundations laid by Howard Kendall, which included the excellent acquisition of giant Irish centre forward Niall Quinn from Arsenal in March 1990. Quinn provided a focal point in the City attack, and scored plenty of goals as the club continued to adjust to life back in the top flight. With Quinn part of a dangerous frontline that also included David White, Peter Reid inspired the Blues to successive fifth place finishes. In 1991 they outdid United by one place and the following year, they increased their points tally from 62 to 70, setting the club up nicely for the start of the first ever Premier League campaign.

United showed flashes of brilliance throughout the 1990-91 season, but again lacked consistency in the league, seemingly saving their best performances for knock-out football. One such example came in the early rounds of the League Cup when the Reds outclassed Arsenal 6-2 at Highbury on a night where young winger Lee Sharpe was in inspired form, grabbing a spectacular hat-trick and tearing the usually solid Gunners back four to shreds. United overcame Southampton in the quarter-finals and Leeds United, a club whose rivalry with the Reds was becoming fiercer, over two legs in the semi-finals, with Lee Sharpe again the goal-scoring hero.

United's second Wembley final in a year was against Sheffield Wednesday, a team managed by former Reds manager Ron Atkinson. The Owls would eventually finish in third and provided a stern task for United in a game played just a few weeks before the European Cup Winners' Cup final. United failed to assert themselves over an extremely hard-working Wednesday side and Owls midfielder John Sheridan scored the only goal of the game with a powerful strike from distance as the Wednesday defence prevented United from playing their usual attacking game.

It was the first Wembley defeat for the Reds under Ferguson, as the League Cup—the only domestic trophy United had never won—continued to elude them. But, with the prospect of another major final to play, there were plenty of reasons to be cheerful despite a serious-looking leg-injury sustained by goalkeeper Sealey during the League Cup Final. The experienced custodian showed great bravery to stay on the pitch with a heavily gashed knee, but there were genuine doubts over his availability for the clash with Barcelona.

The Reds began their European campaign with a comfortable 3-0 aggregate victory over Hungarian side Pesci Munkas, a tie made memorable by a long-range beauty from Clayton Blackmore. Further progress followed as United dispatched Welsh club Wrexham 5-0 over two legs, before Ferguson's men faced a tougher task in the quarter-finals, negotiating a tricky two-legged affair with Montpellier of France. United were drawn against Polish side,

Legia Warsaw in the semi-finals and pretty much guaranteed their progress to the final thanks to a 3-1 away victory, which was followed by a 1-1 draw at Old Trafford.

With the other English teams out of Europe, Manchester United were once again flying the flag for British football on the continent. Les Sealey declared himself fit for the final, but was far from 100 per cent as United faced up to the task of being huge underdogs against Barcelona in Rotterdam. The Catalan giants fielded a side featuring some of the best players in Europe, including Ronald Koeman, Julio Salinas and Michael Laudrup. It was a team that went on to claim the European Champions' Cup a year later, and many expected Johan Cruyff's charges to walk over United.

Bryan Robson was peerless in the middle of the park, disrupting play, dominating the tempo of the game and driving United forward with pride and passion. It was a performance that Robson would go on to describe as one of his greatest in a United shirt, and he wasn't the only man to put in a fantastic display. Mark Hughes, who had previously been discarded by Barcelona, had a point to prove, and his movement, strength and power caused the Spaniard's defence constant problems. Robson and Hughes combined to give United, playing in an unfamiliar all-white kit, a second half lead when Robson's beautifully flighted free-kick was nodded goalward by Steve Bruce before Hughes made sure by slamming the ball into the roof of the net.

Barcelona were shocked and United capitalised again just seven minutes later when Hughes grabbed his second of the night. The Welshman burst onto a superb through-ball by Robson and found himself in acres of space inside the Barcelona half. Hughes had timed his run to perfection, leaving the defenders in his wake before Barcelona keeper, Carles Busquets – the father of future Barca midfielder Sergio Busquets, who would go on to play against the Reds in two European Cup Finals –closed Hughes down a full 25 yards off his line.

The United striker's instinct, balance and quick-thinking took him around the goalkeeper, although a slightly heavy touch forced him wide of the goal with the ball rolling towards the edge of the box and the touchline. Busquets was stranded, but two Barcelona defenders had made up the ground he'd lost, almost reaching the goal line before Hughes slammed an unstoppable right-foot strike into the bottom left corner. Barcelona were shell-shocked, and even though Ronald Koeman forced a goal back from a free-kick, United held out to claim a famous victory and only the second European trophy in the club's history.

While Hughes and Robson received many of the plaudits for the victory, one of the unsung heroes was Brian McClair who had been assigned the role of man-marking Ronald Koeman, and stopping him marking the extra man in midfield, in what proved to be a tactical masterstroke from Alex Ferguson. The deliverance of a European trophy catapulted Ferguson alongside Matt Busby and ensured that the concerns of a year earlier were soon forgotten.

A final league placing of sixth position showed genuine progression as United edged closer to fielding a team capable of challenging for the title. It's said that every great team needs a great goalkeeper, and with all due respect to the stoppers that played under Ferguson in previous seasons the man he brought in during the summer of 1991 was a cut above the rest. Danish giant Peter Schmeichel arrived from Brondby and went on to become one of Alex Ferguson's most important signings and arguably the greatest goalkeeper in the club's history. The manager also invested in Queen's Park Rangers' England defender, Paul Parker, adding further pace and solidity to his backline. Ukraine wing-wizard Andrei Kanchelskis had also been acquired and United appeared to have a team and a squad with good balance and strength in depth.

Things were also changing off the field, as Manchester United was floated on the stock exchange as a public company for the first time, helping to raise funds for the development of the Stretford End. The start of the 1991-92 season signalled the 25-year landmark since Manchester United had last won the league title but the team developed into genuine title contenders throughout the campaign. Their main contenders were Leeds United, a team full of British grit, including tough striker Lee Chapman, and creative flair in the shape of former Red Gordon Strachan, and an intriguingly talented French forward named Eric Cantona – a man who would go on to become a Manchester United legend.

The sale of Strahan proved to be a costly onefor Alex Ferguson as he captained Leeds to victory over his former club and bitter rivals in the 1991-2 league season. United's battle with Leeds proved to be an exhausting season-long contest that eventually ended in bitter disappointment. The Reds again enjoyed Cup success, lifting the European Super Cup after a 1-0 win over Red Star Belgrade and defeating Nottingham Forest in the League Cup Final by the same scoreline, but the team struggled with injuries during the league run-in and faced a punishing schedule following a fixture pile-up. After defeats at home to Nottingham Forest and the already relegated West Ham United handed the initiative to Leeds, the final nails were rammed into the Reds' title coffin with a 2-0 defeat to Liverpool at Anfield, whose home support revelled in United's failure to claim the trophy they had desired for so long.

United's players and fans felt crushing disappointment, but once the dust settled on another largely successful season there was cause for optimism. One of the biggest plusses of the campaign was the emergence of a hugely exciting teenager called Ryan Giggs. Giggs, who had once been on the books at Manchester City, burst onto the scene early in the season and scored his first goal for the Reds against the Blues at Old Trafford. Like Lee Sharpe a few seasons earlier, the young Welshman immediately became a fan favourite and his style of play and physical appearance soon drew comparisons with the great George Best.

As well as displaying an increasingly strong unit on the pitch, Manchester United looked in good shape off it, perfectly preparing themselves for the biggest and most successful rebranding exercise that English football has ever seen, when the First Division became the FA Premier League ahead of the 1992-93 season. Whilst the FA insisted the creation of a new league was to benefit the national team, as they would play less games in order to recover in time for international competitions, it was quite obvious that a new football league would allow the 'big five' (Arsenal, Everton, Liverpool, Manchester United and Tottenham) to create a superior league that could take advantage of a lucrative television rights deal on the table.

After a mooted players' strike was avoided and following a High Court dispute, the FA Premier League was to go ahead and major television networks met at the Royal Lancaster Hotel to bid for the exclusive rights. The shoe-in favourite to secure the rights was ITV, but a Rupert Murdoch-backed BSkyB won the bid with a £304m five-year offer. The move was highly controversial as charging English fans to watch live football was a significant risk, but one that would eventually pay off. As more money was invested into the league, the quality of the football increased and fans became happy to pay for world-class football. The current television rights are worth ten times the original deal.

The format did not change at first, with the 22 teams still in operation, but this was reduced to 20 teams in 1995 after FIFA enforced a rule requiring domestic leagues to reduce their total games. The first FA Premier League kicked off with Arsenal, Aston Villa, Blackburn Rovers, Chelsea, Coventry City, Crystal Palace, Everton, Ipswich Town, Leeds United, Liverpool, Manchester City, Manchester United, Middlesbrough, Norwich City, Nottingham Forest, Oldham Athletic, Queens Park Rangers, Sheffield United, Sheffield Wednesday, Southampton, Tottenham Hotspur and Wimbledon comprising the league.

To accompany the new format would be a new trophy, meaning that United would never again get their hands on the old First Division silverware they had chased for so long. But that would matter little to Reds fans, when Bryan Robson and Steve Bruce finally lifted the new trophy at the end of the season as Ferguson's men ended 26 years of hurt and were crowned Champions at the finale of a campaign filled with memorable attacking displays.

Manchester City began their Premier League campaign and third successive season in the top flight with Peter Reid still at the helm. City's home game against QPR became the first ever Monday night game to be broadcast live on Sky Sports, illustrating the continued Americanisation of the English game. Reid had been given little financial backing to strengthen the team and, like Kendall and Machin before him, he relied upon the continued progression of the 1986 FA Youth Cup winning team. The manager did make a handful of key signings, including a rare foray into the continental transfer market to complete a deal for Dutch centre-back Michel Vonk and paying a club record fee of £2.5m for Wimbledon's pacey defender Keith Curle. The money spent on Curle was a significant investment for City as the club attempted to build on several seasons of consolidation, but that type of deal wasn't the norm, as the Blues mostly looked towards their youth team for new talent, bringing through the likes of Steve Lomas and Mike Sheron, who scored 12 goals during the 1992-93 campaign.

With the windfall of increased television income that followed the introduction of the Premier League, Reid was later afforded a little more leeway in the transfer market, bringing in veteran midfielder Steve McMahon from Liverpool, lightning-quick left-back Terry Phelan from Wimbledon (for £2.5m), Norwegian midfielder Kare Ingebrigtsen and tricky wingers Rick Holden and Fitzroy Simpson.

The signings gave City strength in depth but didn't lead to a significant improvement on the pitch, as the Blues slipped to a ninth place finish in 1993. Many fans weren't impressed with the style of play deployed under Reid, with the long-ball to Niall Quinn used a little too readily for their liking. Seeing their closest rivals playing an increasingly expansive attacking style didn't help matters and Reid was eventually shown the door by Chairman Peter Swales just four games into the 1993-94 season.

Reid's replacement was Oxford United manager Brian Horton, who, despite enjoying relative success in the lower leagues, was hardly the big-name appointment that Blues supporters had hoped for. Continued fan protests against Swales and the way their club was being run led to the City Chairman stepping down in 1994, with former player and huge fan favourite Francis Lee coming in to replace him.

If things had began to stagnate under Reid they soon progressively worsened under Horton as the team struggled for goals – managing a total of just 36 in the league all season and slumping to a disappointing 16th place finish, the club's lowest top flight placing since the 1987 relegation.

At United, having narrowly lost out to Leeds the season before, Ferguson knew that major surgery wasn't required. His only pre-season addition was Cambridge United target man, Dion Dublin, as Mark Robins, a man whose goals had been so crucial to Ferguson's rebuilding, was allowed to join Norwich City. United started the season slowly with shock defeats to Sheffield United and Everton, but gradually found their feet with a home draw against Ipswich Town and a 1-0 win at Southampton, sealed with a last-minute winner from Dublin.

Despite dominating teams and playing effective attacking football, United still struggled to convert their possession into goals, and following the loss of Dublin with a broken leg, Ferguson was keen to add to his attacking ranks. The Scotsman had missed out to Blackburn Rovers for the signing of promising England centre-forward Alan Shearer in the summer and had also been linked with a move for Sheffield Wednesday goal-machine David Hirst. However, a man that certainly hadn't been on the media's radar, who would go on to become the catalyst for the title, was about to arrive at the club, following a fateful telephone conversation between United Director, Martin Edwards and his Leeds United counterpart, Bill Fotherby.

Fotherby was enquiring about the availability of Denis Irwin, and with Alex Ferguson in the room with Edwards he was soon met with a negative response, but Ferguson had another potential deal on his mind. He scribbled a note on a piece of paper and handed it to the Chairman. It said: 'Ask him about Cantona'. Edwards did and after Fotherby discussed the matter with Leeds manager Howard Wilkinson and the two Chairmen had haggled over the price, a £1m deal was agreed to transfer the hugely gifted Frenchman to Old Trafford.

The signing of Cantona was a masterstroke. He proved to be the final figure of flair, a player who had the imagination to unlock a defence with a beautifully weighted pass, a gravity-defying flick or spectacularly timed shot. The fans soon took to the Frenchman, whose physical presence and body language on the pitch portrayed an individual blessed with great confidence that verged on arrogance. As United continued to progress and the fans became accustomed to success, it was an arrogance that they could identify with. Cantona immediately felt a sense of belonging as his talents could be showcased on the stage they deserved. Quite simply, Eric Cantona and Manchester United were a match made in heaven.

The Frenchman had the confidence and strength of character to express his natural talent under the greatest of pressure. It was a quality that would crucially rub off on his team-mates. Cantona's influence on the United playing squad was felt further than on the field of play, as his dedication to training and improving his craft was keenly observed and soon copied by the club's next generation of stars. Memorable moments from Cantona that season came in a 4-1 thumping over Tottenham Hotspur at Old Trafford, where he scored a looping header, but also provided a sumptuous assist for Denis Irwin, a carefully placed header against Manchester City at Maine Road and a world class long-range volley against Crystal Palace in the FA Cup.

As well as Cantona's contribution, one of the crucial elements of United's 1993 title victory came at the end of a tense Premier League contest with Sheffield Wednesday over the Easter period. The Owls had taken a shock lead when John Sheridan, the man whose goal defeated the Reds in the 1991 League Cup Final, converted a penalty conceded by Paul Ince. The referee who had awarded the penalty, Mick Peck, would have an even bigger impact on the game, not through a decision, but through an Achilles tendon injury that forced him from the field of play. Peck was replaced by linesman John Hilditch, eventually leading to six minutes of injury time. As the clock ticked down, the nervous tension around Old Trafford was palpable as the fans began to wonder whether fate would conspire against them once again. Wednesday's England international goalkeeper Chris Woods had been in fine-form, saving anything the Reds threw at him, but he was eventually beaten in the 86th minute when captain Steve Bruce looped a header into the net from a Denis Irwin corner. Bruce wasn't finished there and 10 minutes later, a full six minutes into injury time, the unlikely sight of Gary Pallister drilling in a right-wing cross that was met by a more customary bullet header from Steve Bruce sent the Stretford End wild.

The players and the management realised the significance of the goal and Alex Ferguson and Bryan Kidd couldn't conceal their delight, scampering onto the pitch to celebrate, as Kidd dropped to his knees and kissed the turf. It was a moment, and a game, that set United's title run-in in motion and gave the players, the fans and the manager the belief that the Championship was on its way back to Manchester.

The Reds would eventually be crowned Champions without kicking a ball, as Aston Villa lost 1-0 at home to Oldham Athletic to hand United the title. United's next game against Blackburn Rovers was a celebration of their season as the Reds enjoyed a 3-1 victory. The trophy was awarded to Steve Bruce and Bryan Robson, who fittingly shared the honour of holding it aloft, as two proud Scotsmen, Alex Ferguson and Matt Busby, watched on with great satisfaction.

Ahead of the 1993-94 season, Alex Ferguson only made one major addition to his ranks, with the club record £3.75m capture of Roy Keane from Nottingham Forest. Immediately dubbed the 'new Bryan Robson', big things were expected of the all-action Irishman and he settled quickly, scoring twice against Sheffield United on his home debut and soon developing a good understanding with Paul Ince. The return to fitness of Lee Sharpe, following problems with illness and injury, had the impact of a new signing as the flying winger found his best form and enjoyed a fantastic return in front of goal during the early months of the season.

Another young winger, Ryan Giggs, continued to show his promise and the team, which now had the confidence and belief to match their ability, went from strength to strength.

The 1994 title was wrapped up with something of a canter. Despite another challenge from Aston Villa and the emergence of big-spending Blackburn Rovers, United topped the table for the majority of the campaign, losing just four from 42 games, winning 27 and clocking up 94 points and 80 goals and finished eight points ahead of second-placed Blackburn. The season featured a memorable Manchester derby at Maine Road, which United eventually won 3-2 (after City led 2-0 at half-time), with late goals from Cantona and Keane giving the Reds the points.

United also tasted FA Cup success, defeating Chelsea 4-0 at Wembley to seal the club's first ever league and cup double. The Reds' road to Wembley included a memorable 3-0 victory over Wimbledon, marked by a wonderful long-range volley from Eric Cantona, and a remarkable passing move that was expertly finished off by Denis Irwin. There was also drama in the semi-final against Oldham Athletic when Mark Hughes rescued the Reds with a late extra-time equaliser to force a replay that saw United thump the Latics 4-1. The Wembley final against Chelsea was another one-sided affair inspired by two ice-cool Cantona penalties.

United came close to winning an unprecedented domestic treble when they faced Aston Villa in the League Cup final at Wembley, but the Villans, managed by Ron Atkinson and inspired by a textbook defensive performance by former Red, Paul McGrath, were the better team on the day and won 3-1.

With United now established as the dominant team in England, the club and Ferguson's attention soon turned to conquering Europe. The Reds began their first campaign in the European Cup in 25 years against Hungary's Kispest Honved. Ferguson's men triumphed 5-3 on aggregate to set up a second round tie against Galatasaray of Turkey. The Reds gave themselves a lot to do following a disappointing 3-3 draw with the Turks at Old Trafford, but it was off the pitch events that hampered United further as they faced a white hot welcome in Istanbul, with the team hotel and team bus becoming a target of passionate abuse that verged on hatred.

The hostile atmosphere continued at the Ali Sami Yen Stadium, as the Galatasaray players were in provocative mood and, with the referee providing little protection, Eric Cantona eventually took matters into his own hands. Frustrated by United's inability to break the 0-0 deadlock and the physical treatment being dished out by his opponents, the fiery Frenchman lashed out and was sent off. As Cantona left the pitch he was harassed by the local police, a fate that would follow for his team-mates as they also exited the field of play at full-time. The goalless draw signalled the end of United's interest in the tournament as the club slipped out of the competition before the group stages.

While United were acclimatising to European football, City were still struggling to find their feet in the Premier League. In fact the Reds' continued success throughout the 90s was mirrored by Manchester City's decline as the Blues endured an ominous slump under Brian Horton, setting the scene for a hugely damaging demotion.

8

CONTRASTING FORTUNES

Following his appointment as City manager, Brian Horton moved quickly in the transfer market, attempting to redress City's fortunes by bringing in Nicky Summerbee – son of club legend Mike Summerbee—Everton winger Peter Beagrie, Spurs striker Paul Walsh and German centre forward Uwe Rosler.

While the addition of Summerbee was a romantic nod to the past, one of most iconic elements of Manchester City's history was lost to progress in 1994, as Blues fans had to say farewell to their beloved Kippax Stand, which was demolished and replaced with a more modern alternative, making Maine Road an all-seater stadium in accordance with the requirements of the Taylor Report. A three-tier stand with a 14,000 capacity was eventually unveiled in October 1995 as the club attempted to build an arena to match their neighbours and the rest of the Premier League.

United's only major signing ahead of the 1994-95 season was the capture of Lancashire-born defender David May. Ferguson's men were again one of the most impressive teams in the division, but started to drop a few points as their second successive European Cup campaign took some of the focus.

United were placed straight into the group stages without the need to qualify and were drawn against Barcelona, IFK Gothenburg and the team that had ended their European hopes the previous year, Galatasaray. Hampered by UEFA's selection requirements and a spot of tactical naivety, the Reds struggled away from home, losing to Barcelona and Gothenburg and only managing another 0-0 draw in Galatasaray.

A 2-2 home draw against Barcelona showed the team's potential as a well-taken strike from Lee Sharpe and another Mark Hughes goal against his former employers set up one of the most memorable European nights Old Trafford had seen for decades. But, the corresponding fixture at the Nou Camp was another matter entirely as a United team missing Schmeichel and Cantona was taken apart 4-0. At the time, UEFA had placed restrictions on the number of 'foreign' players—those born outside of the country each club represented.

Only three foreign players were able to be involved in the matchday squad. This included those from other British nations, such as Ryan Giggs, Brian McClair and Mark Hughes, as well as Irishmen Denis Irwin and Roy Keane, ensuring that Alex Ferguson had a huge selection dilemma that forced him to compromise in a number of areas.

Barcelona played with speed and technical brilliance and possessing star strikers, Romario and Hristo Stoichkov, they were rightly dubbed the 'dream team'. The early 90s United squad had nowhere near the strength in depth that became common towards the end of the decade, meaning that a number of youngsters, including Nicky Butt, were included against the Catalan club.

The 4-0 thumping, and other slip-ups away from home, saw United finish third in the group and miss out on qualification for the knockout stages. The Nou Camp drubbing had been a case of men against boys and showed Alex Ferguson just how much work there was to be done in Europe, both tactically and in terms of building a squad capable of coping with the demands of competing at home and abroad.

If the European exit was one of the low-points of a disappointing campaign, the club's lowest ebb came at the end of January when United faced Crystal Palace at Selhurst Park. The Reds went into the game on top of the table, after an Eric Cantona-inspired 1-0 win over Championship rivals Blackburn Rovers, but the Frenchman went on to make headlines for all the wrong reasons just three days later.

United were drawing 1-1 with a Palace side battling against relegation, and the Eagles displayed plenty of fight, and not just metaphorically. A rare David May goal had drawn United level, but the Reds had been largely subdued as an attacking force. Cantona had developed a reputation as a man with a short fuse, who could be easily provoked.

It took some pretty intense and substantial provocation from Palace defender Richard Shaw to cause the Frenchman to snap, but when he did it led to one of the most shocking moments in Manchester United's history. After more man-handling from Shaw, Cantona threw a kick at his marker, right in front of the referee, leading to a straight red card. But the drama didn't end there as Cantona was taunted by the Palace fans as he left the pitch. Some of the chants aimed in Eric's direction could be described as banter, but many of the comments were later alleged by Cantona to be much more venomous. Cantona was clearly incensed and launched himself towards 21-year-old Matthew Simmons, aiming a kung-fu style kick in his direction. The United man had to be restrained by team-mates and club staff to prevent further confrontation, but the damage had been done. The world of football was in shock, prompting media outrage and widespread condemnation of Cantona's actions.

Aware that they needed to take a hard-line against their player's behaviour, within 48 hours Manchester United fined Cantona £20,000 and suspended him from the first team for the rest of the season. However, the FA weren't satisfied with the punishment, fining Cantona a further £10,000 and extending the ban to eight months to include the first two months of the following season.

As well as receiving some of the most severe disciplinary action the football authorities had ever dished out, Cantona faced legal action over the incident and later admitted common assault at Croydon Magistrates Court. He was initially given a 14-day prison sentence and bailed pending an appeal. Thankfully for Cantona, and United and English football in general, the punishment was reduced to a 120-hour community service order on appeal. Cantona spent his community service coaching schoolchildren from Manchester, as the United youngsters he'd already inspired on the training ground began to have more involvement in the first team.

Before the Cantona incident the Reds had bolstered their attacking options by paying a club-record £6m for Newcastle United hotshot Andy Cole. With Cantona's absence, and an injury sustained by Mark Hughes earlier in the season, a lot of pressure was placed on Cole's shoulders. Despite showing glimpses of his class, including five goals in a 9-0 thumping of Ipswich Town and a cute finish against Manchester City at Maine Road, it took the Englishman some time to adjust to being a Manchester United player.

Missing Cantona, and with Cole still finding his feet, United weren't at their ruthless best during the title run-in and found themselves trailing Blackburn by six points at the end of March, but Ferguson's men managed to cut the advantage to two points going into the final fixtures. On what proved to be one of the most dramatic final days of the season in Premier League history, Blackburn faced Liverpool at Anfield while United travelled to West Ham.

Liverpool went on to defeat Rovers 2-1, meaning United just needed to beat West Ham to win the league, but with the Hammers inspired by the fine form of goalkeeper Ludek Miklosko, the Reds only mustered a 1-1 draw and had to face up to another team lifting the Premier League trophy for the first time.

United then faced Everton in their second successive FA Cup Final and, still reeling from losing the title, put in a subdued performance, eventually losing 1-0 as Paul Rideout's winner meant that United ended a season without a trophy for the first time in six years - a statistic that illustrated how much success the club had enjoyed under Alex Ferguson.

It was a level of success that City could only dream of but Brian Horton's new signings did galvanise the team as an attacking force as the front three of Walsh, Rosler and Quinn managed 47 league goals between them. Home-grown younger players began to make their mark on the first team, including midfielder Gary Flitcroft and right-back Richard Edghill. At the beginning of December 1994, City were sixth in the division and looked certainties for a top ten finish but, despite a much-improved goals return, the Blues left the back door open far too regularly, emphasised by a 5-0 thumping against Manchester United at Old Trafford when Andrei Kanchelskis scored an impressive hat-trick, and went on to win just four of their remaining 25 league games. This resulted in a 17th place finish and the avoidance of relegation by just four points.

The fact that City had spent much of the 1994-95 campaign in the lower reaches of the table prompted Francis Lee to show Brian Horton the door before the end of the season and to bring in his former England team-mate Alan Ball from Southampton. Lee wanted his own man at the helm and predicted a bright future for the club under Ball. But, after several mediocre seasons, the City supporters' worst nightmares were confirmed at the end of the 1995-96 campaign when the Blues were relegated from the top flight on the final day of the season.

One of Francis Lee's most important decisions was the signing of Georgian playmaker Georgi Kinkladze, who was brought in before Ball's arrival. Kinkladze was a midfield magician who possessed the close-control and skill to excite the fans and conjure up moments of match-winning brilliance. Alan Ball allowed a number of the club's older performers to depart, but with a team in transition and Ball arguably attempting to change things too quickly, the Blues struggled badly, failing to win any of the opening 12 games of the 1995-96 season. A brief upturn in form during November, including two wins on the bounce, saw the Blues escape the relegation places but it wasn't long before they returned to the danger zone.

City's plight wasn't helped by the enforced sale of talented midfielder Gary Flitcroft in March 1996. With the club's financial problems deepening, Francis Lee and Alan Ball had no choice but to accept a £2.5m offer from Blackburn, meaning a vital driving force was lost ahead of the crucial run-in.

City continued to fight against the almost inevitable relegation right up until a drama-filled final day of the season when a 2-2 draw with Liverpool at Maine Road sent the club down on goal difference. Liverpool had taken the lead through a Steve Lomas own goal and a strike of their own from Ian Rush, ensuring that City ended the first half two goals behind. But inspired by a desperate and vociferous home crowd, the Blues clawed their way back into the game through Uwe Rosler and Kit Symons.

City knew they needed to better the results of Southampton and Coventry to survive and, when word came through that Coventry were behind, the Blues decided to keep possession and attempt to run the clock down to preserve the point they thought would keep them up. This led to the famous scene of a number of players, including Steve Lomas playing 'keep ball' in front of the corner flag to soak up vital seconds, until Niall Quinn, who had been substituted, discovered that Coventry were in fact drawing and not losing and ran down the touchline to pass on the news to his team-mates. City tried to attack and grab a vital winner, but with the momentum lost it was too little, too late. Both sadness and frustration engulfed Maine Road, as the demotion signalled the end of seven successive seasons in the top flight.

Realising that changes needed to be made at United after surrendering the league and cup double, Alex Ferguson acted quickly to overhaul his squad, but rather than add expensive signings the wily Scot allowed three of the club's biggest names to leave. Out went fan favourite Mark Hughes, the dynamic Paul Ince and the increasingly impressive Andrei Kanchelskis, but there were no big name replacements as Ferguson, like the legendary Matt Busby decided to put his faith in youth.

Ryan Giggs had been an established starter for four seasons, and was about to be joined by five other youngsters who had been reared at the club. The talented quintet featured David Beckham, Paul Scholes, Nicky Butt and the Neville brothers, Gary and Phil. Like the Busby Babes before them, the youngsters had enjoyed success in the FA Youth Cup, lifting the trophy in 1992, while a team captained by Phil Neville also won the honour in 1995.

With Cantona still banned at the beginning of the season, United's line-up for the opening day fixture against Aston Villa had a distinctly unfamiliar feel, with many of the younger players selected in the starting eleven. Villa went on to win 3-1, causing many to doubt United's chances that season, including BBC pundit and former Liverpool defender Alan Hansen, who famously claimed: "You'll never win anything with kids."

As the season wore on, the kids began to find their feet and soon showed they were more than capable of performing for the club. The Reds' main challengers for the title were a resurgent Newcastle United side, managed by the enigmatic Kevin Keegan and playing with an attacking style that took the top flight by storm. Ferguson's men had struggled to keep up in the first half of the season, but at the beginning of October the club was buoyed by the long-awaited return of 'The King', as Eric Cantona started his first game in nine months during a 2-2 home draw with Liverpool. Cantona set-up United's opening goal with a cross-field pass for Nicky Butt before converting a late equaliser from the penalty spot.

As the season wore on, Cantona's influence on the team grew stronger, and while the likes of Beckham, Scholes, Butt and the Nevilles showed impressive consistency, it was the Frenchman and Peter Schmeichel who stole many of the headlines as the Reds won a succession of league games by a goal to nil, with the goal invariably coming from Cantona, and Schmeichel often performing heroics to keep a clean sheet.

One such outcome was realised in a huge match between the top two teams at StJames' Park at the beginning of March 1996. Newcastle dominated much of the game, creating a whole host of goal-scoring opportunities, but they were repeatedly denied by Schmeichel who enjoyed one of his best nights between the posts for the Reds. In the 52nd minute Cantona punished the hosts for their wastefulness in front of goal by guiding a beautifully judged volley into the far corner. Newcastle tried to force an equaliser but continued to find the Reds in resolute form and the game ended 1-0.

The Magpies had held a 12 point advantage in January, but United's win reduced the deficit to just two points. The Reds excelled during the run-in, winning seven of their last eight games and eventually claiming the title with a last-day 3-0 victory over Middlesbrough. United and Cantona weren't finished there and went on to defeat Liverpool in the FA Cup Final at Wembley, thanks to another moment of magic from the talismanic striker that ensured a second 'double' in three seasons.

Following the team's relegation, the Manchester City board kept faith with Alan Ball ahead of the 1996-97 season, but feeling his hands were being tied due to the number of players being sold to keep the club afloat financially, the manager tendered his resignation just three games into the Division One campaign.

Ball was immediately replaced by former Manchester United winger, Steve Coppell, who had enjoyed managerial success with Crystal Palace. However, realising the enormity of the job that faced him at Maine Road and feeling the huge pressure associated, Coppell resigned after just six games and 33 days in charge.

City were in a state of flux and turned to Phil Neal, who took charge of the team on a temporary basis but failed to make an impact, losing seven of his 10 matches in charge as the team hovered around the lower reaches of Division One. Former Nottingham Forest manager Frank Clark was brought in to steady the ship and he succeeded in providing some stability at Maine Road, guiding the team to a 14th place finish. However, it proved the briefest of respites as City again struggled during the 1997-98 season.

During the summer of 1996 Alex Ferguson signed five players from the continent, with Raimond van der Gouw, Karel Poborsky, Jordi Cruyff, Ronnie Johnsen and Ole Gunnar Solskjaer joining the club after the Reds had again missed out on Alan Shearer's signature when the England striker opted to join his hometown club Newcastle United. Apart from Cruyff and Poborsky, who had both featured during that summer's European Championships held in England, many United supporters hadn't heard of the new arrivals.

But the least known of the five, Norway striker Solskjaer, would go on to write his name into one of the most memorable chapters in the club's history.

The 1996-97 season proved to be another successful domestic campaign for United, who led the table for long periods and held off the challenges of Newcastle, Liverpool and Arsenal to claim their second successive Premier League title. With Cantona not quite the fulcrum he had been a year previously, other players stepped forward, including David Beckham, who began the season with a famous goal from the halfway line against Wimbledon, Paul Scholes and Ole Gunnar Solsjkaer. Solskjaer top scored in the league with 18 but an unlikely goal-scorer helped The Reds win the game that arguably decided the destination of the Premier League trophy when Gary Pallister scored two first-half headers against Liverpool at Anfield to give United a 3-1 victory that left the Merseysiders adrift in the title race.

United also showed impressive form in the European Cup to that point under Alex Ferguson, reaching the semi-finals where they were knocked out by eventual winners, Borussia Dortmund of Germany. Harsh lessons were learned but the experience was vital to the development of the younger players, who were clocking up plenty of minutes in arguably the toughest club tournament in world football.

Things were ticking along nicely at Old Trafford, with United seemingly getting closer to European success, season by season, but the club was thrown into a state of shock following a surprise announcement at the end of the season from Eric Cantona, who retired from professional football at the relatively young age of 30. Cantona's replacement was England striker, Teddy Sheringham, who endured a tough start to his United career before enjoying a hugely successful few seasons. Roy Keane was appointed captain and David Beckham, a man who was becoming an icon on and off the field, was fittingly awarded the iconic number seven shirt.

In 1997 Manchester City unveiled a new club badge, featuring a design that included the Latin motto 'Superbia in proelio', meaning 'Pride in Battle', and that new philosophy perfectly summed up the battle that the club were facing in their attempts to turn against an increasingly deepening tide of failure and disappointment.

Frank Clark spent heavily during the summer of 1997, adding Portsmouth striker Lee Bradbury for £3m. It was a lot of money to spend on one centre forward, particularly one that was relatively unproven, and the pressure on Bradbury's shoulders affected his form in front of goal. Clark also brought in the versatile Dutchman Gerard Wiekens, amongst other signings, as City boasted one of the biggest squads in the division.

Despite the quality at Clark's disposal, City struggled in Division One and by February, with the team battling against relegation, the manager was sacked and replaced by former

City striker, and previous Everton and Oldham Athletic manager, Joe Royle. Royle added further reinforcements in his battle to beat the drop, including the capture of former Manchester United trainee, Shaun Goater, from Bristol City. A tough striker with aerial strength and an eye for goal, the Bermudan would go on to write his name into Manchester City folklore, but despite his and Royle's best efforts, the team's fortunes took time to turn around and, sadly for City, it was time they didn't have.

In the penultimate weekend of the season they faced Queens Park Rangers at Maine Road in a crucial relegation six-pointer, and like so many times in the past, City were their own worst enemy, as captain Jamie Pollock scored one of most memorable own goals in the history of the English game. The all-action midfielder was bombing back to his own box to intercept the ball, but only succeeded in looping it up into the air, evading both team-mates and opponents, before he planted a header over the on-rushing Martyn Margetson in goal and into the back of the net. Despite its comical nature, the own goal was a tragedy for City as it helped secure a 2-2 draw for QPR and edged the Blues closer to the relegation trapdoor.

Joe Royle's men went into the last day of the season as the most likely candidates for relegation. They faced Stoke City at the Britannia Stadium, needing a win and for their rivals Portsmouth, QPR and Port Vale to all slip-up. But all three teams won, rendering City's 5-2 victory in the Potteries irrelevant as the club faced up to demotion and the prospect of playing in English football's third tier for the first time in their history.

Manchester United played some terrific attacking football at the start of the 1997-98 season, but a serious knee injury for Roy Keane against Leeds United, following a tangle with Alf-Inge Haaland, left the Reds short of their skipper for the majority of the 1997-98 campaign. The second half of the season proved to be one of frustration for United who crashed out of Europe to Monaco on away goals in the quarter-finals and endured a slump in the league as Arsene Wenger's emerging Arsenal side soon narrowed the gap at the top of the table to tee up a potential title-decider at Old Trafford. A win would have probably put United out of sight, but defeat would hand the momentum to the North Londoners, and that's exactly what happened thanks to a late winner from Marc Overmars. The Gunners went on to overtake the Reds and claim their first Premier League crown, signalling the start of what would be a fierce and sustained rivalry between the two clubs.

Despite the ignominy of dropping into Division Two, Manchester City kept faith with Joe Royle as manager, believing his experience of achieving promotion and running a club on a shoestring budget made him suitably equipped to oversee the Blues' return to the second tier. With the required guidance in the dugout, City also had more stability in the boardroom as future FA Chairman, David Bernstein, took up the same role at Maine Road.

Royle didn't make many significant additions during the summer of 1998, opting to put his trust in the existing playing squad and it proved a wise decision, as the attacking pairing of Shaun Goater and Paul Dickov proved a masterstroke. Both strikers were hungry and had a point to prove and their work ethic and competitive nature were vital to City's hopes of promotion. Royle also gave talented young goalkeeper Nicky Weaver his first team debut, and the former Mansfield Town youngster soon justified his manager's faith, becoming a fixture in the side and keeping 26 clean sheets during the season; breaking the club record for the total number of shut-outs in a single campaign.

Another important Joe Royle signing was that of combative centre-back Andy Morrison, who joined City from Huddersfield Town and went on to make his debut for the club at the end of October. A real warrior of a defender, who relished the physical side of the game and never shirked a challenge, Morrison proved an extremely astute signing as his battling qualities, bravery and huge personality played a major role in helping the Blues face up to the enormity of the task that faced them.

Losing the Premier League and again failing to secure three successive titles was hard to take for United, but their failure in Europe caused just as much heartache. Motivated by those disappointments Alex Ferguson made three bold moves in the transfer market, spending over £30m on three established performers who each had plenty to prove, as Dutch defender Jaap Stam, Swedish winger Jesper Gronkjaer and Aston Villa's Trinidadian forward Dwight Yorke all joined the club.

The new investment and the return to fitness of Roy Keane at the start of the 1998-99 season gave the whole United squad a boost. Yorke soon found his scoring form, hitting two on his home debut against Charlton, but it took Stam a little longer to adjust to the pace of English football. The Dutchman suffered a slow start to the campaign, which included a chastening experience in a 3-0 thumping against reigning champions Arsenal at Highbury. But Stam and the team soon found their form, challenging at the top of the Premier League and progressing through the group stages of the Champions League, after topping a tough quadrant of teams that included old foes Barcelona and German superclub, Bayern Munich. There were occasional slip-ups, including a shock 3-2 home reverse to Middlesbrough in December, but following that defeat United went on a peerless run of form, remaining unbeaten in all competitions for the remainder of the season.

Memorable moments in the Premier League included an 8-1 thumping against Nottingham Forest and a 6-2 win at Leicester City, while the Reds also defeated Liverpool in the FA Cup Fourth Round thanks to a 2-1 victory that included two late goals that summed up the belief and never-say-die nature of the team's performances that season. Further progress in the Cup came following a replay victory over Chelsea, setting up an epic semi-final against title challengers Arsenal at Villa Park.

A passionate first game ended in a disappointing 0-0 draw, leading to an evening kick-off three days later. Under the Villa Park floodlights and inspired by a hugely vocal atmosphere, both teams slugged it out in one of the most memorable domestic contests of the decade. United took an early lead thanks to a David Beckham special, when the midfielder curled home a sweeping right-footed strike past David Seaman. Arsenal equalised through a deflected effort from Dennis Bergkamp, before Roy Keane was sent off for a second bookable offence, leaving the Reds under great pressure for the remaining half an hour as Arsenal pressed for a winner.

As the match ticked over into stoppage time, United appeared to have held out until Phil Neville mistimed a challenge in the area, sending Arsenal's Ray Parlour sprawling and prompting referee David Elleray to award the penalty. Dennis Bergkamp stepped up with the chance to fire the Gunners into the Cup Final, but his effort was spectacularly saved by Peter Schmeichel to keep United in the competition.

The game went into extra-time and as both teams tired, the tempo slowed and several passes went awry. One such pass came from Arsenal's defensive midfielder Patrick Vieira, a man who would go on to play for Manchester City. Vieira's slackness was intercepted by substitute Ryan Giggs who began a mazy run forward from inside his own half. The Welshman bobbed and weaved, before bursting into the area and thumping a fierce left-footed drive into the roof of the net, sparking scenes of delirium as Giggs ran off with a smile of disbelief etched across his face and his hastily removed shirt swinging around in the air. The Welshman's wonder-goal proved to be the winner, sending the Reds to Wembley and striking a major psychological blow in the title race.

That famous FA Cup victory came just seven days before a crucial Champions League semi-final second leg against Juventus. The Reds had reached the last four following a quarter-final victory over another Italian side, Inter Milan, and went on to draw the home leg against Juventus 1-1. The Turin club's away goal gave them the edge going into the decisive match on home soil, where things went from bad to worse for United as Juventus took an early two-goal lead thanks to a brace from Filippo Inzaghi. United looked dead and buried, but knowing two goals would take them through, and inspired by a man on a mission in captain Roy Keane, the team soon steadied themselves after their opponents' opening salvo and began to control the tempo of the game.

Keane drove the team forward, dominating a midfield that also contained the considerable talents of Zinedine Zidane, Edgar Davids and Didier Deschamps, and eventually dragged United back into the tie with a powerful near-post header from a David Beckham corner before Dwight Yorke added a second to ensure the teams went in level at the interval, but with United holding the away goal advantage. The Reds began the second half where they left off in the first, as Yorke's direct dribble through the heart of the Italians' defence provided the chance for Andy Cole to stroke the ball home and send United into their first European Cup Final since 1968.

Amid the joyous scenes of celebration there were moments of sadness for two of United's most talented performers. The influential midfield pair of Roy Keane and Paul Scholes had to come to terms with the knowledge that they wouldn't play a part in the biggest game in the club's recent history, having both received yellow cards that meant they were suspended for the final.

Meanwhile Manchester City were one of the strongest teams in the Second Division but couldn't find the necessary consistency to finish in the top two automatic promotion places, as big spending Fulham, managed by future Blues boss Kevin Keegan, steamrollered the Division, sealing the title with 101 points. Second place went to Walsall, a smaller club with a much lower budget than City, meaning the Blues had to rely on the lottery of the play-offs to gain promotion.

Manchester United faced Bayern Munich in the Champions League Final, in a match held at Barcelona's iconic Nou Camp Stadium. With the Premier League title in the bag, following a last-day home victory over Tottenham, thanks to a delcious Andy Cole lob, and a routine FA Cup Final win over Newcastle, Alex Ferguson's players were on the verge of making history. No British team had ever won a treble of the three major trophies, but the Reds were now just 90 minutes, and perhaps a little bit of stoppage time, away from achieving that feat.

With Keane and Scholes out of contention, Ferguson had to reshuffle his pack for the final; selecting David Beckham in a more central role, bringing Jesper Blomqvist in on the left wing and shifting Ryan Giggs to the right. The adjustments and perhaps the nerves of the occasion unsettled United in the opening exchanges and Bayern took an early lead when Mario Basler's deflected free-kick left Peter Schmeichel stranded.

The Reds struggled to make an impression on the game and went in behind at half-time. During the interval Alex Ferguson's motivational speech famously included the line, "At the end of this game, the European Cup will be only six feet away from you and you'll not even able to touch it if we lose. And for many of you that will be the closest you will ever get. Don't you dare come back in here without giving your all."

The manager's words and his second half substitutions eventually did the trick as replacement Teddy Sheringham grabbed a close-range equaliser in the first minute of stoppage time. The goal came when a David Beckham corner, which goalkeeper Peter Schmeichel had joined the attack for, was cleared to the edge of the box. The ball was met by a miss-kicked Ryan Giggs shot which fell perfectly into Sheringham's path for the Englishman to stroke the ball home.

The Reds weren't finished there and when another corner was won two minutes later, there was a feeling engulfing both sets of players that it might be United's night. Beckham whipped in another beautiful delivery, which was flicked on by Sheringham and prodded into the roof of the net by the other substitute, Ole Gunnar Solskjaer. The bench erupted in celebration while the Bayern players fell poleaxed to the floor in devastation. Schmeichel went on to lift the trophy, providing the perfect ending to his glorious United career, as the Reds reclaimed the title of Europe's premier club.

The final fell on what would have been Sir Matt Busby's birthday (Busby passed away in 1994, aged 84). As well as producing his famous, post-match comments, "Football, bloody hell", Alex Ferguson, a man who would also soon be knighted, paid tribute to his countryman, saying that Busby had probably been "kicking a few balls" that night.

On 15 May, the day before Manchester United would wrap up the Premier League title and begin their three steps to heaven, City kicked-off a play-off semi-final tie against Wigan Athletic.

A credible away 1-1 draw against the Latics gave City a good platform for the home tie, which the Blues eventually won in front of a nervy Maine Road crowd thanks to a solitary goal from Shaun Goater that set up a Wembley play-off final date with Gillingham. In between the semi-finals and the final, Manchester United added both the FA Cup and the European Champions League to their trophy cabinet, but City fans and players had to focus on their big day out at Wembley; a game that proved to be one of the most important in the club's history.

Defeat would mean another season in the Second Division, continued loss of revenue, further disenchantment from the fans and the possibility of another managerial change, but victory would help set the club on the long road to recovery. The Blues walked out under the twin towers just four days after Manchester United had lifted the European Cup. The last time the Reds had tasted success in that particular tournament, the Blues had recently been named Champions of England, illustrating how times had changed and the depths that City had plummeted.

In typical City fashion, Joe Royle's men eventually ensured the right outcome, but only following the most theatrical of circumstances, as, perhaps with the last-gasp exploits of their red neighbours still fresh in their minds, the Blues produced some late drama of their own.

The final was a tense encounter played in pouring rain and City found a well-organised Gillingham side in determined form, under the guidance of future Premier League boss

Tony Pulis. Gills goalkeeper Vince Bartram, who was later voted man of the match, was in inspired form and kept the Blues at bay for the majority of the game. City looked the most likely to score, but when the deadlock was eventually broken, the goal came from Gillingham striker Carl Asaba in the 81st minute. Royle's charges were in a state of shock and matters worsened just six minutes later when Robert Taylor extended the Kent club's advantage.

With three minutes left on the clock City were two goals behind and needed a miracle. The fans didn't see it coming and many, unable to face the enormity of the disappointment, began to leave the ground. But the players continued to fight and when the ball fell kindly to Kevin Horlock in the 90th minute he drove a low shot into the back of the net. There were still five minutes of stoppage time to play and the goal revitalised City, giving the players something to cling to, while filling their opponents' heads with doubt.

Gillingham attempted to keep the ball in the City half to run down the clock, but the Blues knew they had time to create at least one more golden chance. As the clock ticked into the 95th minute it was now or never and defender Gerard Wiekens thumped the ball into the heart of the Gillingham defence. Following a scramble and some excellent work from Shaun Goater, the ball fell to Paul Dickov just inside the box. Despite being tightly marked, Dickov shrugged off his defender and slammed an unstoppable strike into the roof of the net, leaving Bartram – his close friend and the best man at his wedding – completely stranded. It was Dickov's 15th goal of an extremely productive campaign and it proved to be the most important and memorable strike of his City career.

Although Dickov had been a hero in normal time, he was almost the villain when the final went to penalties following a goalless half an hour of extra-time, missing his spot-kick. But thanks to a missed penalty from the Gills and two saves from goalkeeper Nicky Weaver, including the decisive stop from Guy Butters's spot-kick, Dickov's blushes were spared. The Blues scored through Horlock, Richard Edghill and former Manchester United winger Terry Cooke, ensuring a 3-1 victory and passage back to the second tier of English football.

Following his crucial save, Weaver embarked upon a euphoric celebratory run as his response matched the unbridled delight of the City fans. With the way the club has progressed since that famous day at Wembley, many Blues fans see Dickov's equaliser and the subsequent penalty shootout victory as a seminal moment in Manchester City's history.

While United had shown they meant business on the pitch, the club had developed into a huge worldwide brand and was attracting the interest of major investors who wanted a slice of the power and financial rewards associated with the Reds. One of those interested parties was Australian media mogul Rupert Murdoch, whose British Sky Broadcasting company attempted a takeover in September 1998.

Negotiations between United and BSkyB had begun during the summer, but later stalled, before a final bid of £623.4m was accepted. However, following the protestations of several fans groups, including the recently formed Shareholders United against Murdoch (now known as the Manchester United Supporter's Trust) and IMUSA (Independent Manchester United Supporters Association), the proposed takeover was referred to the UK's Monopolies and Mergers Commission in October by Trade Secretary Peter Mandelson.

There were concerns that a huge conflict of interest existed as BSkyB—a company that had revolutionised the broadcasting of English football and played a huge part in establishing the Premier League as a worldwide brand – would own the biggest club in the Division. Questions were raised about the potential for United to receive increased and more positive coverage and a greater share of the Premier League cash pot. Supporters all over the country feared for the long-term future of the English game. Eventually the Mergers Commission's report, finalised in April 1999, blocked BSkyB's bid.

It meant that United would not be owned by a multi-national company with a hugely powerful figurehead, but the attempted takeover was an indication of the times and continued development of the business of football. Having floated on the Stock Exchange, United were no longer an independent entity, leaving themselves open to a takeover from wealthy investors, including those based on the other side of the globe with little knowledge of the game and no emotional attachment or genuine loyalty to the club. It wouldn't be the last time that such a takeover was attempted.

United went on to defend their Premier League crown in 2000 in devastating fashion, clocking up a record 91 points in a 38 game season and a record 97 goals. The Reds also claimed the Intercontinental Cup for the first time in their history, thanks to a Roy Keane-inspired 1-0 victory over Brazilian side Palmeiras, but their FA Cup crown was lost without having the chance to defend the trophy, as the Reds were controversially coaxed into competing in the inaugural World Club Championship held in Brazil half-way through the season, at the expense of competing in their domestic cup.

As in the 1950s under Matt Busby, the Reds were pioneers in new-look international competition, but in truth the club, and the competition could never hope to have the same impact as that of the Busby Babes and the early European Cup. The Reds' defence of that particular trophy eventually ended in disappointment following a quarter-final exit at the hands of eventual winners, Real Madrid. The task of reigning in Europe was also made even harder that season by the introduction of a second qualifying group stage to the Champions League.

Capitalising on the momentum and the buzz of the play-off winning glory, Joe Royle's

Manchester City enjoyed an extremely impressive 1999-2000 Division One campaign, competing at the top of the table for the majority of the season and eventually gaining automatic promotion after finishing just two points behind Charlton Athletic in second place. Royle had kept largely the same squad, adding a few shrewd additions, including flying left-winger and assist-machine Mark Kennedy and dependable defender Spencer Prior.

Other players came to the fore, such as Australia midfielder Danny Tiatto, and The Blues boasted the best defensive record in the division, conceding just 40 goals in 46 games. But the real star of the show was Shaun Goater, who hit an impressive 29 goals in all competitions, including 23 in the league, to fire the Blues back into the top flight.

9

A RIVALRY FOR THE 21ST CENTURY

Manchester United began the 21st century in the way they'd ended the 20th, dominating the domestic game and eventually winning the 2001 Premier League at a canter to ensure a third straight league title for the first time in the club's history. Further development at Old Trafford during the summer of 2000 saw the capacity increase to 67,500. There was less investment on the playing side, with charismatic French goalkeeper Fabin Barthez the club's only major signing, as Sir Alex Ferguson continued to search for an adequate replacement for Peter Schmeichel. But Barthez was helpless to prevent United eventually crashing out of the Champions League at the quarter-final stage as Bayern Munich avenged their defeat in the 1999 final with a 3-1 aggregate victory.

City's return to the Premier League in 2000 ensured the first Manchester derby in four years took place at Maine Road. In the Blues' absence from the top flight, United's rivalries had intensified with Liverpool, Leeds United and Arsenal, but for City fans the Manchester derby was far and away the biggest game of the season. It had been the longest absence of the famous fixture since the Second World War and, by the time match day came around, both sets of supporters were desperate for kick-off. There was plenty of hype in the build up to the game, but the action on the pitch didn't live up to the expectation and the match was settled by a David Beckham free-kick after just 90 seconds.

The second Manchester derby of the season is one remembered for a seemingly premeditated foul challenge and a red card rather than a goal or moment of magic. During a 1-1 draw that was petering out at Old Trafford, Roy Keane went in studs first on City midfielder Alf-Inge Haaland. The full-force of Keane's right boot slammed into the Norwegian's knee and sent him sprawling on the turf. As Haaland lay injured, the red-carded Keane gave him both barrels, finally releasing the festering resentment that had been suppressed inside since a cruciate ligament injury he sustained during a tangle with the same player in 1997. In his book, entitled *Keane - The Autobiography*, the United legend revealed his views on the feud with Haaland, detailing how the Norwegian had accused him of faking injury in the previous incident and how he responded four years later: "I'd waited long enough. I hit him hard. The ball was there (I think). Take that you ****. And don't ever stand over me sneering about fake injuries. What goes around, comes around. He got his just rewards. He f***** me over and my attitude is an eye for an eye."

It was a tackle and an outburst that was more reflective of an individual rivalry, rather than that of the two clubs, but it remains one of the most significant and controversial events to have taken place in a modern-day derby.

While the Reds went on to wrap up the title with the comfort of a 10-point margin in 2001, City's season proved much more of a struggle. In the intervening five seasons since their last appearance in the Premier League, the gulf between the top two divisions had increased significantly.

At the beginning of the season, Joe Royle added to his squad with the signings of Liberia striker George Weah, Costa Rica forward Paulo Wanchope, the afore-mentioned Haaland and the energetic Darren Huckerby, but City still edged towards the drop zone, eventually finishing third from bottom and slumping to relegation.

Sir Alex Ferguson was much busier in the transfer market in the summer of 2001, completing a £19m deal for Dutch striker Ruud van Nistelrooy and the signing of Argentinian midfield maestro Juan Sebastian Veron from Lazio for a club record £28.1m. With the extra demands placed upon his squad by the increased format of the Champions League, Ferguson knew he needed strength in depth and now boasted one of the finest midfield and forward lines in the world. However, the same couldn't be said about the United backline, particularly after Jaap Stam was allowed to leave to club to sign for Lazio.

Stam's autobiography had been serialised in a national newspaper and included allegations that Sir Alex Ferguson encouraged the players to go down and had asked Stam to speak to his fellow Dutch international team-mates about joining United. Stam later revealed that the Reds told him he had to move on to balance the books. Whatever the reason for his departure, the commanding defender didn't last long at Old Trafford following the publication of the book and it left the Reds with a gaping hole at the centre of defence.

Ferguson's response was to bring in veteran French World Cup winner Laurent Blanc, a man he had tried to sign in the past. Blanc had a shaky start, not helped by a drop in form from Fabien Barthez, as United endured their worst opening to a season for a number of years. Old Trafford was no longer a fortress as United suffered five defeats in seven league games during November and December, including three losses in a row to Arsenal, Chelsea and West Ham, contributing to the club's worst home record since the 1977-78 season.

There was an air of uncertainty surrounding the club, which had begun to translate into performances on the pitch after Sir Alex Ferguson had announced, at the beginning of the campaign, that it would be his last as he intended to walk away from professional football at the end of the season, aged 61. Now, some 10 years later and with Sir Alex as feisty and hungry for success as ever, it's difficult to conceive that the Scotsman could have even considered such a decision back in 2001, but he had seemingly made up his mind and the announcement was made.

The final of that season's Champions League would be played in Glasgow and, ever the romantic, Ferguson possibly envisioned another European Cup victory in his hometown as the perfect crowning glory to his managerial career. However, that wasn't to be the case as United were sent crashing out of Europe in the semi-finals by Bayern Munich, and Sir Alex later announced that he'd had a change of heart and wanted to continue at the Old Trafford helm well into his 60s.

Perhaps many of the existing United squad began to fear for their futures at the club, concerned that a new manager might not rate them, but the announcement certainly seemed to have a destabilising influence that ensured the campaign could not be rescued despite the manager's eventual u-turn and an improved second half of the season.

After their mid season blip, the Reds only lost three more league games but had given themselves too much to do to catch a rampant Arsenal and finished 10 points behind their London rivals. The title was eventually conceded in the most painful of fashions as Arsenal came to Old Trafford for United's penultimate fixture of the season, knowing that victory would seal their second Premier League crown in four years. Sylvain Wiltord forced home the only goal of the game to give the Gunners the title. Reds fans had to stomach watching Arsenal players and fans celebrating the Championship on their patch and things got worse on the last day of the season as a disappointing scoreless draw against Charlton Athletic, again at Old Trafford, saw Liverpool leapfrog United into second place and leave Ferguson's men in third. It was the first time the Reds had finished outside of the top two since 1991, but with Ferguson in place for the 2002-03 campaign United would soon be back on track.

The Reds fared better in Europe, reaching their most advanced stage since lifting the trophy three years earlier, as the likes of Veron and Van Nistelrooy enjoyed the different style of play and helped The Reds to qualify through both group stages and defeat Deportivo La Coruna of Spain in the quarter-finals. United were paired with Germany's Bayer Leverkusen in the semi-final and a disappointing 2-2 draw at Old Trafford set up a nervy second leg in Leverkusen. United took an early lead through Roy Keane, a man hell-bent on lifting the Champions League trophy having missed the 1999 final, but a whole host of presentable chances were squandered before the Germans grabbed an equaliser and the Reds slumped out on away goals.

Following City's relegation and the removal of Joe Royle as manager, Kevin Keegan took charge at the start of the 2001-02 season and soon assembled a team filled with attacking flair and hard-working players, ideally suited to achieving success in the second tier. A man never afraid to splash the cash, Keegan soon added to his City squad, snapping up established international performers like Eyal Berkovic, Ali Benarbia and Stuart Pearce.

The Blues enjoyed a hugely successful season, with the finishing abilities of Shaun Goater and Darren Huckerby contributing to the team's 99 points and 108 goals. Keegan's team had achieved a new club record points tally, firing themselves into the top flight in style.

In the summer, City added further new blood as Champions League winning striker Nicolas Anelka signed in a club record £13m deal, Cameroon international midfielder Marc-Vivien Foe came in on loan and French defender Sylvain Distin and Manchester United's legendary goalkeeper, Peter Schmeichel, joined on permanent deals.

The investment in the team ensured that City adapted better to the top flight than they had during their previous season in the Premier League, and eventually finished in ninth place, with the highlight of the season being a 3-1 victory over Manchester United at Maine Road. The win was the Blues' first over the Reds in 13 years and striker Shaun Goater was the hero of the hour, scoring twice - the second being his 100th for the club - adding to Nicolas Anelka's opener.

A lot of focus had been made over the years on United being the more global club, while City had more local roots and Manchester-born players. This had been the case in the late 1980s and early 90s but the first matches at the turn of the new millennium provided a contrasting truth. While United fielded a team featuring many home-grown players, including locally raised youngsters like Ryan Giggs, Paul Scholes, Nicky Butt and Gary Neville, the City side took on a much more international feel, as manager Keegan selected a team without a single English or British player.

Following their memorable win against United, the Blues also earned a credible draw at Old Trafford later in the season when another goal from Goater sealed a 1-1 draw. As well as a sound mid-table finish, the Blues also qualified for the UEFA Cup after topping the 'Fair Play' league, ensuring the club's first involvement in European football for 24 years.

The 2002-03 season was Manchester City's last at Maine Road, as the club's 80-year history at the ground ended in a disappointing 1-0 defeat to Southampton on the final day of the season. City's last goal at Maine Road was scored by Marc-Vivien Foe, who bagged a brace in a 3-0 victory over Sunderland.

City moved from Maine Road into the City of Manchester Stadium, which had been built to host the 2003 Commonwealth Games. There had been plans to further expand Maine Road, but with a purpose built sporting arena already being constructed, the Club decided to move to the council owned facility. Many fans were heartbroken by the idea of moving away from a ground that held such significant memories, both happy and sad, and one that possessed such a special atmosphere, but the club needed to progress off the field to keep pace with matters on it, and the move was accepted as a necessary evil by many.

It meant the club returned to its original east Manchester roots, with the City of Manchester Stadium located a mile outside of the city centre. Having been used for athletics during the Commonwealth Games, the stadium had to be converted for football, with sections of the track removed and re-laid at other venues. The ground level was also lowered to make way for increased seating and temporary stands were replaced with permanent structures, adding a further 23,000 to make the overall capacity 47,805.

United's only major signing during the summer of 2002 was the club record £29.1m capture of England defender Rio Ferdinand from Leeds United. Ferdinand went on to impress in defence, but it was at the other end of the pitch that United enjoyed their best form, with the goal-scoring exploits of Ruud Van Nistlerooy, who hit 25, and a revitalised Paul Scholes, who scored 14, proving key as the Reds reclaimed the Premier League title. United played plenty of free-flowing attacking football, including a 6-2 victory over Newcastle United at St James' Park and a 4-0 thumping of Liverpool at Old Trafford in successive matches.

The Merseysiders did beat United in the League Cup final, however, and Ferguson's men crashed out of the FA Cup at home to Arsenal, in a game made more famous by a post-match incident involving David Beckham and Sir Alex Ferguson. During an argument about one of the conceded goals, Beckham reacted to his manager's criticism, leading the Scotsman to lose his temper and take a swing at a discarded football boot. The boot flew up and hit Beckham in the head, causing a small cut, but once the press got hold of the story it took on whirlwind proportions. Many blamed the incident on Beckham's eventual departure at the end of the season to Real Madrid. There was probably much more to it than that, but the incident certainly didn't help a seemingly strained relationship.

The Reds once again exited the Champions League at the quarter-final stage, with the Galacticos of Real Madrid—including the likes of Zinedine Zidane, Luis Figo, Ronaldo and Raul—proving too strong over two-legs, despite a hard fought 4-3 home victory for United.

As well as Beckham's high-profile summer departure of other significant transfers from

Old Trafford in 2004 included those of Laurent Blanc, Dwight Yorke and Juan Veron, who moved on to big-spending Chelsea. The London club had recently been taken over by Russian oil tycoon, Roman Abramovich, and the summer of 2004 was their first statement of intent in the transfer market.

Ferguson once again opted for youth to replace such established performers, bringing in the highly-rated but extremely raw Portuguese teenager Cristiano Ronaldo from Sporting Lisbon. Joining Ronaldo at the club were Brazilian midfielder Kleberson, tough-tackling Cameroonian Erik Djemba-Djemba, young French forward David Bellion and American goalkeeper Tim Howard. All five were unproven in the Premier League and it would take them time to adapt, with only Ronaldo going on to live up to the heavy expectations placed on those wearing the red shirt.

Ferguson did sign proven Premier League quality in January 2004, splashing out £12.82m for Fulham's French striker Louis Saha as the Reds desperately tried to keep pace with an almost peerless Arsenal side, which remained unbeaten in the league. United were a team in transition, as Ferguson attempted to lower the average age of his squad and blend a mixture of youth and experience. The Reds' chances of success weren't helped by an enforced eight-month absence for Rio Ferdinand, who was severely punished by the FA for forgetting to take a routine drugs test after training.

Manchester City and their supporters were stunned and saddened during the summer by the tragic news that Marc-Viven Foe, the Cameroon midfielder who had spent the 2002-03 campaign on loan at the club, collapsed on the pitch while on international duty for his country against Colombia. Attempts to revive the midfielder failed and he later died at the stadium having suffered from a hereditary heart condition. City fans flocked to the recently vacated Maine Road to leave floral tributes and football shirts in honour of Foe, and the club later retired the 23 shirt the midfielder had worn during his time with the Blues.

City moved into their new stadium for the start of the 2003-04 season and Kevin Keegan again bolstered his squad, bringing in several established internationals, including Steve McManaman, Claudio Reyna and Michael Tarnat. Despite the experience of the new arrivals, who helped provide balance to a team that was also beginning to feature home-grown players like Shaun Wright-Phillips and Stephen Ireland, and the platform of playing at a new stadium, City found the campaign one of frustration despite a bright start, which included three wins in five games. The team's form faltered following a 3-0 home defeat to Leicester City and Keegan's men started to slip down the table, enduring a run of just one win in 18 league and cup games and becoming embroiled in a relegation battle. The Blues eventually ensured their Premier League survival with two games to spare, ending the campaign in 16th position following a 5-1 home thumping of Everton.

Progress into the second round proper of the UEFA Cup was secured following victories over the New Saints and Lokeren, but the Blues eventually exited the competition on away goals after two disappointing draws with Polish minnows, Groclin. In a season of few highs, one of the most memorable moments came in a fourth round FA Cup replay against Tottenham Hotspur at White Hart Lane. City trailed 3-0 at the interval, losing Nicolas Anelka to injury and Joey Barton – another player to have graduated through the Manchester City academy–to a red card. It meant that The Blues were a man down and starved of their most dangerous attacking talent in the second half, but miraculously they clawed their way back into the game before eventually winning 4-3, thanks to a later winner from former Manchester United youngster, Jon Macken. The win set up an FA Cup fourth round tie against United at Old Trafford but this time, against 10 men (following a Gary Neville dismissal for a head-butt on Steve McManaman), City failed to progress after a 4-2 loss to their neighbours.

However, the Blues got their revenge in the league later that season, as the first ever Manchester derby to be held at the City of Manchester Stadium ended in a humiliating 4-1 defeat for the red half of Manchester. City's goals game from Macken, Fowler, Wright-Phillips and Trevor Sinclair, with Paul Scholes providing United's solitary response.

While rivals Arsenal were the model of consistency, United struggled to find the winning formula of recent seasons, losing six and drawing nine, eventually conceding the league by a significant 15-point margin and being beaten into second place by an ever-improving Chelsea side. United didn't fare any better in the Champions League, exiting at the quarter-final stage to FC Porto, managed by Jose Mourinho, a man the Reds would become accustomed to competing against once he left Portugal for Chelsea having won the European Cup.

The FA Cup provided some solace for United, as the Reds stormed to the Millennium Stadium final thanks to a 1-0 semi-final win over Arsenal at Villa Park. If the build up to the contest brought back memories of the classic 1999 semi-final between the two sides, the match failed to live up to the billing. United out-fought the Gunners, with young Scotland midfielder Darren Fletcher putting in one of his most impressive shifts in a United shirt, before Paul Scholes smashed in a first-half winner. The Reds faced Championship side Millwall in the final and duly outclassed their opponents thanks to a Cristiano Ronaldo opener and two goals from Ruud van Nistelrooy. The United players donned specially made shirts to celebrate the victory, in tribute to youth team forward Jimmy Davis, who had died in a car accident before the start of the season.

City struggled in the cup competitions during the 2004-05 season, including a shock

FA Cup defeat to Oldham Athletic, but managed to find more consistency in the league, eventually finishing eighth in the table. Despite an upturn in league form, Kevin Keegan had stepped down as manager in March 2005, leaving former England international Stuart Pearce to take over as caretaker boss. Pearce had an instant impact and the team enjoyed an impressive end of season run, only narrowly missing out on qualification for Europe on the final day, during a memorable contest against Middlesbrough at the City of Manchester Stadium.

With the game tied at 1-1 and City needing a win to qualify for the UEFA Cup, Pearce took the drastic action of replacing midfielder Claudio Reyna with substitute goalkeeper Nicky Weaver, in order to put first-choice stopper David James up front in an attempt to use his height and physical presence to cause problems for their opponents. It was seen as a strange decision by many, particularly as the Blues had £5m centre forward Jon Macken on the bench, but Pearce's ploy almost worked. James' presence in the Middlesbrough area during corners and other set pieces caused plenty of disruption and when defender Franck Queudrue handled the ball, City were awarded a last minute penalty and the chance to fire themselves into Europe. However, Robbie Fowler failed from 12 yards and the Blues missed out.

Despite his temporary role ultimately ending in disappointment, Stuart Pearce did enough to impress the City board and was awarded the job on a permanent basis during the close season. The new manager wasn't given as much freedom in the transfer market as his predecessor due to the club's dwindling finances. Pearce brought in former Manchester United striker Andy Cole on a free transfer and began to give more opportunities to the club's younger players, including Micah Richards and Nedum Onuoha.

Later in the season, Pearce made a significant investment in Greek centre-forward Georgios Samaras, who commanded a £6m fee from Dutch side Heerenveen. But the tall striker struggled to make an impact and the manager's judgement in the transfer market came into question. City enjoyed a good start to the season, but fell away badly, losing nine of their last 10 games and finishing 15th.

Things got worse the following season as The Blues were embroiled in a relegation scrap as well as being eliminated from the League Cup by a League One side for the second successive season, with Chesterfield following the example of Doncaster Rovers to overcome City.

Pearce significantly invested in the playing squad, bringing in the likes of Ousmane Dabo, Bernardo Corradi and Andreas Isaksson, but failed to achieve consistent results in the Premier League. Blues fans struggled to endure some of the football being served up at the City of Manchester Stadium, as their team managed a poultry 10 goals at the ground all season, failing to hit the back of the net on home soil after New Year's Day, 2007. City's home goals return was a record low in the top flight of English football, and with the team finishing in a lowly 15th position, the club took action and sacked Pearce. It had been one of the least eventful and dramatic campaigns in the club's history, but all of that was about to change as the Blues were about to enter a period of transition both on and off the pitch.

Despite new signings during the summer of 2004 in the shape of Alan Smith from Leeds United and Gabriel Heinze from Paris Saint-Germain, Manchester United's summer business was dwarfed by Chelsea's efforts in the transfer market (with Jose Mourinho now at the helm, Chelsea spent over £70m). Despite United's status as one of the most profitable clubs in the world they simply couldn't compete with that level of investment, as Chelsea had the capability to build a championship winning squad in a single summer.

The Reds did make one bold move after the season had kicked off, spending an initial £25.6m on Everton youngster Wayne Rooney. The Liverpool-born forward had taken Euro 2004 by storm with England and clearly had a bright future in the game. It was a signing that excited United fans and the teenage powerhouse made an instant impression on his debut, scoring a memorable hat-trick against Turkish side Fenerbahce at Old Trafford in the Champions League. It was a sign of things to come as Rooney topped the club's scoring charts with 17 in all competitions that season and claimed the 2005 PFA Young Player of the Year Award.

The 2004-05 campaign proved to be one of the most painful in living memory for many United fans. Not only was the league lost to big-spending Chelsea, as converting draws into wins continued to be a problem for Ferguson's men, but they were beaten on penalties in the FA Cup final by Arsenal in a game they had dominated. Wayne Rooney and Cristiano Ronaldo gave a glimpse of the Reds's future with a sumptuous attacking display at the Millennium Stadium, but United failed to press home their advantage and eventually lost on spot-kicks after Paul Scholes's penalty was saved and Patrick Vieira scored with what turned out to be his last kick in an Arsenal shirt.

But worse was to come for Reds fans, as hated rivals Liverpool miraculously won the 2005 Champions League final after defeating AC Milan on penalties. It meant that Liverpool had now won five European Cups to United's two, and made all of the recent frustrations in the competition even harder to bear.

It had been only United's fourth trophyless campaign in seven seasons, but struggling on the pitch and seeing each of their rivals taste success was hard to take for Reds fans. However, what concerned them even more that year was the takeover of the club by the Glazer family, headed up by US tycoon Malcolm Glazer.

Glazer had initially bought a stake in the club in 2003 and gradually increased his shareholding over the years until pushing his ownership of the club to around 57% in May 2005. As the American owned over 30% of the club, he could launch a full takeover bid and soon took control 75% of the club's shares. It meant that Glazer could de-list Manchester United from the stock exchange and he soon took 98% ownership of the club through his Red Football parent company, forcing a compulsory buy-out of the remaining 2%. His total purchase of the club totalled almost £800 million but the biggest concern for United fans was that the majority of Glazer's investment had come from borrowed finance, secured against the club's assets, meaning that Manchester United was plunged into millions of pounds worth of debt overnight.

The debt taken on by the Glazers to finance the club was in the region of £660m and split between the club and the family, leading to interest payments of around £62m a year. Glazer indicated that his family intended to run the club for a number of years, considering it a major long-term project and appointed his sons, Joel and Avram, as Chairmen, and his other two sons Kevin and Edward and daughter Darcie to the Manchester United board as non-executive directors.

Reds fans bitterly opposed the takeover. Having seen their club run in a profitable debt-free manner for so many years, the amount of money United owed to banks and other investors was a huge concern. The Manchester United Supporters Trust was one of the most ardent rivals to the Glazers, and continues to be to this day, asking questions about how the debt will be repaid and the continued increase in ticket prices at Old Trafford.

A fan campaign known as 'Love United, Hate Glazer' has seen supporters regularly protest at the ground, both vocally and passionately but also with more subtlety, including the 'Green and Gold until We're Sold' campaign, which involved supporters donning green and gold colours—in homage to the original identity of Newton Heath. Other protests have included the boycott of many sponsors' products in an attempt to dissuade large brands from associating with Manchester United. These campaigns have enjoyed varying degrees of success, with many supporters only becoming more vocal when things aren't going as well on the pitch, but the Manchester United Supporters Trust has maintained their stance from day one and continues to oppose the Glazers's takeover of the club.

Led by the passionate yet pragmatic Duncan Drasdo, the Manchester United Supporters Trust is in it for the long-term, constantly lobbying for more transparency surrounding the Glazers's ownership and the level of debt associated with the club, while focusing on a future where the club could potentially be owned and run in a viable way by the supporters.

Another result of the takeover was the creation of a new club by a group of disgruntled supporters called FC United of Manchester. The club was soon accepted into the North West Counties Football League Second Division, six divisions from the Football League, and the club continues to progress up the football ladder, currently playing in the Northern Premier League.

The establishment of the new club wasn't just in direct reaction to the Glazers's ownership, it was also proof of the increasing disconnect between genuine football fans and the global brands their clubs had become. Football was big business and ticket prices continued to increase season on season, making what was once a traditional working-class form of entertainment something now out of reach for many. Fans became consumers and their loyalty to support their club was exploited financially. Supporters could cope with the principle of paying more money to help build the club and fund new signings but the notion of parting with their hard earned cash to pay off the millions of pounds worth of debt that had been saddled onto the club, proved too much for many.

Manchester City have their own supporter-led club called Maine Road FC. The club was originally founded by a group of Blues supporters under the name of City Supporters Rusholme and initially played Sunday League football before changing their name to Maine Road FC and joining the Manchester League in 1972. The club is based in Chorlton-cum-Hardy in Manchester and play their home games at Brantingham Road.

While Maine Road FC wasn't set up in the same circumstances as FC United, they still enticed a number Blues supporters who have become disgruntled with modern day football and crave a return of the formative elements of the game that they previously enjoyed the most.

On Saturday November 4, 2006, Maine Road FC and FC United of Manchester met for the first time in a game that was christened the 'little derby'. FC United had recently joined the North West Counties Division One and were top of the table, with Maine Road lying eight points behind in third. The teams lined up in the traditional red and blue colours of United and City in a match that was played at Stalybridge Celtic's 6,500 capacity Bower Fold Stadium and eventually ended 2-1 to FC United. Both clubs give the fans a taste of football in its purest form, providing a welcome escape from the money-obsessed business that the professional game had become, for a fraction of the price.

Since the Glazers's 2005 takeover, ticket prices at Old Trafford have increased by over 42%, illustrating that many of the fans' fears have come to pass, with supporters pointing out that the club's net transfer spend is continually lower under the new owners. In defence of the Glazers, despite the huge levels of debt, the club's commercial success has thrived, as long-term deals with American companies like Nike, AIG, AON, DHL and Chevrolet have provided plenty of investment and enhanced the club's reputation and presence all over the world, helping United to retain its position as the globe's most profitable football club.

But it can be argued that these achievements could have been realised without enforcing so much debt on the club, leaving the Reds in an extremely healthy financial position and able to constantly compete in the transfer market when deemed necessary by the manager.

The Glazers have also established a good and trusted working relationship with Sir Alex Ferguson and Chief Executive David Gill, which has continued to provide stability at the club. In fact, both Ferguson and Gill have continued to defend the Glazers over the years, which in many ways is to be expected. The trophies have also continued to roll into the Old Trafford cabinet, but many believe that this maintained success is in spite of the American's presence, rather than because of it.

In March 2010, a group led by Goldman Sachs' chief economist Jim O'Neill, which became known as the Red Knights, announced it was preparing a bid to buy the club from the Glazer family. However, a spokesperson for the club said that the Glazers were not interested in selling, and this stance was backed up in 2011 following a rumoured £1.6 billion from the Qatari royal family.

Amidst the concerns over the club's finances, United continued to invest in the squad during the summer of 2005 as Sir Alex brought in vastly experienced Dutch goalkeeper Edwin van Der Sar and promising South Korean midfielder Park Ji-Sung, who both proved excellent investments, as did the mid-season additions of two uncompromising defenders, Nemanja Vidic and Patrice Evra.

The biggest departure during the 2005-06 campaign came when club captain Roy Keane left United in November, joining Celtic on a free transfer. Keane had spent 12 years at the club and been one of most influential performers under Alex Ferguson, but following a controversial appearance on United's in-house television channel, MUTV, during which the Irishman was critical of a number of the club's younger players after a insipid 4-1 defeat to Middlesbrough, it became clear that Keane's days at Old Trafford were numbered.

On November 25, 2005, just seven days after Roy Keane left the club, United fans mourned the death of legendary former player George Best, who died at the age of 59 following a long battle with alcoholism. Fitting tributes were held in United's match at West Ham and at Old Trafford, as the world of football remembered one the game's true greats.

Following Keane's departure, Gary Neville was appointed captain as Ferguson tried to build a team to compete with a powerful Chelsea side that retained the Premier League title in 2006. It was an improved league showing from United, who claimed runners-up spot. But in truth they never truly challenged the Londoners. The biggest disappointment for United came in Europe as the Reds crashed out of the competition in the group stages.

The only glimmer of hope for United came in the 2006 League Cup, which they lifted at the Millennium Stadium following a routine 4-0 victory over Wigan Athletic. It was another game in which Rooney and Ronaldo excelled and gave Ferguson and the fans hope for the future. The increasing influence of the younger players saw Ruud van Nistelrooy marginalised and join Real Madrid at the end of the season.

As Van Nistelrooy left United, the club's only move in the transfer market saw Spurs and England midfielder Michael Carrick join the club. Carrick soon formed a terrific partnership with the evergreen Paul Scholes as United started the season in fine form, maintaining consistency for the whole of the campaign and eventually pipping Jose Mourinho's Chelsea to the 2007 Premier League title.

It was the season that the Reds also put their European demons behind them, reaching the semi-final of the Champions League, where they were eventually outclassed by AC Milan in the San Siro. Chelsea also claimed revenge for losing the league, by defeating United 1-0 in the first ever FA Cup final to be held at the new Wembley Stadium, but it was the Premier League trophy that United fans and Sir Alex Ferguson had craved the most. Reclaiming the title after a four-year absence, having rebuilt a team and contended with the riches of Chelsea, the 2007 success was labelled by many as the manager's greatest ever achievement. It came at a time when fans were learning to deal with not taking winning the Premier League for granted, and with it being the first title for many of the players, it was celebrated with even greater gusto.

Meanwhile, Manchester City had issued a statement regarding a possible takeover during the previous season and a number of interested parties soon came forward, including former City player Ray Ranson and the former Prime Minister of Thailand, Thaksin Shinawatra. It was Shinawatra whose bid eventually proved successful despite the Thai Government freezing over £800m of his assets during an investigation into allegations of corruption.

In June 2007 the takeover was eventually complete, as the Manchester City board accepted Shinawatra's £81.6m bid, meaning the Thai family acquired 75% of the club and were able to take full control. Keen to make an immediate impact by raising the profile of the club and giving the team the best chance of success, Shinawatra's first move was to bring in former England manager, Sven-Goran Eriksson as manager. With a combination of Shinawatra's investment and Eriksson's ability to entice players, the Blues began an aggressive recruitment drive in the transfer market; something the club's supporters would soon become accustomed to.

Eriksson spent over £40m during the summer of 2007, signing the likes of Martin Petrov, Elano and Geovanni. It was a statement of intent from The Blues and many tipped the club to challenge for a top four finish and Champions League qualification, something that had been unimaginable before the takeover.

The Reds strengthened ahead of their title defence, bringing in England international midfielder Owen Hargreaves from Bayern Munich for £17m, spending around £30m to secure the promising talents of Brazilian middle man Anderson from FC Porto and Portuguese winger Luis Nani from Sporting Lisbon, and tying up a loan deal for Argentina striker Carlos Tevez.

Such significant investment gave Ferguson the platform to challenge both at home and in Europe, and United went on to successfully defend their Premier League title and reach the final of the Champions League following a tense 1-0 two-legged semi-final victory over a hugely talented Barcelona team, thanks to a wonder strike from Paul Scholes.

Under Eriksson, the season began well for City who opened the campaign with an impressive away victory over West Ham. The Blues went on to claim a rare league double of Manchester United, as City defeated the Reds by a single goal at Maine Road and a shock 2-1 victory in one of the most unique Manchester derbies of all-time.

In February 2008, United commemorated the 50th anniversary of the Munich air disaster by holding a memorial service at Old Trafford and renaming the tunnel under the South Stand as the 'Munich Tunnel'. The club also marked the anniversary during the Manchester derby at Old Trafford with a minute's silence that saw both sets of supporters hold aloft scarves bearing their club's colours. The silence was impeccably observed by the City fans who behaved with genuine class on a day when many feared that minority elements of their following, who had previously sung sickening chants about the tragedy and referred to their United counterparts as 'Munichs', would hijack the moment of respect.

United also marked the derby by wearing a retro home kit, reminiscent of the one worn by the 1958 team, made up of plain red shirts, white shorts and black socks without a club badge or any sponsorship logos. The usual squad numbers were also replaced with the traditional one to 11, in an approach that was mirrored by City.

While the occasion was a fitting tribute to the Busby Babes and those that lost their lives in Munich, including former City goalkeeper Frank Swift, United's performance on the pitch was below par. Many of the players later admitted that the emotion of the week building up to the game and the pressure they felt to win the match had weighed heavy on their shoulders. However, City performed admirably and were worthy winners, thanks to two goals from Zimbabwe striker Benjani that sealed a 2-1 win.

Despite the team's attacking flair and vastly improved results, City were still prone to conceding and suffered a couple of hammerings, including a 6-0 reverse to Arsenal and a final day 8-1 defeat to Middlesbrough, in a game that proved to be Eriksson's last game in charge after months of speculation surrounding his future.

The Swede had guided City to a ninth place finish and secured UEFA Cup qualification via the Fair Play League. Eriksson's replacement was named just two days after his departure as Manchester United legend Mark Hughes took over. Hughes had fashioned an excellent reputation following impressive spells in charge of Blackburn Rovers and the Wales national team, but with the huge finances at his disposal the pressure he faced at City was on another level.

United were paired with Chelsea in the first ever all-English European Cup Final and the match was played in appropriate conditions in Moscow, as torrential rain engulfed the stadium throughout the evening. Ferguson's men began the game well and took a deserved lead through Cristiano Ronaldo, who guided a powerful header into the net following good work on the right wing from Paul Scholes and Wes Brown. The Reds had further chances to extend their lead, with Tevez, Ronaldo and Rooney looking particularly lively, but Chelsea came into the game in the second period and levelled the scores through Frank Lampard.

The game went into extra-time and United gained an advantage when Didier Drogba was sent off for aiming a slap at Nemanja Vidic. But neither team added to their tally and the game went to penalties. Carlos Tevez successfully converted the first kick for the Reds with Michael Ballack doing the same for Chelsea. Michael Carrick and Juliano Belleti both scored before Cristiano Ronaldo stepped up, but after a delayed run-up the Portuguese ace saw his penalty saved by Petr Cech. Chelsea immediately capitalised, scoring their next two kicks from Frank Lampard and Ashley Cole, in between successful United attempts from Owen Hargreaves and Luis Nani – who had to score to keep the Reds in the contest – meaning Chelsea captain John Terry had the chance to win the trophy for his team with one kick of the ball.

Terry looked confident before taking the kick, but slipped just before connecting with the ball and his effort came crashing back off the post. Invigorated by the miss, United converted their next penalty as Anderson crashed the ball home in emphatic style. Salomon Kalou then levelled matters, before Ryan Giggs, who was breaking Bobby Charlton's appearance record for the club, having equalled it against Wigan Athletic a week earlier – an occasion he marked by scoring the goal that sealed the Premier League title – calmly stroked the ball home to put United within touching distance of further glory. Nicolas Anelka was the man that needed to score to keep Chelsea in the tie, but Edwin van Der Sar read his intentions, diving the right way and tipping the ball to safety to secure the trophy for Manchester United for the third time in their history.

During the season, Cristiano Ronaldo had elevated his standing to one of most effective attacking talents in world football. Scoring 31 goals in the league and 42 in all competitions, the Portugal magician was influential and showed excellent combination play with Wayne Rooney and Carlos Tevez.

Rumours about the Portugal star's future were rife during the summer of 2008, but the Reds managed to keep hold of their prized asset, eventually adding to their attacking options with the deadline day signing of Dimitar Berbatov from Spurs, who joined in a club record £30.75m deal. Comparisons were made between the attacking talents that Ferguson had at his disposal – Ronaldo, Rooney, Tevez and Berbatov – and the holy trinity of Best, Law and Charlton that had starred during the 1960s, and the extra firepower helped United retain their title, winning the Premier League for the third consecutive season – making the Reds the first team to have achieved the milestone on two occasions, as they also equalled Liverpool's overall record of 18 English league titles.

The team also came close to making history in Europe as they again reached the Champions League final, having dismissed Arsenal in devastating fashion in the semi-final thanks to a Ronaldo-inspired 3-1 victory at the Emirates Stadium. United faced Barcelona in Rome for the chance to become the first English team to retain the European Cup since Nottingham Forest in 1980. But United were dominated by a Barcelona team filled with the outstanding talents of Lionel Messi, Andres Iniesta, Xavi and Samuel Eto'o, and lost the game 2-0.

Further trophies were added, as the Reds became the first English club to win the FIFA World Club Cup in December 2008, after defeating Ecuadorian side LDU Quito 1-0 in the final thanks to a Wayne Rooney goal, and went on to lift the League Cup in March 2009, following 4-1 penalty shootout victory over Tottenham Hotspur.

Over at City, like Eriksson before him, Hughes was backed in the transfer market by Shinawatra and brought in players such as Tal Ben Haim, the returning Shaun Wright-Phillips and Belgium defender Vincent Kompany for £5m. Kompany would go on to prove Hughes's best buy, eventually confirming his role as the team's first choice centre-back and becoming club captain.

Despite City's continued investment, the controversy surrounding their owner continued and, with Shinawatra's assets frozen in Thailand, he was reluctant to return to his homeland to clear his name. During the summer, rumours persisted about City's finances, leading to speculation that Hughes was close to walking away from the club. City supporters, still saddened at the departure of Eriksson, and wary of the headlines surrounding the club's new owners, began to turn against Shinawatra.

Many Blues fans were probably suspicious following another takeover that summer by an Arab consortium called the Abu Dhabi United Group. At the top of the group was Sheikh Mansour bin Zayed Al Nahyan, a multi-billionaire whose family had made their money from the United Arab Emirates oil industry. With Mansour in charge it meant that Manchester City had the richest owner in world football. Khaldoon Al Mubarak was eventually named

Chairman, having a more hands-on role at the club than Mansour and regularly attending games.

City now had almost unlimited transfer funds and the long-term vision and commitment to invest in all aspects of the club. Mark Hughes would no longer have to worry about finances; his biggest concern would be dealing with the huge expectation surrounding every move he made in the transfer market and how quickly his team were progressing.

On taking over at the club, Mansour was keen to reassure supporters that he was the real deal and had the club's best interests at heart, saying, "I am a football fan, and I hope that you will soon see that I am also a Manchester City fan. But I am also a long-term investor and that is probably more important to the club and to you because it means we are here for the long haul."

The day the takeover was confirmed, September 1, 2008, proved to be one of huge drama. It was also the final day of the summer transfer window and, now flush with cash, the Blues were keen to make their mark. Manchester United had been in lengthy negotiations with Tottenham Hotspur for their hugely gifted Bulgarian striker Dimitar Berbatov, but City came in with a late bid and almost succeeded in snatching the striker from under the noses of United. City weren't finished there and went on to make the biggest signing in the club's history to that point, spending a club and British record £32.5m on Real Madrid's Brazil star, Robinho. Other deadline day bids for the likes of David Villa and Mario Gomez were rejected as Manchester City showed that they meant business.

The club now had the money and the intent to compete with the biggest and most successful clubs in Europe in terms of player investment. The next task was to match their rivals on the pitch, but it remained to be seen whether Hughes would be given the time to achieve those ambitions, as questions began to circulate about whether the Welshman was a big enough name to take the club forward.

Since taking charge of the club in 2008, Sheik Mansour has spent close to £500m on new signings for Manchester City and, while this kind of investment and transformation of the club has been met with delight by many Blues fans, there are elements of the club's longer-term supporters that find it hard to digest exactly what the newly branded Manchester City has come to represent. Blues fans with vivid memories of Maine Road, and City's struggles and romance associated with the club's history, have been troubled by the developments and become disenchanted with what their club has become.

While in many ways their wildest dreams have come true, the reality of how this has been realised has concerned many Blues fans, particularly those that have retained great pride in the more traditional approach adopted as the club retained its local identity. This identity has been kept, while Manchester United developed into a global brand; attracting supporters all over the world and were transformed into a consumer-led business rather than a sporting institution solely reliant upon its roots.

The views of many Blues fans are perfectly summed up in City supporter Colin Shindler's 2012 book, *Manchester City Ruined My Life*—a follow up to his hugely successful *Manchester United Ruined My Life*, which acted as a love letter to his club, covering the memories associated with following them and how those memories are intertwined with personal emotion, in the way that only the beautiful game can.

Shindler's later title delves into the media obsessed transformation of sport into business, exposing the views that many modern day's fans are reluctant to reveal, particularly when their teams are enjoying success. Feeling a lack of connection with the club he loves, Shindler began to view the Blues with disinterest, as he details in his book: "I know what it is like to be in love. I also know that it is like to be disappointed in love. Manchester City in their current guise feel like the end of a love affair, a bereavement of unique nature. Just like the end of a love affair I understand rationally why it had to end but emotionally I remained confused."

Despite losing fans like Shindler emotionally, if not literally, City were focused on a successful future that would entice new followers. But the Blues were in inconsistent form at the start of the 2008-09 campaign, losing seven of their opening 12 games, as the new signings took time to settle and Hughes tried to find a winning combination. Defeats in the Manchester derby, both at home and away, didn't aid their cause and the Blues could only manage a disappointing 10th place, a full 40 points behind Champions Manchester United.

City were linked with further signings during January 2009, with a mooted £100m deal for AC Milan's Brazil star Kaka eventually breaking down. Hughes was able to strengthen in January, signing Dutch international midfielder Nigel de Jong from Hamburg for £16m, West Ham's Craig Bellamy for £14m, Wayne Bridge of Chelsea for £10m and spending £5.9m on Newcastle United stopper Shay Given.

A return of 14 goals from record signing Robinho was satisfactory, but the team needed further strengthening to close the gap on the clubs competing for the top four positions. One bright point in the campaign was City's progress in Europe as Hughes guided the Blues into the quarter-finals of the UEFA Cup, where they eventually lost to Hamburg over two legs.

Manchester City were progressing, but not as quickly as the new owners wanted and the pressure was on Hughes to at least challenge for a Champions League place during the 2009-10 season. Further high-profile acquisitions followed as the likes of Gareth Barry, Emmanuel Adebayor and Kolo Toure all joined the club for significant transfer fees, but the biggest signing of the summer was the capture of Carlos Tevez in a permanent deal, after the Argentina striker's loan spell at Manchester United ended.

The signing was seen as a significant blow to United as City proved they could attract players on the same level as the Reds. The move also hurt United fans, who loved Tevez's all-action and committed displays, as the Argentinian's style of play was reminiscent of his new manager at City during his time at Old Trafford.

It was a signing that delighted the Manchester City fans, particularly when the club used Tevez's image as part of a provocative marketing campaign, erecting a huge sky blue billboard at the top of Deansgate in the City centre, with the Argentinian in a City kit accompanied by the words 'Welcome to Manchester'. Many Blues fans revelled in the fact the campaign made reference to their widely-held belief that theirs was the true Manchester club, as United were based in Salford, and that Manchester itself was filled with more Blues than Reds – an assertion that anybody who has visited the City would accept as inaccurate.

It was an act that summed up the new-found confidence of Manchester City as the Blues captured an Old Trafford fans' favourite, ensuring that Tevez would become an icon of City's progression as he became one of the first truly world class players to join the Citizens ranks and make an immediate impact at the club.

In direct response to the billboard, Alex Ferguson claimed City had a "small club mentality", believing the Blues to be obsessed with United, and later in the season Sir Alex would refer to City as "noisy neighbours." Maybe City were obsessed with United, but there was no harm in that. The Reds were at the level that they wanted to reach and perhaps Ferguson's decision to comment on them revealed more of his concerns about the Blues' continued progression.

But that progression wasn't instant and the City board finally lost patience with Mark Hughes who was sacked in December 2009 after just 18 months in charge. The Blues had started the campaign well, winning their opening three games and clocking up an impressive 4-2 victory over Arsenal. Next up was the Manchester derby at Old Trafford and it proved to be one of the most entertaining clashes between the two clubs for years. United had stormed to a 3-1 lead, before two late goals from Craig Bellamy drew City level. With the game seemingly destined for a draw and ticking into the sixth minute of injury time, United conjured up one final chance to win it, when Ryan Giggs's beautifully judged through-ball found substitute Michael Owen in the box, and the former England striker calmly prodded his shot past Shay Given before celebrating in front of a jubilant Stretford End.

In 90 minutes Manchester City had illustrated how close they were getting to United, showing the fight and ability to take on their great rivals on their home patch. But it was a case of close, but not close enough for Hughes, as his team later won just two games in 11 Premier League matches, and Italian coach Roberto Mancini was appointed as his replacement.

The manner of Hughes's dismissal showed a genuine lack of respect as a statement announcing his departure was issued just two hours after the 4-3 home win over Sunderland, with the Welshman seemingly aware of his fate before the game kicked off. His replacement, Roberto Mancini, was already in the stands watching the match, having been in discussion with the City hierarchy for several weeks.

United manager Sir Alex Ferguson branded City's treatment of Hughes as 'unacceptable' and the Blues' controversial Chief Executive, Garry Cook, later tried to defend the club's behaviour by repeatedly denying any conspiracy had taken place behind Hughes's back, but it was clear to many that Hughes had been shabbily treated by a club intent on success.

10

THE HEROES

Part 2

In this second focus on some of the finest footballers to perform for the Manchester giants, the players lining up for the clubs between 1970 and the present day are covered, including a number of stars from the Sir Alex Ferguson era at United and a collection of cult heroes who are held in equally high esteem by City supporters.

Manchester United

Sammy McIlroy

POSITION:

Striker

BORN:

August 2, 1954 in Belfast, Northern
Ireland

UNITED CAREER:

1971-1982

APPEARANCES:

419

GOALS:

71

HONOURS:

Second Division Title (1975), FA Cup
(1977)

CITY CAREER:

1985-1986

APPEARANCES:

13

GOALS:

1

A hugely skilled striker or winger who enjoys the distinction of being the last ever youngster signed by the legendary Matt Busby, Sammy McIlroy experienced a brilliant 11-year career with Manchester United. An expert finisher who linked up play well with excellent close-control and varied passing range, the Northern Irishman made a memorable debut for the Reds when, aged just 17-years-old, he scored one and created another in a Manchester derby at Maine Road. After leaving Old Trafford for Stoke City in 1982, Sammy returned to Manchester three years later to spend a single season with Manchester City.

TRIVIA

Sammy McIlroy played in all of Northern Ireland's games at the 1982 and 1986 World Cup finals.

Martin Buchan

POSITION:
Defender
BORN:
March 6, 1949 in Aberdeen, Scotland
UNITED CAREER:
1972-1983
APPEARANCES:
456
GOALS:
4
HONOURS:
Second Division Title (1975), FA Cup (1977)

A reliable defender who brought authority and assurance to the United backline after joining the club from Aberdeen for a club record fee, Martin Buchan went on to show excellent leadership skills, calmness and ability on the ball. He held an often shaky defence together and was a rare constant during an unsettled period for the Reds. The Scotsman was crucial as the team bounced back to the top flight at the first time of asking in 1975 and lifted the FA Cup at Wembley two years later.

TRIVIA

Martin Buchan is the only player to captain both Scottish and English cup winning sides, lifting the FA Cup with United in 1977 and the Scottish equivalent with Aberdeen in 1970.

Lou Macari

POSITION:
Striker
BORN:
June 4, 1949 in Largs, Scotland
UNITED CAREER:
1973-1984
APPEARANCES:
400
GOALS:
97
HONOURS:
Second Division Title (1975), FA Cup
(1977, 1983)

TRIVIA

The 'Lou Macari Chip Shop' on Chester Road near Old Trafford is extremely popular with United fans on matchdays.

A real fans' favourite during his seven-year spell at Old Trafford, Lou Macari was a fiery and hugely skilled forward, who used his strength and vision to hit the target and create countless opportunities for team-mates. The Scotsman was an expert at holding up the ball as a striker but, when moved into a midfield role by Tommy Docherty, he enjoyed a greater influence over the game. Many will remember Macari for his part in the winning goal against Liverpool in the 1977 FA Cup Final, when a combination of the Scotsman's determined strike and Jimmy Greenhoff's chest saw the ball hit the back of the net and end the Merseysiders' dreams of the treble.

Arthur Albiston

POSITION:
Left-back
BORN:
July 14, 1957 in Edinburgh, Scotland
UNITED CAREER:
1974-1988
APPEARANCES:
485
GOALS:
7
HONOURS:
Second Division Title (1975), FA Cup
(1977, 1983, 1985)

A top class defender who showed great energy and enthusiasm to bomb forward and supplement the attack, Arthur Albiston was one of United's most consistent performers for over a decade. A three-time FA Cup winner with a great appetite for the game, Albiston went about his business in a calm and assured way, much like future United left-back Denis Irwin. Arthur shared many of Irwin's attributes and was an excellent servant to the club.

TRIVIA

Arthur Albiston was a youth coach at Manchester United between 2000 and 2004.

Bryan Robson

BORN:

January 11, 1957 in Chester-le-Street, England

UNITED CAREER:

1981-1994

APPEARANCES:

461

GOALS:

99

HONOURS:

FA Cup (1983, 1985, 1990), European Cup Winners' Cup (1991), European Super Cup (1991), League Cup (1992), Premier League (1993, 1994)

THEY SAID ...

"He was a miracle of commitment, a human marvel who could push himself beyond every imaginable limit on the field. Of all the players I have worked with, he ranks among the three or four who have impressed me the most. As a competitor he had no superior." Alex Ferguson.

The driving force of Manchester United throughout the 1980s and early 90s, Bryan Robson could be relied upon to produce the goods whether the team was struggling or in full-flow and no matter whether he was 100 per cent fit or hampered by injury. Rightly christened 'Captain Marvel' due to his inspirational performances as United skipper, the super fit, tough-tackling, engine room of the Reds midfield was also highly-skilled, with great vision, a wand of a left foot and the ability and desire to arrive late in the box to score countless crucial goals. 'Robbo' was the fans' favourite and gave the Red Army reason for great pride, even during an era where the team often failed to live up to expectations.

Norman Whiteside

BORN:
May 7, 1965 in Belfast, Northern Ireland
UNITED CAREER:
1982-1989
APPEARANCES:
274
GOALS:
67
HONOURS:
FA Cup (1983, 1985)

THEY SAID ...
"As a player he was close to the genius category." Alex Ferguson.

After the impressive impact that Norman Whiteside made on the United first team following his debut as a preciously talented teenager, comparisons to the great George Best were made, due to Whiteside's birthplace and the fact that he had been spotted by the same man that recommended Best to Matt Busby, club scout Bob Bishop. Strong for his age, with the skill and vision to dribble past defenders, play inch-perfect passes and score from all ranges and angles, Norman soon became a crucial part of the Reds' first eleven during the 1980s. Sadly, injury robbed Whiteside of much of his career and from fulfilling his true potential, but he was still a top class performer for United.

Mark Hughes

POSITION:
Striker
BORN:
November 1, 1963 in Ruabon, Wales
UNITED CAREER:
1980-1986 and 1989-1995
APPEARANCES:
467
GOALS:
163
HONOURS:
FA Cup (1985, 1990, 1994, 1996), European Cup Winners' Cup (1991), European Super Cup (1991), League Cup (1992), FA Premier League (1993, 1994)

THEY SAID ...

"Physically and technically, he was equipped to trouble any defence and he had the heart to thrust his sturdy body in where it hurt." Alex Ferguson.

A warrior of a striker, whose strength on the ball, ability to hold off defenders and penchant for powerfully-struck spectacular goals made him a huge fans' favourite during his two spells at Old Trafford, Mark Hughes gave cause for optimism and pride during the late 80s when the team was struggling, and provided crucial goals and a fantastic link-up with Eric Cantona once Alex Ferguson's men found their Championship-winning form. 'Sparky' was the man for the big occasion, scoring goals when it mattered in cup finals and semi-finals. The Welshman's bravery and the passion he showed for the United badge were evident from his first kick for the club to his last.

Brian McClair

POSITION:
Striker, Midfielder
BORN:
December 8, 1963 in Bellshill, Scotland
UNITED CAREER:
1987-1998
APPEARANCES:
471
GOALS:
127
HONOURS:
FA Cup (1990, 1994, 1996), European Cup Winners' Cup (1991), European Super Cup (1991), League Cup (1992), FA Premier League (1993, 1994, 1996, 1997)

An ice-cool finisher who combined fantastic work-rate with an intelligent football brain, Brian McClair proved to be one of Alex Ferguson's most important early additions at Manchester United. Able to drop deeper into midfield when required, the Scottish international was an accurate passer of the ball and strong in the air. McClair formed a devastating strike partnership with Mark Hughes as both men helped transform the Reds from a mid-table cup team to a side able to compete for the league title. Brian is now Director of Manchester United's Youth Academy.

TRIVIA

In his first season for Manchester United Brian McClair scored 24 league goals, becoming the first United player to score 20 in one league campaign since George Best in 1968.

Steve Bruce

POSITION:
Central Defender
BORN:
December 31, 1960 in Corbridge, England
UNITED CAREER:
1987-1996
APPEARANCES:
414
GOALS:
51
HONOURS:
FA Cup (1990, 1994, 1996), European Cup Winners' Cup (1991), European Super Cup (1991), League Cup (1992), FA Premier League (1993, 1994, 1996)

TRIVIA

Steve Bruce scored an impressive 19 goals in all competitions during the 1990-91 season. He was also United's joint leading goal-scorer in the league, as he and Brian McClair hit the target on 13 occasions.

A fiercely competitive defender who regularly placed his head where other players would hesitate to put their feet, Steve Bruce gave absolutely everything for the Manchester United cause. Signed from Norwich City in 1987, Bruce was never known for his pace, but his ability to read the game and communicate with his fellow defenders ensured that the Reds had an extremely solid backline for the best part of a decade. A monster in the air and a tenaciously tough-tackler, Bruce also showed composure in possession and from the penalty spot as the team's designated spot-kick specialist for a number of seasons. Reds fans will always remember the late brace of headers Bruce bagged against Sheffield Wednesday in 1993 to help end the Championship jinx.

Gary Pallister

POSITION:
Central Defender
BORN:
June 30, 1965 in Ramsgate, England
UNITED CAREER:
1989-1998
APPEARANCES:
437
GOALS:
15
HONOURS:
FA Cup (1990, 1994, 1996), European Cup Winners' Cup (1991), European Super Cup (1991), League Cup (1992), FA Premier League (1993, 1994, 1996, 1997)

TRIVIA

Gary Pallister formed an excellent partnership with Steve Bruce, which lead to the pair famously being given the nickname of 'Daisy and Dolly' by Alex Ferguson.

Having signed for United as a highly-rated, yet raw defender, Gary Pallister developed into one of the finest defenders of his generation at Old Trafford. Pallister was uncompromising in the air and strong in the tackle, but also possessed the pace and reading of the game to sniff out danger and keep even the most dangerous opponents at arm's length. Like Bruce, Pallister was comfortable with the ball at his feet and helped United develop their free-flowing passing style from the backline.

Peter Schmeichel

POSITION:

Goalkeeper

BORN:

November 18, 1963 in Gladsome, Denmark

UNITED CAREER:

1991-1999

APPEARANCES:

398

GOALS:

1

HONOURS:

FA Cup (1994, 1996, 1999), European Super Cup (1991), League Cup (1992), FA Premier League (1993, 1994, 1996, 1997, 1999), European Cup - Champions League (1999)

CITY CAREER:

2002-2003

APPEARANCES:

29

GOALS:

0

HONOURS:

None

Widely considered as the finest goalkeeper in Manchester United's history, Peter Schmeichel was one of the most important acquisitions of Sir Alex Ferguson's early reign at Manchester United. The Denmark international had a phenomenal presence between the posts, as well as lightning-quick reflexes, excellent anticipation and top class distribution. When the Red Devils' defence was breached, opposing strikers faced the unenviable task of trying to beat the giant goalkeeper, and more often than not he intercepted the ball or put them off their stride. Peter left United after lifting the 1999 European Cup, opting to join Sporting Lisbon in Portugal. However, it wasn't long before he returned to England, playing for Aston Villa and spending a single season with Manchester City, where he helped the Blues consolidate their position in the Premier League under Kevin Keegan.

TRIVIA

During his eight years with Manchester United and single season with City, Peter Schmeichel was never on the losing side in a Manchester derby.

Ryan Giggs

POSITION:

Winger, Central Midfielder

BORN:

November 27, 1973 in Cardiff, Wales

UNITED CAREER:

1991-Present Day

APPEARANCES:

910

GOALS:

163

HONOURS:

FA Cup (1994, 1996, 1999, 2004), European Super Cup (1991), League Cup (1992, 2006, 2009, 2010), FA Premier League (1993, 1994, 1996, 1997, 1999, 2000, 2001, 2003, 2007, 2008, 2009, 2011), European Cup - Champions League (1999, 2008), Intercontinental Cup (1999), World Club Cup (2008)

THEY SAID ...

"He can leave even the best defenders with twisted blood." Alex Ferguson

A true one club man and an outstanding servant to Manchester United, the longevity of Ryan Giggs's career is almost as remarkable as his considerable footballing talent. The club's record appearance holder, the most decorated man in the history of British football, and a 12-time Premier League champion, the Welsh wizard has enjoyed phenomenal success. Having broken through as a hugely exciting winger, possessing pace, flair, flicks and tricks, Giggs went on to refine his game into that of a play-making midfielder, capable of sitting deeper or operating in the hole behind a central striker. Wherever and whenever he has played for Manchester United, Ryan has shown a level of consistent brilliance that most players would struggle to achieve throughout a single season, let alone over two decades.

Denis Irwin

POSITION:
Left-back
BORN:
October 31, 1965 in Cork, Ireland
UNITED CAREER:
1990-2002
APPEARANCES:
529
GOALS:
33
HONOURS:
FA Cup (1994, 1996, 1999), European Super Cup (1991), League Cup (1992), FA Premier League (1993, 1994, 1996, 1997, 1999, 2000, 2001), European Cup - Champions League (1999), Intercontinental Cup (1999)

TRIVIA
Sir Alex Ferguson often refers to Denis Irwin as the best pound for pound signing he ever made for Manchester United.

One of the most dependable performers ever to play for Manchester United, Denis Irwin quietly made a huge contribution to the Reds' success during the 1990s. Two-footed, quick, strong in the tackle and with the ability to join the attack and whip in devastating crosses and score a few memorable goals of his own, the Irish full-back was a top drawer all-round footballer. Irwin was also a dead-ball specialist who showed composure and class from both penalties and free-kicks, regularly scoring memorable long-range efforts until the emergence of a certain David Beckham. Viewed by many as the best left-back to have graced the turf at Old Trafford.

Eric Cantona

POSITION:

Striker

BORN:

May 24, 1966 in Marseille, France

UNITED CAREER:

1992-1997

APPEARANCES:

185

GOALS:

82

HONOURS:

FA Cup (1994, 1996), FA Premier League (1993, 1994, 1996, 1997)

THEY SAID ...

"I'm so proud the fans still sing my name, but I fear tomorrow they will stop. I fear it because I love it. And everything you love, you fear you will lose." Eric Cantona.

The final figure of flair in Alex Ferguson's Championship-seeking side of the early 1990s, Eric Cantona provided the skills, composure, big-game mentality and sheer belief that inspired those around him to take the final step to becoming champions of England. A hugely gifted natural footballer whose vision and imagination to create something beautiful, helped tear defences apart and brought smiles to the faces of millions of United fans, Cantona made a bigger impact on Old Trafford than any player before or after him. In many he ways he changed the philosophy and outlook of the club and its supporters, who still sing his name at matches, some 15 years since his last appearance in a red shirt.

Roy Keane

POSITION:
Central Midfielder
BORN:
August 10, 1971 in Cork, Ireland
UNITED CAREER:
1993-2005
APPEARANCES:
480
GOALS:
51
HONOURS:
FA Cup (1994, 1996, 1999, 2004), FA Premier League (1993, 1994, 1996, 1997, 1999, 2000, 2001, 2003), European Cup - Champions League (1999), Intercontinental Cup (1999)

Roy Keane was quite simply the heartbeat of Manchester United during his 12-year stay at Old Trafford. Billed as 'the next Bryan Robson' upon his arrival, Keane went on to equal the influence and importance of 'Captain Marvel', eventually becoming skipper himself and leading by an almost peerless example. The Irishman tackled with intent, passed with unerring accuracy and drove the side forward both physically and vocally. If the team was below par or up against it, Keane would drag them to victory or back into games, demanding excellence and maximum effort from himself and those around him.

THEY SAID...

"If I was putting Roy Keane out there to represent Manchester United on a one against one, we'd win the Derby, the National, the Boat Race and anything else. It's an incredible thing he's got." Alex Ferguson.

Paul Scholes

POSITION:
Central Midfielder - Striker
BORN:
November 16, 1974 in Salford, England
UNITED CAREER:
1993-2011 and 2012-Present day
APPEARANCES:
698
GOALS:
154
HONOURS:
FA Cup (1996, 1999, 2004), League Cup (2006, 2009, 2010), FA Premier League (1996, 1997, 1999, 2000, 2001, 2003, 2007, 2008, 2009, 2011), European Cup - Champions League (1999, 2008), Intercontinental Cup (1999), World Club Cup (2008)

THEY SAID ...
"You rarely come across the complete footballer, but Scholes is as close to it as you can get." – Zinedine Zidane.

Nicknamed 'Sat Nav' by his team-mates, Paul Scholes's passing range and consummate ease in possession of the ball has seen him dictate the tempo and direction of play at Old Trafford for almost 20 years. Born in Manchester, and one of the graduates of United's hugely successful youth team, Scholes began his career as a striker and was an excellent natural goal-scorer before Alex Ferguson moved him into midfield, where he went on to become one of the most talented and respected players of his generation. After initially hanging up his boots at the end of the 2010-11 campaign, Paul returned to action in January 2012 and effortlessly slipped back into the United rhythm; the United rhythm that he dictated.

David Beckham

POSITION:
Right-midfielder
BORN:
May 2, 1975 in Leytonstone, England
UNITED CAREER:
1993-2003
APPEARANCES:
394
GOALS:
85
HONOURS:
FA Cup (1996, 1999), FA Premier League (1996, 1997, 1999, 2000, 2001, 2003,), European Cup - Champions League (1999), Intercontinental Cup (1999)

TRIVIA

David Beckham is the third highest assist provider in the Premier League, with 152 in 265 appearances for Manchester United.

Probably the most famous footballer on the planet, David Beckham developed his sporting ability and his profile during a hugely successful 10-year stay at Old Trafford, as brand-Beckham and brand-United seemingly grew in equal measure. Joining the club as a youngster after being spotted at a Bobby Charlton soccer camp, the Londoner went on to establish himself on the United right-wing where he provided countless assists with his lethal right-footed delivery into the box. A deadball expert who scored some truly memorable free-kicks for the Reds, Beckham could also take a mean corner, illustrated by the two in-swingers that led to both goals in the 1999 Champions League final.

Andy Cole

POSITION:
Striker
BORN:
October 15, 1971 in Nottingham, England
UNITED CAREER:
1995-2001
APPEARANCES:
275
GOALS:
121
HONOURS:
FA Cup (1996, 1999), FA Premier League (1996, 1997, 1999, 2000, 2001) European Cup - Champions League (1999), Intercontinental Cup (1999)

Goal king Cole endured a slow start to his United career, struggling for form and to adapt to his new team's style of play, but once the England striker settled into his rhythm he became one of the most deadly centre forwards to have represented the club. Later developing an almost telepathic partnership with Dwight Yorke, Cole's movement and anticipation in the area led to plenty of chances, most of which he put away with an ice-cool finish while drenched in composure.

TRIVIA

Andy Cole is the second-highest goal-scorer in Premier League history. Only former Manchester United target Alan Shearer scored more in the division.

Ole Gunnar Solskjaer

POSITION:
Striker

BORN:
February 26, 1973 in Kristiansund, Norway

UNITED CAREER:
1996-2007

APPEARANCES:
366

GOALS:
126

HONOURS:
FA Cup (1999, 2004), FA Premier League (1996, 1997, 1999, 2000, 2001, 2003, 2007), European Cup - Champions League (1999), Intercontinental Cup (1999)

A consummate professional who was rewarded for his patience and acceptance at starting the majority of his career from the substitutes bench, Ole Gunnar Solskjaer wrote his name into Manchester United history by scoring the stoppage winner that sealed the 1999 European Cup. Nicknamed the 'Baby-faced assassin', the Norway international regularly came off the bench to score crucial goals, but was equally dangerous when starting games, either up front or on the wing. A deadly finisher in front of a goal, who linked up well with his team-mates, Solskjaer proved one of the best value for money acquisitions of Alex Ferguson's Old Trafford tenure.

TRIVIA

During the 1998-99 season, Ole Gunnar Solskjaer famously netted four goals in 12 minutes after coming on as a second half substitute against Nottingham Forest.

Cristiano Ronaldo

POSITION:
Winger, Striker
BORN:
February 5, 1985 in Madeira, Portugal
UNITED CAREER:
2003-2009
APPEARANCES:
292
GOALS:
118
HONOURS:
FA Cup (2004), League Cup (2006, 2009, 2010), FA Premier League (2007, 2008, 2009), European Cup - Champions League (2008), World Club Cup (2008).

THEY SAID ...

"I think he is the best player in the world. He can play with both feet, he has fantastic skill, strength and bravery, and he's a greater headerer of the ball." - Sir Alex Ferguson.

During his six-year spell at Old Trafford, United fans ran out of superlatives to describe Cristiano Ronaldo. The Portuguese star displayed incredible technique and moments of match-winning brilliance either playing on the wing or through the middle. After joining the Reds as a teenager who possessed immense ability, Ronaldo developed into the finished article and one of the world's finest players during his time in Manchester, adding devastating end-product to the tricks and flicks that overflowed during his early years at the club. Cristiano starred during the 2008 campaign when the Reds won a league and European Cup double and goes down in history as one of the club's very best.

Alan Oakes

POSITION:

Midfielder

BORN:

September 7, 1942 in Winsford, England

CITY CAREER:

1959-1976

APPEARANCES:

678

GOALS:

4

HONOURS:

Second Division Title (1966), First Division Title (1968), FA Cup Winner (1969), European Cup Winners' Cup (1970), League Cup (1970, 1976)

Manchester City's all-time record appearance holder and a key element of their successful team of the 1960s and 70s, Alan Oakes was a terrific all-round footballer, whose energetic and committed displays provided an excellent foil for the creative talents of Colin Bell. He played in all but one of the Blues games during the title winning 1967-98 campaign, offering consistency and drive, and was named as the club's Player of the Year in 1975.

TRIVIA

Alan Oakes is the cousin of former City team-mate Glyn Pardoe, while his son Michael Oakes was also a professional footballer, playing in goal for Aston Villa.

Mike Doyle

POSITION:
Midfielder, Central Defender
BORN:
November 25, 1946 in Ashton-under-Lyne, England
DIED:
June 27, 2011
CITY CAREER:
1965-1978
APPEARANCES:
558
GOALS:
40
HONOURS:
Second Division Title (1966), First Division Title (1968), FA Cup Winner (1969), European Cup Winners' Cup (1970), League Cup (1970, 1976)

TRIVIA
In the club's official magazine, Blues supporters once voted Mike Doyle as Manchester City's hardest player.

Manchester-born and a lifelong Blues fan, Mike Doyle once famously claimed that there were only two clubs in Manchester: Manchester City and Manchester City reserves! A tough centre-back who could also play in midfield, Doyle remains the club's most decorated player and one of the heroes of the Blues' golden era. Famed for antagonising United players and supporters, Doyle seemed to raise his game for the Manchester derbies and lost just one of the 16 games he played against the Reds.

Joe Corrigan

POSITION:
Goalkeeper
BORN:
November 18, 1948 in Manchester,
England
CITY CAREER:
1967-1983
APPEARANCES:
604
GOALS:
1
HONOURS:
European Cup Winners' Cup (1970),
League Cup (1970, 1976)4

TRIVIA

Joe Corrigan made 592 appearances for Manchester City; a Blues' club record for a goalkeeper.

A giant of a man, both in terms of stature and presence, Joe Corrigan succeeded in the almost impossible task of following the legendary Bert Trautmann between the posts at Maine Road. Another Manchester-born player, Corrigan joined the Blues as a youngster and went on to play over 600 times for the club. The committed goalkeeper was extremely brave and strong in the air, but also possessed good reactions. After hanging up his gloves, Joe became a successful goalkeeping coach, working at Liverpool and West Bromwich Albion amongst others.

Dennis Tueart

POSITION:

Winger

BORN:

November 27, 1949 in Newcastle, England

CITY CAREER:

1974-1978 and 1979-1983

APPEARANCES:

224

GOALS:

86

HONOURS:

League Cup (1976)

A skilful winger with an eye for goal, Dennis Tueart was extremely popular with the Maine Road faithful during his two spells at the club. He scored a spectacular overhead kick in the 1976 League Cup Final and possessed a bit of magic that would get supporters off their seats in anticipation of a goal. Tueart later became a director at Manchester City and was heavily involved in the managerial appointments of Joe Royle and Kevin Keegan.

TRIVIA

Dennis Tueart's winning goal against Newcastle United for Manchester City in the 1976 League Cup Final was later voted as the greatest moment in the competition's history.

David White

POSITION:
Striker - Winger
BORN:
October 30, 1967 in Urmston, England
CITY CAREER:
1985-1993
APPEARANCES:
339
GOALS:
96
HONOURS:
None

TRIVIA

David White's best goal-scoring season for Manchester City came in 1991-92 when he hit the target on 18 occasions and guided the Blues to a second successive fifth place finish.

Another Manchester-born youngster who made the grade at Manchester City, David White was a powerful and speedy winger or striker, who became one of the stars of the Blues' promotion winning team of 1989 and also showed his class in the top flight. White mostly operated on the right wing and enjoyed an impressive scoring return for a wide-man, prompting a call up and full cap for the England team. Blues fans were dismayed when David was transferred to Leeds United in 1993 in exchange for fellow winger David Rocastle.

Niall Quinn

POSITION:

Striker

BORN:

October 6, 1966 in Dublin, Ireland

CITY CAREER:

1990-1996

APPEARANCES:

245

GOALS:

78

HONOURS:

None

TRIVIA

During a game against Derby County in 1991, Niall Quinn amazingly scored and saved a penalty in the same match, after going in goal for City following usual stopper Tony Coton's red card.

A giant of a striker who led the City line with passion and poise during his six-year stay at Maine Road, Niall Quinn was a talismanic figure for Blues fans during a time when their team often struggled for consistency. Strong in the air, with plenty of ability on the ground, Quinn relished the physical side of the game and enjoyed several fierce battles with Manchester United defender, Steve Bruce and Gary Pallister, in the early 1990s. He left the club for Sunderland in 1996, following City's relegation, but is still fondly remembered by the club's supporters.

Uwe Rosler

POSITION:
Striker
BORN:
November 15, 1968 in Altenburg, East
Germany
CITY CAREER:
1994-1998
APPEARANCES:
176
GOALS:
64
HONOURS:
None

A powerful striker who showed good timing in the air and predatory finishing skills in the box, Uwe Rosler was one of the few bright sparks of a disappointing mid-1990s spell for Manchester City. The German worked extremely hard and had plenty of ability, forming an excellent striking partnership with Paul Walsh. Rosler's goals were unable to keep City in the top flight, but he remained at Maine Road for two more years following the 1996 relegation and continues to enjoy great affection from Blues supporters.

TRIVIA
Uwe Rosler is currently the manager of English League One club Brentford.

Georgi Kinkladze

POSITION:

Central Midfielder

BORN:

July 6, 1973 in Tiblisi, Georgia

CITY CAREER:

1995-1998

APPEARANCES:

121

GOALS:

22

HONOURS:

None

TRIVIA

Georgi Kinkladze was a two-time Georgian Player of the Year and also won Manchester City's Player of the Year award twice.

One of the only bright points of Alan Ball's disastrous reign at Maine Road, the Georgian magician provided a brand of flair, cheek and technical brilliance that hadn't been seen at the club since the days of Rodney Marsh. While Kinkladze often struggled for fitness and had the capacity to drift out of games, when he was in the mood he could produce moments of match-winning brilliance, using expert balance and technique to dribble past players and create chances for himself and others. At a time when Manchester United had Eric Cantona, Kinkladze was City's answer to the Frenchman and proved to be a talismanic creative force in his own right.

Paul Dickov

POSITION:
Striker

BORN:
November 1, 1972 in Livingston, Scotland

CITY CAREER:
1996-2002 and 2006-2008

APPEARANCES:
199

GOALS:
41

HONOURS:
Second Division Play-Offs (1999), First Division Title (2002)

In his two spells at Manchester City, Paul Dickov's work-rate and never-say-die attitude endeared him to the Blues' supporters. The diminutive Scotsman will eternally be remembered for his crucial stoppage time equaliser during the 1999 Second Division Play-Off Final, which sent the game into extra-time and helped City gain promotion. It's often speculated where the club would be now if it hadn't been for Dickov's late show at Wembley.

TRIVIA
Paul Dickov's stoppage time equaliser against Gillingham in the 1999 Second Division Play-Off Final was previously voted as the greatest goal in Manchester City's history by the club's supporters.

Shaun Goater

POSITION:

Striker

BORN:

February 25, 1970 in Hamilton, Bermuda

CITY CAREER:

1998-2003

APPEARANCES:

212

GOALS:

103

HONOURS:

Second Division Play-Offs (1999), First Division Title (2002)

Although Shaun Goater began his career at Manchester United, he never made a first team appearance for the Red Devils and went on to become a legend on the other side of Manchester after joining City in 1998. Famed for his goals, excellent work-rate and infectious smile, the chant 'Feed the Goat and he will score' was often sung around Maine Road, as the Bermudan front man became a cult hero and a vital element of the team that helped return the Blues to where they belonged following the struggles of the late 1990s.

TRIVIA

Shaun Goater was awarded an MBE in 2003 for services to sport and young people in Bermuda.

11

HEAD TO HEAD FOR THE PREMIER LEAGUE

The December 2009 sacking of Mark Hughes as manager had shown the ruthlessness of the new regime at Manchester City. The club's owners were striving for excellence and couldn't wait any longer for Hughes to achieve it. His replacement, Roberto Mancini, had won the Italian 'Serie A' title on three occasions with Inter Milan, showing he could deal with the pressure of winning trophies at a big club, and was expected to be competing for honours with City sooner rather than later.

Brian Kidd, the former Manchester United player and assistant manager, who had been working in the Blues' academy, was promoted to assistant manager and Mancini's former Sampdoria team-mate David Platt, an England international as a player who had began his career on the books at United, also joined the backroom staff.

Having persuaded Cristiano Ronaldo to stay some 12 months earlier, Sir Alex Ferguson had to face up to losing his prized asset in the summer of 2009 as the Portuguese match-winner joined Real Madrid in a world record £80m transfer. Ferguson only invested a small proportion of the Ronaldo money, signing the hard-working and lightning quick Ecuador winger Antonio Valencia from Wigan Athletic for an undisclosed fee, as well as former Liverpool striker Michael Owen on a free transfer.

Roberto Mancini went on to guide City to an impressive fifth place finish, securing a place in the Europa League and narrowly missing out on the top four and qualification for the Champions League, following a home defeat to fellow top-four contenders Tottenham Hotspur. City also reached their first semi-final since 1981, facing Manchester United in the League Cup over two-legs. The first game at Maine Road saw United take the lead after just 17 minutes through Ryan Giggs, but City equalised just before half-time through Carlos Tevez who found the net against his former club for the first time after converting a penalty and controversially celebrating the goal in front of the United fans. The Argentinian grabbed his second in the second half, ensuring the Blues took a 2-1 advantage into the second leg at Old Trafford.

The return match was every bit as entertaining as the league contest between the two at the Theatre of Dreams earlier in the season and again produced plenty of late drama. Paul Scholes levelled the tie early on before Michael Carrick put United further ahead after 20 minutes, but just five minutes later that man Tevez hauled City level. The contest was tied with 90 minutes on the clock, but as The Reds had proved on so many occasions in the past, stoppage time was one of their most dangerous periods of the game, and a powerful header from Wayne Rooney whistled past Shay Given into the net to send United through and knock City out.

In the absence of Ronaldo, Wayne Rooney stepped up to the mark, enjoying his most prolific season in front of goal-hitting 34 in all competitions but the Reds narrowly missed out on the 2010 title to Chelsea. United exited the Champions League against Bayern Munich in the quarter-finals but didn't end the season empty-handed after securing a second successive League Cup, following a 2-1 victory over Aston Villa.

The 2010-11 campaign was another battle between United and Chelsea, but this time the Reds had the upper hand, finishing top of the pile to seal a record 19th English League Title and defeating the Blues in the semi-final of the Champions League. One of the stars of the season was diminutive Mexican striker Javier 'Chicharito' Hernandez who had joined the club in the summer and went on to form a great partnership with Wayne Rooney, scoring important goals at crucial times.

Rooney's future at Old Trafford had been in doubt earlier in the campaign, when contract negotiations between the club and their star-striker stalled and Rooney announced that he wanted to leave United. The news was greeted with shock by Reds fans and that shock turned to anger when it appeared as though Rooney's likely destination if he left the club would be the Etihad Stadium. Seeing a talented and popular player like Carlos Tevez defect to the other side of Manchester had been bad enough, but potentially losing their star-man, and the player that Alex Ferguson had built his latest United team around, was too much to bear. A mob of 30 young supporters reportedly assembled outside Rooney's family home in Cheshire carrying a banner that stated, 'Join City and Die'. Rooney, the club and the manager soon addressed their differences and the England striker signed a lucrative long-term deal with the Reds. It had been another painful reminder of how City could compete with United off the pitch as the Blues continued to improve on the field.

Carlos Tevez had justified the hype that surrounded his arrival at the Etihad Stadium, scoring 29 goals in his debut season and becoming the fulcrum of the team. Mancini added further additions to his squad during the summer of 2010, splashing over £100m on the likes of the sublimely talented David Silva, powerhouse midfielder Yaya Toure, the unpredictably brilliant Mario Balotelli and the steady and reliable James Milner. The Italian also invested another £27m in Edin Dzeko in January as the Blues built arguably the strongest squad in the division.

With such investment came added pressure for Mancini, who knew that a top four finish and qualification for the Champions League was the minimum requirement for the 2010-11 campaign. The Italian went on to achieve that by guiding City to third place and securing the club's first major trophy in 34 years, when they claimed the 2011 FA Cup after a straightforward victory over Stoke City at Wembley, thanks to a winning goal from the increasingly influential Yaya Toure. Wembley had also been the venue for the semi-final, which had seen the Blues paired with Manchester United. In an absorbing tactical encounter that produced few chances, City came out on top with a 1-0 win thanks to another Yaya Toure goal.

The 2011 Champions League final took place at Wembley and saw United once again pitted against the might of Barcelona after a relatively straight forward European campaign for the Reds. The silky Spaniards again dominated possession and took an early lead through Pedro. United rallied and a well-worked move from Rooney and Giggs was finished off by the Englishman. The scores were level at half-time, but Barcelona blew the Reds away in the second half, as goals from Lionel Messi and David Villa ensured a 3-1 victory.

Despite comfortably winning the title, United now had to face up to the significant challenge of competing with a team heralded as one of the best the world had ever seen. If Barcelona were the target for United, a more pressing concern was the continued growth and improvement of their City neighbours and the 2011-12 season would see the return of a meaningful rivalry between Manchester United and Manchester City.

City's FA Cup success meant that the famous rolling banner that had adorned the Stretford End at Old Trafford, which acted as a rolling ticker that was increased for every year that the Blues went without a major trophy, had to be removed; much to the delight of Roberto Mancini and the City supporters.

The response from the United faithful was to add a new banner celebrating the record 19 titles the club had achieved. It would take City some time to reach the milestone, but the club appeared to be in the best position possible to finally challenge for the league title the following season.

* * * *

Not since the 1967-68 campaign had Manchester United and Manchester City gone head to head for the league title. The Reds' dominance of the 1990s and throughout the first decade of the new Millennium had catapulted the club light-years away from their city rivals and as money became an increasingly crucial factor in the success of a football club, it had taken drastic intervention from Manchester City's billionaire owners to create a team capable of once again competing with United and ensure a re-ignition of the rivalry between the clubs. Further reinforcements were added in the summer of 2011 as City once again smashed their transfer record with the £38m signing of Argentina striker Sergio Aguero while adding two of Arsenal's Frenchmen, Samir Nasri and Gael Clichy, to their squad.

The 2011-12 season proved to be one filled with twists and turns, as each club boasted the upper hand and surrendered the initiative on numerous occasions. Many believed that the experience of Sir Alex Ferguson and his serial Premier League winners would be crucial in deciding the destination of the trophy, but as the campaign progressed it was clear that the title would be settled by the finest of margins. It was the 20th Premier League season since the English top flight was re-branded in 1992 and would prove to be one of the most memorable.

Before the league action got underway, both clubs slugged it out at Wembley in the Community Shield in what proved in many ways to be a microcosm of the forthcoming season, as both clubs spent time in the ascendancy, looked dangerous going forward and showed the type of commitment and persistence that ensured late drama. City stormed into a two-goal lead in the first half, thanks to strikes from Joleon Lescott and Edin Dzeko, but United showed equal dominance after the interval with goals from Chris Smalling and Luis Nani drawing them level, before the Portugal winger burst clear in the 94th minute to score his second and win the game 3-2 for United.

The Reds had put a marker down by lifting further silverware, but the Blues had shown they meant business. There was little between the teams during a one-off game, but it remained to be seen how closely matched they would be over the course of a gruelling 38-game season.

Both teams started the campaign in positive fashion as United stormed to early victories over Tottenham and Arsenal at Old Trafford, including a surprise 8-2 victory over the Gunners, while City picked up equally convincing early wins against Swansea City and Spurs.

Both teams remained unbeaten going into the first Manchester derby of the Premier League season, played on October 23 at Old Trafford. United had won six of their first eight games, with Blues winning seven of theirs and an extremely tight encounter was expected at Old Trafford, and for the first 45 minutes that was the case. Despite the Reds' superiority in terms of possession, City took the lead on 22 minutes through controversial Italian striker Mario Balotelli, who famously celebrated his goal by unveiling a message on his t-shirt that proclaimed 'Why always me?' in reference to the headline-grabbing nature of his Blues career to date.

One nil down at the interval, United came out for the second half in determined mood, but their chances of getting back into the game were dealt a severe blow when defender Jonny Evans was sent-off for a professional foul on Balotelli. City soon capitalised on their numerical advantage, storming to a 3-0 lead as Balotelli grabbed his second of the afternoon and Sergio Aguero his first. The Blues then took their foot off the pedal, content to keep possession and secure the three points. But admitting defeat is a trait not accepted in the DNA of Manchester United and the Reds grabbed a late goal back through Darren Fletcher, which inspired them to surge forward in an attempt to score again. In response, City slipped up through the gears before ruthlessly exposing the space left behind the United defence to score a further three goals in stoppage time. The thumping 6-1 victory shocked Old Trafford and reverberated around the world of football.

As Blues fans stayed behind in an otherwise empty stadium, Roberto Mancini struggled to conceal his delight in his post match interviews as Sir Alex Ferguson attempted to put into words the humiliation he was feeling. The statistics being reeled off after the game emphasised the size of the victory and were even more painful for Ferguson, his players and Reds fans. The landmarks realised by the result included: Manchester United's heaviest defeat in the Premier League, the club's worst loss at Old Trafford since 1955 and the first time United had conceded six goals at home since 1930. It was also the biggest winning margin in a Manchester derby since City won by the same scoreline in 1926.

The win put City five points clear at the top of the table and significantly increased their goal difference in relation to their rivals. Sir Alex Ferguson had always feared losing the league title by such a margin and was desperate for his team to catch the Blues and exceed their points total.

The Reds' response was to shut up shop in the league games that followed, winning four out of five by a single goal, to keep the pressure on City. Buoyed by the nature of their victory at Old Trafford, Roberto Mancini's men also won four of their next five fixtures before suffering their first defeat of the season in a 2-1 loss at Chelsea, as United closed the gap to two points.

Both teams matched each other's form during the remainder of 2011 and the beginning of 2012 after a run of positive results was followed by poor displays over the Christmas period, as United first lost successive games to Blackburn Rovers and Newcastle United and City dropped points at West Brom and lost at Sunderland.

During December both United and City crashed out of the Champions League in the group stages with something of a whimper as the Premier League and their rivalry seemed to be dominating their focus. City retained top spot for the opening weeks of 2012, winning three games on the bounce as United continued to clip at their heels. In fact, both sides were matching each other for victories and the run-in for the title race was well and truly on.

City and United met in the third round of the FA Cup in January and United gained a little revenge for the embarrassment of Old Trafford by beating the Blues 3-2 on their own patch. The Reds took an early lead through Wayne Rooney before a harsh red card for City captain Vincent Kompany helped the visitors go three ahead. United fans dreamt of properly avenging the earlier 6-1 reversal with a similar score at the Etihad, but City rallied and made the eventual scoreline more respectable. The cup-tie was also significant due to the return of Paul Scholes, who reneged on his decision to retire at the end of the 2010-11 campaign, returning to the heart of the action as a second half substitute.

Scholes's first league game back in the red of United saw him score the opening goal in a home victory over Bolton Wanderers that maintained the pressure on City. Further victories against Arsenal and Stoke followed before United came back from 3-1 down against Chelsea at Stamford Bridge to grab a 3-3 draw.

Then a 2-1 home victory over Liverpool, in a match that will be remembered for the resurrection of hostilities between United's Patrice Evra and Liverpool striker Luis Suarez, sent the Red Devils back to the top of the table.

City soon pegged United back, but a shock 1-0 defeat at Swansea in the second week of March, on the same day as a United victory at West Brom, handed the title initiative back to the Reds. The gap at the top of the table became three points when City drew with Stoke and Sunderland at the end of March and United went on to beat Blackburn Rovers at the beginning of April, and opened up a five point lead with just seven games remaining.

It was a lead that many observers saw as unassailable, particularly considering United's ruthless displays during previous title run-ins and the club's vast experience in such situations. Many started to rule City out of the race, with Blues manager Roberto Mancini even questioning his side's chances in what appeared to be the sort of psychological ploy often used by Sir Alex Ferguson.

Things went from bad to worse for the Blues in April when a 1-0 defeat at Arsenal on the same day that United had defeated QPR at Old Trafford gave the reigning champions an eight-point advantage at the top of the table. City were written off in most quarters, and if Mancini had been deliberately downplaying his team's chances before the Arsenal defeat he seemed to be genuinely pessimistic in his television interviews following the game. It wasn't just the defeat that led to many ruling out City's chances of a comeback, but more the manner of the loss as Mario Balotelli picked up another red card much to the visible annoyance of his team-mates and his manager.

On paper, United's final six games looked easier than City's and many expected the Reds to cruise to the title, but the race for the Premier League had plenty of further twists on the horizon as United put in an abject performance away at Wigan Athletic before showing suicidal defending against Everton at Old Trafford, squandering 3-1 and 4-2 leads before eventually drawing 4-4. In the meantime their local rivals had won three games on the bounce, including a 6-1 away thrashing of Norwich City, cutting United's points advantage to three and increasing their own already superior goal difference.

The Reds' late wobble set up the next Manchester derby of the season perfectly. City knew that victory in the game, held at the Etihad Stadium, would see them go level on points with United and return to the top of the table by virtue of their better goal difference. The Monday night kick-off was the biggest of the season, but didn't live up to that billing as a spectacle as both teams began cautiously, particularly United who seemed content with a draw that would maintain their three point advantage with just two games remaining.

As the game wore on, City were doing most of the running and began to dominate both possession and territory. Their more positive outlook was rewarded on the stroke of half-time when influential skipper Vincent Kompany powered home a header to give the hosts the lead. United tried in vain to get a foothold in the game following the interval but the power and physical presence of the likes of Kompany, Yaya Toure and Nigel de Jong proved too much for the Reds and City's slender advantage remained intact.

Blues fans greeted the final whistle as though the championship had already been secured. Although there was still much to do, the momentum was now with the Blue half of Manchester and with just two games to go would prove crucial, as would City's superior goal difference.

With the teams level on points in the penultimate weekend of the season, City faced the toughest looking fixture of the run-in as they travelled to play an in-form Newcastle United. The fixture brought back memories of the Blues last title triumph in 1968 when Joe Mercer and Malcolm Allison's charges sealed the Championship with a memorable last-day victory over the Magpies at St James' Park, and reference to that achievement in the build up to the game only added to the pressure on the current crop of players. However, they held their nerve and won 2-0 with a match-winning performance by Yaya Toure, who scored both goals.

United did all they could to keep the race going by beating Swansea 2-0 at Old Trafford later that day but the mood inside the theatre of dreams was a subdued one as Reds fans began to accept that their local rivals had at least one hand on what they believed was 'their' trophy.

The Reds went into the final day knowing they would have to better City's result to win the title. If City won their game, at home to relegation-threatened Queens Park Rangers, whatever United did in their away clash at Sunderland would prove irrelevant as their rival's goal difference was seemingly unassailable.

The United fans retained little optimism, fully expecting City to stroll to victory against a team that had struggled all season. But their own players gave them a boost when an early goal from Wayne Rooney put them ahead and kept the pressure on their neighbours, who were playing at the same time, in a match that would fray the nerves of everybody concerned.

City's fixture against QPR was a game filled with drama within the drama, captivating coincidence and both subtle and significant subtext. The relegation-threatened West Londoners were under the stewardship of former Manchester City boss and Manchester United striker Mark Hughes, a Reds legend who had been shabbily treated by City and shown the door by Chief Executive Garry Cook.

Lining up on the field against their former club was headline-grabbing midfielder Joey Barton-a man who would have a significant impact on the game-and central defender Nedum Onuoha, who had left the club in controversial circumstances following a terrible misjudgement in communications by the afore-mentioned Cook. The City Chief Executive had mistakenly sent an email to Onuoha's mother that contained hugely offensive reference to her terminal cancer, meaning his career at the club ended in disgrace.

On the pitch Onuoha played his part in an absorbing contest, but he and the Manchester United fans keeping track of the score at the Etihad Stadium would have feared the worst when Argentina full-back Pablo Zabaleta put City ahead in the 39th minute.

Scenes of delirium enveloped the Etihad and were matched by dejection at the Stadium of Light as news of the goal filtered through to the United support. At half-time, both games were 1-0, meaning that the title would remain in Manchester, but this time in the Blues' trophy cabinet if the scores remained the same.

But just three minutes into the second half the picture changed completely when Djibril Cisse capitalised on a mistake by Joleon Lescott to fire QPR level. The goal was met with disbelief at the Etihad, but joy in Sunderland as United's supporters were given a glimmer of hope. That glimmer grew wider when Rangers went further ahead 20 minutes later through Jamie Mackie, stunning the City fans into silence.

In between both goals, there had been further drama at the Etihad when QPR captain and former City skipper, Joey Barton, was sent off after striking Carlos Tevez, kicking out at Sergio Aguero and then attempting to head-butt Vincent Kompany. It was an unsavoury incident and the last thing that the visitors needed in such a crucial game, and led to four minutes of stoppage time being added at the end of the contest.

The United fans couldn't believe what they were hearing. With their team still leading and City capitulating under the pressure, the most unlikely of final day title victories seemed to be within their grasp.

As the clock ticked down, the scenes at the Etihad Stadium became increasingly desperate as City players who had shown such skill and composure throughout the season began to fall to pieces in front of goal. The pressure continued to build, and the anxiety inside the stadium translated from the pitch to the stands and vice versa. Even the usually calm Roberto Mancini cut an agitated, panic-filled figure.

As both games entered the final 10 minutes, City still trailed by two goals and United were in control at the Stadium of Light. The City fans were seeing their worst nightmares unfolding in front of them. Having led United for so much of the season, before slipping behind and fighting back to the top the of the table, their team appeared to be choking on the biggest stage possible. Many players appeared burdened by the psychological barrier of winning that first Premier League title, and thoughts no doubt began to turn to the future if the team blew their chance in such a manner ... would they ever recover? Would it signal the end of Mancini at the club?

It was too much for many Blues fans who failed to hide their nerves vocally, with the groans that met every miss-placed pass or wasted chance; and physically, with many nails bitten, faces covered in anguish and some fans taking their frustrations out on the stadium's fixtures and fittings.

At the Stadium of Light, and with both games entering the 90th minute, United supporters dared to dream, believing for the first time that week that the title would be heading to Old Trafford. As the final whistle sounded the fans were caught between a mixture of celebration and anticipation of what was happening at City ...

The Blues were continuously knocking on the door, severely testing the resilience of a tiring, 10-man QPR. With so many shots blocked and openings squandered, City then grabbed an equaliser seemingly out of nowhere when substitute Edin Dzeko headed home in the 92nd minute. There was still two minutes of stoppage time left and City needed another goal, but with their confidence now boosted there seemed an inevitability about the outcome.

The news had filtered through to Sunderland as the United fans and players, many of whom were on the pitch waiting to celebrate the title, and everybody connected with the

Reds began to fear the worst.

Their fears and the dreams of thousands of City fans were soon realised when Segio Aguero smashed home a 94th minute winner following some excellent work by Mario Balotelli to send the Etihad Stadium wild. The immediate emotion of those connected with Manchester City was relief that they hadn't blown such a fantastic chance to win the title, before the realisation of their achievement and huge pride at finally reclaiming the league title began to sink in.

Devastation had well and truly sunk-in at the Stadium of Light as United players and supporters cut dejected and forlorn figures. It had been the most memorable final day in Premier League history and a fitting conclusion to one of the most dramatic title races since the division's inception. City became just the fifth club in 20 years to win the Premier League, with United's 12 titles illustrating the Reds' dominance of the division.

But both clubs will not be content with living in the past and, with one of the most memorable seasons in the history of Mancunian football ending in such dramatic fashion, United and City will be determined to be the city's and the country's number one for the months and years ahead.

* * * *

The competition between the Blues and the Reds will not simply be waged on the pitch, but also in the transfer market and commercial market, with every top class player who becomes available seemingly linked with a move to Manchester, and both City and United lining up increasingly lucrative deals with worldwide companies attempting to maximise their global brand.

United reacted to their rivals' increased investment by significantly adding to their squad during the summer of 2012, capturing Dutch international striker and the 2011-12 Premier League top scorer, Robin van Persie for a reported £24m deal. The 29-year-old had interested City but, in what appears to signal a change of transfer policy at the Etihad Stadium, Roberto Mancini wasn't able to simply throw money at the player to secure his signing. On the contrary, it seems that van Persie had his heart set on United, as the club's history, reputation and standing in the game all over the world appealed to him.

The Reds also added Japan midfielder Shinji Kagawa as they attempt to bolster their attacking options in a bid to ensure that they will not lack in the goals difference column in future seasons. Manchester City, perhaps conscious of the financial fair-play guidelines being brought in by UEFA, have invested less than has been customary in recent years, capturing young English talent like Jack Rodwell and Scott Sinclair and cheaper foreign alternatives like Javi Garcia to bolster their ranks.

Whoever lines up for United and City this season and in the years to come, the memories of the 2011-12 season, and the unique sporting and cultural rivalry between both clubs, will continue to remain entirely relevant as the 'Battle for Manchester' continues to intensify in the years ahead.

STATISTICS

Manchester United

Founded: 1878 as Newton Heath LYR, changing their name to Manchester United in 1902.

Nickname: The Red Devils, the Reds, United

Stadium: Old Trafford

Capacity: 75,811

Manager: Sir Alex Ferguson

Club Captain: Nemanja Vidic

Record Signing: £30.75m for Dimitar Berbatov from Tottenham Hotspur (2008)

Record Fee Received: £80m for Cristiano Ronaldo to Real Madrid (2009)

Record Appearance Holder: Ryan Giggs (909 at the start of the 2011-2012 season)

Record Goal-scorer: Sir Bobby Charlton (249)

Honours:

English First Division/Premier League: 19 (1908, 1911, 1952, 1956, 1957, 1965, 1967, 1993, 1994, 1996, 1997, 1999, 2000, 2001, 2003, 2007, 2008, 2009, 2011)

European Cup-UEFA Champions League: 3 (1968, 1999, 2008)

European Cup Winners' Cup: 1 (1991)

FA Cup: 11 (1909, 1948, 1963, 1977, 1983, 1985, 1990, 1994, 1996, 1999, 2004)

League Cup: 4 (1992, 2006, 2009, 2010)

Intercontinental Cup: 1 (1999)

World Club Cup: 1 (2008)

European Super Cup: 1 (1991)

FA Community Shield: 19 (1908, 1911, 1952, 1956, 1957, 1965, 1967, 1977, 1983, 1990, 1993, 1994, 1996, 1997, 2003, 2007, 2008, 2010, 2011)

Manchester City

Founded: 1880 as St. Marks (West Gorton), changing their name to Manchester City in 1894

Nickname: The Citizens, the Blues, City

Stadium: Etihad Stadium

Capacity: 47, 726

Manager: Roberto Mancini

Club Captain: Vincent Kompany

Record Signing: £38m for Sergio Aguero from Athletico Madrid (2011)

Record Fee Received: £21m for Shaun Wright-Phillips to Chelsea (2005)

Record Appearance Holder: Alan Oakes (680)

Record Goal-scorer: Eric Book (176)

Honours:

English First Division -Premier League: 3 (1937, 1968, 2012)

European Cup Winners' Cup: 1 (1970)

English Second Division: 7 (1899, 1903, 1910, 1928, 1947, 1966, 2002)

Third Division Play-off Winners: 1 (1999)

FA Cup: 5 (1904, 1934, 1956, 1969, 2011)

League Cup: 2 (1970, 1976)

FA Community Shield: 3 (1937, 1968, 1972)

List of Managers: Manchester United

A.H. Albut	1892-1900	Walter Crickmer	1931-1932
James West	1900-1903	Scott Duncan	1932-1937
Ernest Mangnall	1903-1912	Walter Crickmer	1937-1945
John Bentley	1912-1914	Matt Busby	1945-1969
Jack Robson	1914-1922	Wilf McGuinness	1969-1970
John Chapman	1922-1926	Matt Busby	1970-1971
Lal Hilditch	1926-1927	Frank O'Farrell	1971-1972
Herbert Bamlett	1927-1931	Tommy Docherty	1972-1977

| Dave Sexton | 1977-1981 | Alex Ferguson | 1986-present |
| Ron Atkinson | 1981-1986 | | |

Manchester City

Frederick Hopkinson	1880-1882	Tony Book	1974-1979
Unknown	1882-1884	Malcolm Allison	1979-1980
Edward Kitchen	1884-1887	Tony Book	1980-1980
Walter Chew	1887-1889	John Bond	1980-1983
Lawrence Furniss	1889-1893	John Benson	1983-1983
Joshua Parlby	1893-1895	Billy McNeill	1983-1986
Sam Omerod	1895-1902	Jimmy Frizzell	1986-1987
Tom Maley	1902-1906	Mel Machin	1987-1989
Harry Newbould	1906-1912	Tony Book	1989-1989
Ernest Mangnall	1912-1924	Howard Kendall	1989-1990
David Ashworth	1924-1925	Peter Reid	1990-1993
Albert Alexander	1925-1926	Tony Book	1993-1993
Peter Hodge	1926-1932	Brian Horton	1993-1995
Wilf Wild	1932-1946	Alan Ball	1995-1996
Sam Cowan	1946-1947	Asa Hartford	1996-1996
Wilf Wild	1947-1947	Steve Coppell	1996-1996
Jock Thomson	1947-1950	Phil Neal	1996-1996
Les McDowall	1950-1963	Frank Clark	1996-1998
George Poyser	1963-1965	Joe Royle	1998-2001
Joe Mercer	1965-1971	Kevin Keegan	2001-2005
Malcolm Allison	1971-1973	Stuart Pearce	2005-2007
Johnny Hart	1973-1973	Sven-Goran Eriksson	2007-2008
Tony Book	1973-1973	Mark Hughes	2008-2009
Ron Saunders	1973-1974	Roberto Mancini	2009-present

A Foot in Both Camps:

Players and Managers to Have Represented Both City and United

Bob Milarvie	(Newton Heath-MU-1890-1891; Ardwick-MC-1891-1896)
Frank Barrett	(Newton Heath-MU-1896-1900; MC-1901-1902)
Horace Blew	(MU-1906; MC-1906)
George Livingstone	(MC-1903-1906; MU-1909-1915)
Ernest Mangnall	(MU-1903-1912; MC-1912-1924)
Billy Meredith	(MC-1894-1906, 1921-1924; MU-1906-1921)
Sandy Turnbull	(MC-1902-1906; MU-1906-1915)
Jimmy Bannister	(MC-1902-1906; MU-1906-1909)
Herbert Burgess	(MC-1903-1906; MU-1906-1910)
Matt Busby	(MC-1928-1936-Player; MU-1945-1969-Manager)
Harry Rowley	(MU-1928-1937; MC-1932-1933)
Bill Dale	(MU-1926-1931; MC-1931-1937)
Denis Law	(MC-1960-1961, 1973-1974; MU-1962-1973)
Brian Kidd	(MU-1967-1974; MC-1976-1979)
Wyn Davies	(MC-1971-1972; MU-1972-1973)
Sammy McIlroy	(MU-1971-1982; MC-1985-1986)
Peter Barnes	(MC-1974-1979, 1987-1988; MU-1984-loan, 1985-1987)
Steve Coppell	(MU-1975-1983-Player; MC-1996-Manager)
Mark Hughes	(MU-1980-1986, 1988-1995-Player; MC-2008-2009-Manager)
Peter Beardsley	(MU-1982-1983; MC-1998-loan)
John Gidman	(MU-1981-1986; MC-1986-1988)
Mark Robins	(MU-1986-1992; MC-2001-loan)
Tony Coton	(MC-1990-1996; MU-1996)
Andrei Kanchelskis	(MU-1991-1995; MC-1999-loan)
Terry Cooke	(MU-1994-1999; MC-1999-2002)
Peter Schmeichel	(MU-1991-1999; MC-2002-2003)
Andy Cole	(MU-1995-2001; MC-2005-2006)
Carlos Tevez	(MU-2007-2009; MC-2009-)
Owen Hargreaves	(MU-2007-2011; MC-2011-12)

Respective Premier League Positions (1992-2012)

Year	Champions	Manchester United	Manchester City
1992-1993	Manchester United (1)	1st	9th
1993-1994	Manchester United (2)	1st	16th
1994-1995	Blackburn Rovers (1)	2nd	17th
1995-1996	Manchester United (3)	1st	18th *
1996-1997	Manchester United (4)	1st	Division One
1997-1998	Arsenal (1)	2nd	Division One *
1998-1999	Manchester United (5)	1st	Division Two
1999-2000	Manchester United (6)	1st	Division One
2000-2001	Manchester United (7)	1st	18th *
2001-2002	Arsenal (2)	3rd	Division One
2002-2003	Manchester United (8)	1st	9th
2003-2004	Arsenal (3)	3rd	16th
2004-2005	Chelsea (1)	3rd	8th
2005-2006	Chelsea (2)	2nd	15th
2006-2007	Manchester United (9)	1st	14th
2007-2008	Manchester United (10)	1st	9th
2008-2009	Manchester United (11)	1st	10th
2009-2010	Chelsea (3)	2nd	5th
2010-2011	Manchester United (12)	1st	3rd
2011-2012	Manchester City (1)	2nd	1st

* relegated

Respective FA Cup Competition Positions (1993-2012)

Year	Champions	Manchester United	Manchester City
1992-1993	Arsenal *	Fifth Round	Sixth Round
1993-1994	Manchester United	WON	Fourth Round
1994-1995	Everton	Finalist	Fifth Round
1995-1996	Manchester United	WON	Fifth Round
1996-1997	Chelsea	Fourth Round *	Fifth Round
1997-1998	Arsenal	Fifth Round *	Fourth Round
1998-1999	Manchester United	WON	Third Round
1999-2000	Chelsea	Did not compete #	Fourth Round
2000-2001	Liverpool	Fourth Round	Fifth Round
2001-2002	Arsenal	Fourth Round	Fifth Round
2002-2003	Arsenal	Fifth Round	Third Round
2003-2004	Manchester United	WON	Fifth Round
2004-2005	Arsenal	Finalist	Third Round
2005-2006	Liverpool +	Fifth Round	Sixth Round
2006-2007	Chelsea ^	Finalist	Sixth Round
2007-2008	Portsmouth	Sixth Round	Fourth Round
2008-2009	Chelsea	Semi-Finals +	Third Round
2009-2010	Chelsea	Third Round	Fifth Round *
2010-2011	Manchester City	Semi-Finals	WON
2011-2012	Chelsea	Fourth Round	Third Round

* replay ^ extra-time + penalty shootout
# Manchester United became the first FA Cup winners not to defend their title when they opted to take part in the 2000 FIFA World Club Challenge in South America.

In 2012, the Premier League celebrated its second decade by holding the 20 Seasons Awards.

Fantasy Team of the 20 Premier League Seasons:

Manchester City-United representatives: Panel Choice: Peter Schmeichel (MU-MC), Gary Neville (MU), Tony Adams, Rio Ferdinand (MU), Ashley Cole (MU-MC), Cristiano Ronaldo (MU), Roy Keane (MU), Paul Scholes (MU), Ryan Giggs (MU), Thierry Henry, Alan Shearer.

Public Vote: Peter Schmeichel (MU-MC), Gary Neville (MU), Tony Adams, Nemanja Vidið (MU), Ashley Cole, Cristiano Ronaldo (MU), Steven Gerrard, Paul Scholes (MU), Ryan Giggs (MU), Thierry Henry, Alan Shearer.

Best Manager: Sir Alex Ferguson
Best Player: Ryan Giggs
Best Team: 2003-04 Arsenal
Best Season: 2011-12 season
Best Save: Craig Gordon, 18 December 2010, Sunderland v Bolton Wanderers
Best Goal: Wayne Rooney, 12 February 2011, Manchester United v Manchester City
Best Match: Manchester United 4-3 Manchester City, 20 September 2009
Best Goal Celebration: Eric Cantona, 21 December 1996, Manchester United v Sunderland
Most Appearances: Ryan Giggs (598)
Top Goal-scorer: Alan Shearer (260)
Most Clean Sheets: David James (173)

ABOUT THE AUTHOR

Jon Reeves has been a freelance writer for over seven years. During this time he has written a number of fiction and non-fiction football books for Shoot, Parragon Publishing and Pedigree Publishing, and regularly contributed to the Shoot Monthly magazine.

He contributed to the 2008 Shoot Annual, the best-selling football annual in the UK, as well as a series of other football-themed titles for Shoot and Pedigree Publishing. Jon was also responsible for writing and editing ten titles developed as part of the FA's Official England series, including an in-depth trivia book and four children's fiction stories.

A 2004 graduate from the University of Lincoln, Jon combines his freelance writing career with a role as Communications Executive for a UK Sports Media and Marketing Agency called Soar Media.

Originally from Dorset on the South Coast of England, Jon now lives in Leicester with his wife Katie. Throughout his work, Jon aims to transmit his lifelong passion for the beautiful game into print.

Dedication
This book is dedicated to my wife Katie, 'baby' Reeves,
Mum, Dad and Em.

First published in 2012 by
New Holland Publishers Pty Ltd
In association with Shoot
London • Sydney • Cape Town • Auckland

Garfield House 86-88 Edgware Road London W2 2EA United Kingdom
1-66 Gibbes Street Chatswood NSW 2067 Australia
218 Lake Road Northcote Auckland New Zealand
Wembley Square First Floor Solan Road Gardens Cape Town 8001 South Africa

www.newhollandpublishers.com
www.newholland.com.au

A record of this book is available at the British Library and the National Library of Australia

ISBN 9781780093420

Publisher: Fiona Schultz
Project Manager: Alan Whiticker
Designer: Kimberley Pearce
Proofreader: Jon Mahoney
Cover photograph: Shoot
Production director: Olga Dementiev
Printer: CPI Books UK

10 9 8 7 6 5 4 3 2 1

Keep up with New Holland Publishers on Facebook and Twitter http:--www.facebook.com-
NewHollandPublishers
Twitter: @NewHollandAU